ORACLE

A Comprehensive Reference and guide

on

Literary Criticism

(Based on the FYUGP syllabus of BA 3RD SEMESTER

Dibrugarh University)

By

Purabjyoti Gogoi

PREFACE

Literary criticism as a subject in literature is the art and way of understanding literature. It focuses on teaching how to analyze, interpret, and evaluate texts, helping to uncover the layers of meaning within a piece of literature. Instead of merely reading a work for its plot or characters, literary criticism encourages readers to dive deeper into the underlying themes, symbols, cultural messages, and authorial choices that shape the work.

With "ORACLE" my purpose is to offer the students of English literature a comprehensive and approachable reference guide to literary criticism; a resource that not only explains the major theories and approaches but also demonstrates how these methods can enrich our reading experience to facilitate in the concerning exams. Being a student of English literature, the subject of literary criticism has been always a matter fascination, which I regard as the motivation that drove me to compose this comprehensive reference based on the (FYUGP) syllables of Dibrugarh University.

I would like to express my gratitude to my beloved parents who have always supported me. I would extend my words of gratitude to my companion Biplab Khanikar who organised my writings and helped me in the journey of 'ORACLE'. I would also extend my regards to my teachers who have helped me. Lastly, I would like to extend my regards to all my loved ones who have helped me in any either way at the different stages.

~Purabjyoti Gogoi .

<u>SYLLABUS (FYUGP)</u>
<u>AS PER DIBRUGARH UNIVERSITY</u>

Title of the Course: Literary Criticism
Course Code: C-4
Nature of the Course: Major
Total Credits:04
Distribution of Marks: 60 (End Sem) + 40 (In-Sem)

Course Objectives:
- acquaint the learners with the art of criticism of literary texts as have been practiced from the classical period to the early twentieth century
- provide the learners a broad survey of the history and development of literary criticism in Western culture from Plato and Aristotle to the eighteenth century
- Familiarize learners with significant ideas such as mimesis, representation, tragedy, republic, nature, the sublime, the text and so forth.

UNITS	CONTENTS	L	T	P	TOTAL HOURS
I (15 MARKS)	Plato: *The Republic Book 10* Aristotle: *Poetics*	12	02		14
II (15 MARKS)	Horace- *Ars Poetica* Longinus- *On the Sublime*	14	02		16
III (15 MARKS)	Phillip Sidney- *An Apology for Poetry* John Dryden- *An Essay of Dramatic Poesy*	12	02		14
IV (15	Alexander Pope- An Essay on Criticism	14	02		16

MARKS)

Samuel
Johnson-
"On
Metaphysical
Wit"
from*Life of*

Cowley

60   TOTAL   12   08   60
MARKS

Modes of In-Semester Assessment:**40 Marks**
01. Two Sessional tests:**10x2-20 Marks**
02.Any two of the following activities listed below:**10x2-20 Marks**

- Seminar/ Group discussion/ Assignment related to the Course content.
- Presentation of seminar papers.
- Assignments.
- Quiz.

Final Examination: 60 Marks
Unit 1: 1 LAQ+1 SA=(10+5)=**15 marks**
Unit 2: 1 LAQ+1 SA=(10+5)=**15 marks**
Unit 3: 1 LAQ+1 SA=(10+5)=**15 marks**
Unit 4: 1 LAQ+I SA= (10+5)=**15 marks**
*LAQ= Long Answer Question; SA= Short Answer

Suggested Readings:

Abrams, M.H. The Mirror and the Lamp: Romantic Theory and the Critical
Tradition. London: Oxford University Press, 1971.

Abrams, M.H., and Geoffrey Galt Harpham. 4 Glossary of Literary Terms. 10th
ed. USA: Wadsworth, Cengage Learning, 2012.

Adams, Hazard. Critical Theory Since Plato. 2nd ed. California: Harcourt Brace
Jovanovich College Publishers, 1992.

Barton, Edwin J., and Glenda A. Hudson. A Contemporary Guide to Literary
Terms with Strategies for Writing Essays about Literature. Boston, USA: Houghton
Mifflin, 2004.

Brooks, Cleanth, and Paul Rand. The Well Wrought Urn: Studies in the Structure
of Poetry. California: Harcourt Brace, 1947.

D.J. Enright, and E.DeChickera. English Critical Texts. London: OUP, 1962.
Daiches, David. Critical Approaches to Literature. 2nd ed. London: Orient

Longman Pvt. Ltd, 2005.

Guerin, Wilfred L. A Handbook ofCritical Approaches to Literature. 4th ed.
London: Oxford University Press, 1999.

Hudson, WH. An Introduction to the Study of Literature. New Delhi: Atlantic
Publishers and Distributors Pvt. Ltd, 2006.

Leitch, Vincent B., ed. The Norton Anthology of Theory and Criticism. London:
W. W. Norton and Company, 2001

M. A.R Habib. A History ofLiterary Criticism and Theory: From Plato to the
Present. Malden, MA: Blackwell Publishing, 2008.

Preminger, Alex. Princeton Encyclopedia of Poetry & Poetics. New Jersey:
Princeton University Press, 1972.

51/116

S. RamaswamiandV. S. Sethuraman. The English Critical Tradition: Volumel&
2. New Delhi: Macmillan, 2014.

Waugh, Patricia. Literary Theory and Criticism. London: OUP, 2006.
Wellek, Rene, and Austin Warren. Theory of Literature. London: Penguin, 1980.

CONTENTS

UNITS	INDEX	PAGE NO
1	**Plato**: *The Republic Book 10* **Aristotle**: *Poetics*	1-24 25-65
2	**Horace-** *Ars Poetica* **Longinus-** *On the Sublime*	66-113 114-154
3	**Phillip Sidney-** *An Apology for Poetry* **John Dryden-** *An Essay of Dramatic Poesy*	155-194 195-239
4	**Alexander Pope-** An Essay on Criticism **Samuel Johnson-** "On Metaphysical Wit" from *Life*	240-292 293-319

UNIT – I

PLATO: THE REPUBLIC, Book X

1. **About Plato**

2. **The Republic**

3. **The Republic Book X**

   a. Introduction

   b. Synopsis

   c. Analysis

4. **Probable questions:**

   a. Analyze Plato's views on mimesis, nature of poetry and the role of art in society.

   b. Analyze Socrates' allegory of the myth of Er in Book X.

5. **References and suggested readings**

1. **About Plato**

Plato born around 437 BCE was an ancient Greek philosopher, best known for his works on ethics, politics, metaphysics and epistemology, often written in the form of dialogues. As a pioneer of western philosophy, Plato introduced foundational concepts that shaped critical areas of thought.

Plato was born in Athens, Greece to an aristocratic family and later was under the mentorship of Socrates, till he finally emerged as a profound figure in the development of western philosophy. Plato's philosophical approach was notably shaped by his mentor, Socrates. He was closely associated with Socrates' methodology of questioning and pursuit of

---

Socrates

Socrates was an ancient Greek philosopher who lived from around 469 to399 BCE, belonging to the classical era. He is one of the pioneers who had immense contributions in the development of Western philosophy. He is best known from his 'methos' of questioning and dialogue which is referred to as- 'Socratic Method'. Much about Socrates' and his philosophical aspects is known from his students, especially through, Plato. Socrates was subjected to trial by three of fellow citizens on the ground of corrupting the youth of Athens and hence was imprisoned and executed.

---

truth extensively, which influenced his own approach to his own approach to philosophical aspects related to art, life and society.

Plato's philosophical aspects are primarily conveyed through his numerous dialogues in the form of conversations between different characters. These dialogues are central to understanding his thoughts; have been instrumental in shaping western philosophy. His dialectical approach using dialogues and critical examination to uncover deep truths and resolve intellectual conflicts has been formative in philosophical discourse.

In his philosophical discourse Plato constantly employs his mentor Socrates as a central character who through conversations with other characters seeks to explore various themes ranging from critics, politics, art to metaphysics and epistemology and more. Plato's central character 'Socrates' in his works acts as the speaker who leads the other characters and the readers or his audience to Plato's structured ideas as well as his mentor's, regarding the various concepts.

Plato's contributions extend beyond his own writings. His establishment of the Academy in Athens in around 387 BC is considered as one of the first institutions of higher learning in the western world as it marked the beginning of the institutionalized philosophical inquiry. In addition to his philosophical pursuits, Plato was also involved in Athenian politics through he grew disillusioned with the city's political climate following

Socrates' trial and execution. Socrates' death was a turning point in Plato's life. After it, he left Athens and travelled for some years before starting to write dialogues in which Socrates was mostly the central figure. His later years were dedicated to writing and teaching at the Academy until his death around 348 or 347 BCE.

Plato's influence through his compositions extends far beyond his own time. His ideas have shaped subsequent philosophical traditions from Neo-Platonism in late antiquity to Renaissance Humanism and beyond.

His Notable works:

1. *The Republic*
   Plato's most famous work, in the form of dialogues, explores themes like justice, the ideal state' and the role of philosopher king includes a wide range of philosophical topics including the theory of forms' the allegory of the cave' etc.

2. *Phaedo*
   Focused on the final hours of his mentor, Socrates before his execution. Written in dialogic form it explores themes like immortality of the soul, nature of death & afterlife, etc.

3. *The Symposium*
   Written in dialogic form, Plato examines the nature of love Eros through a series of speeches by different characters including Socrates at a

banquet. The idea of love as a pursuit of beauty and truth is discussed here.

4. *Phaedrus*

   In these dialogues, Plato addresses topics like rhetoric love & soul, includes a discussion on the nature of true love and role of rhetoric in persuasion.

5. *Timaeus*

   Here Plato dives into the nature of the physical world and the creation of the cosmos. Plato here lays down the discourse of the natural of the physical world and its relationship of the ideal forms; presents a cosmological account of the origins and structure of the world

---

2. The Republic

- **Introduction**

The Republic composed round 380-370 BCE by Greek philosopher Plato is an influential philosophical text that explores the fundamental nature of justice, the ideal state and the role of the philosopher in the society, among the other such ideas. The republic is considered as a significant ext of the utopian literary genre.

The title republic is derived from Latin which is attributed to Cicero who called the text 'De re Publica' meaning about affairs or even called it as 'De Republica' which created a confusion as to its true meaning. A second title 'Peri Dikaiou' on justice was also included later.

The text is divided into 10 books that cover various discussions of social political and literary importance. The first Book deals with the subject of justice and its nature; in the next two subsequent books – Book II and Book III deals with the exploration of the theory of the ideal state; Book IV and V deal with the concept of justice and the identification of he soul in three parts respectively; Book VI and VII deal with the importance of knowledge and enlightenment; Book VIII and IX deal with the types of government and state while the last one Book X concludes with a critique off poetry and arts, the idea of immortality, truth, culminating in the myth of Er, which depicts the soul's journey after death.

Throughout the text several characters engage through dialogues led by the central character Socrates who can be regarded as reflective of the reflective of Plato himself. The character of Socrates through the discourse questions notions of justice and seeks to uncover deeper truths about mortality, governance and literature. The other characters include namely- Hesiod, Thrasymachus, Glaucon, Cephalus, Polemarchus and others.

The text opens with the characters gathering at Cephalus' place. It starts with Cephalus who introduces traditional notion of justice suggesting that it revolves around honesty and the fulfillment of obligations. He gives the perspective that justice provides a peaceful life, a perspective that gets soon challenged by Socrates. Socrates concerns that justice is simply of more advantage of the stronger person or people but he refrains from providing his own notion of justice. He proposes the idea of an ideal state that would be based on the concept of justice. The discourse takes a provocative turn with Thrasymachus, who asserts that justice is merely the advantage of the stronger. His bold assertion raises fundamental questions about power and morality arguing that rules often manipulate concepts of justice to maintain control. Socrates counters this view by articulating a more nuanced understanding insisting that true justice serves the common good and ultimately benefits the individual. Socrates within the discourse develops his idea of an ideal state where education, social structure, specialization art will prevail with people having specialization in any of the specific form of occupation chosen by them. Base on their abilities. Socrates emphasizes on the role of education to be supreme which would civilize the people. He defines the role of art to reflect good conduct and puts a ban on imitative literature. In his ideal state 'Kallipolis' he envisions a society composed of rulers as "philosopher kings", guardians, producers and as well as warriors etc. each class corresponding to a different aspect of the soul which Socrates classifies as reason, spirit and appetite. He appoints the philosophers as the rulers of the ideal state.

A vital moment occurs in the text with the allegory of the cave that Socrates provides to illustrate the philosopher journey from ignorance to enlightenment. Throughout the text the theme of education emerges as crucial for cultivating virtues and ensuring the stability of the ideal state. Socrates emphasizes that a rigorous educational system is vital for producing wise leaders who can govern justify the discourse concludes with the myth of Er by Socrates. It serves as an allegory for the soul's journey after death. The myth serves to illustrate he immortality of the soul suggesting that its condition is influenced by one's ethical behavior and philosophical understanding.

3. The Republic, Book X

• Synopsis

Socrates takes on the subject of the nature of art. The nature of art is recognized a being imitative. To uphold the argument, he illustrates through the allegory of 'beds and tables". He describes that artistic works and poetry are a third steps away from the Forms and Truth. By forms here he means the ideas that are at the root of reality. The artist as he considers carries no knowledge of the real forms, and he simply represents and replicates. Such kind of poetic and artistic works mislead the individuals in a society and take away their intellectual capability.

Socrates asks for a ban on imitative art for the well-being of the ideal society and the philosophers. However, he provides the relief to some extent and allows he kind of poetry like hymns to gods and paeans in praise of good men. Other than these he considers all of the other forms as deceptive and deviated from truth which can corrupt the morals of men.

Socrates and Glaucon then shift the discussion to consider the nature of the soul and at how just soul is rewarded. The soul is acknowledged as being immoral in nature which can't be destroyed even after death. On the other hand, they also focus on the reward of goodness of man in life for being just and virtuous. A just soul they assert is never left unrewarded by the divine.

Socrates concludes the discussion by narrating the myth of Er, brave soldier who died in a battle but returned to life after experiencing the process of eternal justice in the afterlife. Er although dead war appointed as a messenger between the two realms. When he returned back to life, he shared what he witnessed. He saw the souls facing the trial after death. The unjust soul who committed sins and caused suffering to others were punished ten times more for each of the crime they did. After the trial and sufferings but the unjust souls they are provide the chance to choose their next life, since the soul being immortal cannot be destroyed. Er asserts that while some souls choose the just life based on their process alludes that the soul is immortal and one must survive the consequences of the actions done.

- **Analysis**

Book X of 'The Republic' can be classified into two arts - while the former focuses on the theory of mimesis and the nature of poetry; the latter focuses on justice through the myth of Er.

The character of Socrates begins by reaffirming the banishment of poetry from the ideal city. Art is recognized as imitative in nature that presents a dittoed reality. He accuses the tragedians and the dramatic poets of falsehood as their distorted representation harm the minds of their audiences and ultimately detaches them the knowledge of truth as the truest form. (Line 595(a)-(c) Book X)

Plato provides his theory of forms or ideas through the analogy of bed and tables. He accuses the artists to imitate and make poor copies of the idea. The persona of Socrates provides the allegory of beds and table to illustrate the different forms.

'For example, there are many particular beds and tables". (Line 596 (b) Book X)

He acknowledges the idea to be the ultimate form which takes material for at the hands of an efficient craftsman. The latter artisans who replicate the material form are charged with poor imitation, who have no knowledge of the real form. The imitation through art only provides likeness of a thing in concrete and likeness is always less than the real.

"...his product is not "what is", but something which resembles "what is" without being it..." (Line 597 (b) Book X)

He categorizes the words of forms the perfect, the unchangeable the material world; and the imperfect copies of former through art.

The artist is criticized to simply represent and replicate with true knowledge. The poetic endeavor while aesthetically compelling serves to mislead, promoting audiences to embrace emotional expressions that threaten the intellectual and moral conduct of the individuals.

"So, the artists have neither knowledge nor correct opinion about the goodness or badness of the things he represents.... the poet too, as the artist will beautifully ill-informed about the subjects of his poetry" (Line 602(a)-(b) Book X)

Plato assertion that imitative art or mimesis is inherently inferior to the realm of true knowledge is rooted in the forms- abstract, immutable ideals. The artist according to Plato represents something which is far detached from the ultimate reality of the form or ides.

"...this process of representation deals with something at third, remove from the truth..." (Line 602(c) Book X)

He accuses the works of art and poetry to corrupt the souls as they are detached from the truth. Imitative art is charged with spreading falsehood and making its audiences less reasonable.

"...the work of the painter and all other representative artists was far removed from the truth and associated with elements in.... without health or truth." (Line 603 (b) Book X)

Plato goes to the extent of considering imitative art as inferior child born inferior (Line 603(b)). His criticism here is harsh against art as well as poetry.

Plato's critique extends to the portrayal of gods and heroes within the spectrum of dramatic poetry by the poets and the tragedians like Homer. He is particularly troubled by the representation of immoral actions and flawed characters which can corrupt the minds of the individuals of the society and manipulate their ethical considerations. He approves for the censorship of such poetry that fails to uphold morals, ideals that constitute the ideal state

"The dramatic poet will...represent character that is unstable and refractory" (Line 605 (a) Book X)

Plato recognizes the nature of poetry to be rebellious which desires to command the mind of the audiences. He takes it to be a threat to the philosophical capability of the individuals of the society to apprehend the truest forms. The "ideal society" he contends must prioritize the cultivation of virtues through philosophical education and administer the philosophers as defenders against the corrupting influences of imitative art.

The only form of poetry that Plato considers should be allowed is the hymns to the gods' and men of character and virtues.

"The only poetry that should be allowed in a satire is hymns to the gods and paeans in praise of good men..." (Line 607 (c) Book X)

He attributes poetry with the role to promote educations and morality among the audiences.

The discussion then shifts to the next section where Socrates and Glaucon engage regarding the nature of the soul. The soul they conclude is immortal that cannot be destroyed.

"Then if there's no evil that can destroy it, either its own or another's... it must be immortal" (Line 611(d) Book X)

They also shed light on the rewards of goodness in life that is the reward of excellence and just could achieve.

Socrates in the second half of Book X examines the nature of the soul and justice through the myth of Er. In the concluding section of the text, Socrates provides a vivid illustration of the soul being immortal and that one must suffer the consequences even after death through the myth of Er.

Socrates narrates that Er, who was the son of Armenius, a native of Pamphylia, was killed in a battle. When he was about to be cremated on the twelfth day after his death he came back to life. He narrated what he witnessed and experienced in the realm of souls. Er provides an explicit description of the process of justice that continues even after life in the other world the realm of dead. He although was dead was spared from the trial and instead was asked to witness the entire process so that he can pass on the knowledge of it to the living men when he regains his life. He was treated as the messenger between the two realms of life and death.

Er mentions of the "thong of souls" that appeared for trial and face the consequences of their choices and actions. The souls are sentenced to suffer ten times for each wrong they did to others.

"For every wrong he has done to anyone a man must pay the penalty in turn, ten times for each that is to say…" (Line 615(a)-(b) Book X)

ER asserts that no soul is exempted from the process of justice. When the souls are done from suffering for their sins, they are offered choices to choose their next life. (Line 619(a)-(b) Book X)

While some choose well others committed the same mistakes driven by desire and greed.

"For the most part they followed the habits of their former life…" (Line 620(a) Book X)

The aspect of justice being eternal and 'free will' provided to the soul or the individuals to make their choices and be accountable for them is depicted in this concluding section. The myth appears as a brilliant literary device which summarizes all the previous discussions occurred throughout the discourse regarding the 'ideal state' and justice.

4. Probable Questions

1. Analyze Plato's views on mimesis, nature of poetry and the role of art in society.

Answer:

'The Republic' by Greek Philosopher, Plato composed around 380 - 370 BCE, is a fundamental text that contributed in the development of western philosophy. The text explores the ideas regarding justice, role of philosophies, art, etc. among the others, and proposes for the establishment of an "ideal state". In book 10 of the text, Plato through his characters presents an explicit discussion on art, its nature and role.

Plato in book 10 proposes an intricately linked discussion of his theory of forms. The concept of mimesis or imitation is subjected to rigorous scrutiny, leading Plato to a comprehensive critique of poetry and the arts. Plato in his theory of 'mimesis' asserts that all art is mimetic (imitative) by nature and argues that 'idea' is the ultimate reality. The persona of Socrates in the discourse illustrates the argument of art being imitative through the analogy of beds and tables. He introduces two forms as an example.

"For example, there are many particular beds and tables." (Line 596(b))

He introduces the 'idea' to have come first to the carpenter who gave shape to his idea through his craftsmanship. Plato then poses the question about another craftsman who can "make all the objects produced by other particular crafts." Plato explains that the objects that were created by the latter craftsman are mere imitations of the former's 'idea'. The objects created by the latter have deviated from the original 'idea' as the latter has added his own perspective while crafting. He declares a painter to be belonging to the latter kind who paints the objects that 'resembles' the idea of the real.

"For a painter is a craftsman of just this kind…" (Line 596(c))

The implication here that Plato provides is that art being imitative in nature deviates from truth, and only provides likeness of a thing in concrete and likeness is always less than the 'real'.

"his product is not 'what is' but something which resembles 'what is' without being it." (Line 597 (b))

3. Plato tends to establish the distinctions between the world of forms - the perfect, unchangeable and the material world on the other side which contains imperfect copies of the ideal forms. This threefold hierarchy- form, physical object and artistic imitation underscores his agreement that artistic representation is inherently inferior and distanced from truth. The artist according to his argument only captures the appearance thereby further detaching the representation of the ultimate reality of the form 'idea'. The analogy of bed

here represents the 'form' that is at the top of the hierarchy.

"So painter, carpenter and God are each responsible for one kind of bed."
(Line 597(b))

Plato characterizes the artist to simply represent and replicate.

"'And what about the artist? Does he make or manufacture'
'No'
'Then what does he do?'
'I think that we may fairly claim that he represents what the other two makes' "
(Line 597(c))

For him, art merely copies a copy; is twice removed from reality.
Plato classifies all artistic representation to be far from "the throne of truth" (Line 597 (e)). This positioning underscores Plato's concern that the average individual can be seduced by the allure of artistic representation and so may confuse these imitations with authentic understanding of the truth. He gave the argument that imitative art possess the potential to corrupt the soul by appealing primarily to the emotions rather than the intellect. He accuses the poetic works, especially tragedies; invoke a 'catharsis' that ultimately detracts from the noble pursuit of wisdom. The 'ideal' society that Plato proposes in the text, he argues for the

cultivation of virtue through philosophical education, positioning the philosophers as defenders against the potentially corrupting influences of imitative art. Plato's vision of an 'ideal' state necessitates careful regulations of artistic expression, ensuring that it serves the promotion of truth and virtue rather than undermining them. For Plato, it is only philosophers who engage in the real mimesis of the forms for providing a sufficiently qualified representation.

For Plato, the ultimate reality is in the world of ideas, and the material world is but an imitation of it. It can be interpreted that Plato was reacting not only against the disordered and mythical vision of the world offered by the artists or the poets but also against the skepticism of individuals regarding the philosophers. According to Plato, the world of Forms, being changeless and eternal alone constitutes reality. He seeks to create an intimate connection between his aesthetics of ideal state and his formulation to art and poetry. Through the characters of Socrates, Plato constantly provides the argument that art and poetry have failed to examine justice as poetic knowledge is confined to the world of appearance. He tries to establish the hegemony of the philosophers as the guardians of the ideal state by banishing the poets.

Plato in book x of the text, alleges the nature of poetry to establish a "vicious constitution" in the soul, which sets up emotions as rulers in place of reason.

"The dramatic poet produces a similarly bad state of affairs in the mind of the individual by encouraging the unreasoning part of it." (Line 605(c))

He further recognizes the nature of poetry to make the individual less reasonable who "cannot distinguish greater and less." Due to the unreliable presentation of truth and reality-"by creating images far removed from the truth." (Line 605(c))

Plato further puts the allegation on poetry that is:

"has a bad effect on its audiences, who learn to admire and imitate the fault it represents." He based on this argument reaffirms the decision of banishment of the poets. Poetry is charged with spreading falsehood.
"It has terrible power to corrupt even the best characters...."
(Line 605(d))

Through the character of Socrates, he contends here that poetry fosters such emotional manipulation which can lead to moral decay.

Despite acknowledging his admiration for poets like Homer, Plato critiques Homer for failing to engaging in politics or philosophy. He condemns Homer for presenting dramatic poetry which is far from reality. Plato questions the moral implications of his narratives. He argues that Homer's portrayal of the heroes and the godly figures promotes immorality and are unsuitable for the 'ideal state'. Plato prioritizes philosophical discourse over artistic expressions through dramatic poetry.

".... you may agree with them that Homer is best of poets and first of tragedians."
(Line 607 (a))

Plato considers that the role of poetry should be to promote education and morality for the "just", "ideal" society. It should serve a constructive role in society. It should present reason, truth and ideals rather than emotional appeal through imitation. He provides the relief to the argument that poetry must be banished from the proposed 'ideal' state by asserting that poetry that provides praise to the Gods and man of character can be allowed.

"The only poetry that should be allowed in a state is hymns to the Gods and paeans in praise of good men..."
(Line 607(a))

But he is adamant to the idea of eliminating poets that engage in dramatic poetry seeking to appeal the audience like Homer and the tragedians. It can be said the Plato throughout his entire argument regards poetry as having the complex role with society which is capable of both enriching and endangering human experiences. While he mostly condemns it for its imitative and manipulative nature but at the same acknowledges its merit to promote truth and virtue. He recognizes the nature of poetry to be rebellious with the desire to rule, posing threat to the throne of philosophy and reason; his suspicion of literature is guided by his intuition of the potential of poets and poetry to move and charm the individuals of the society.

In conclusion, Plato's theory of mimesis - i.e. art being imitative in nature remains central to the text - "The Republic". His skepticism towards the poets for being worshipped as the ideal personas is reflective throughout, particularly in book X. He remains adamant to his assertion that poetry have no definable function in an 'ideal state' and thus labels it to spread immorality which is why it should either be banished or put under censorship under the rulers of the 'ideal state'. Plato aligns the ability of poetry with degradation of political and philosophical discourse. Thus, his criticism of the nature of poetry reaffirms his idea of the necessity of cultivating a 'just' and 'ideal society'.

2. Analyze Socrates' allegory of the myth of Er in Book X.

OR

3. Significance of the myth of Er as the concluding section of text.

Answer:
Book X of the text 'The Republic' by Plato serves as a powerful allegory about the soul, the afterlife, and the consequences of moral choices by the individuals. It serves as a culmination of the dialogues between the characters on the various aspects.

Socrates by the end of the discourse provides a vivid illustration of the consequences one must suffer even after death through the myth of Er. He narrates the myth that Er, the son of Armenius was a brave man who was killed in a battle but returns to life and then shares his experiences in the afterlife. Er tells that he witnessed a grand process of judgment in the realm of soils where souls face the trial and are evaluated on their earthly lives. The souls are given verdict according to their earthly lives, as "just" souls are rewarded whereas unjust face the punishment in a pit of retribution. After their judgment the souls get the opportunity to choose their next Lives m, which signifies their 'free will'. Er observes that this chorus reflects the soul's past experiences and their understanding of virtue. Some choose wisely, while others, lacking foresight repeat their past mistakes.

"...when he had spoken, the man with the first lot came forward and choose the greatest tyranny he could find. In his Folly and greed, he chooses it without examining it fully." (Line 619 (c) Book X)

Plato employs the myth in an elaborate manner through Socrates to emphasize that souls are immortal and that an individual must face the consequences of actions; one should reflect on their experiences to live a life of virtues in the pursuit of truth and judgment.

In the myth, Er's eyes serve as the witness at the site of a judgment that is always in motion and beyond the customs of mankind; with the theme as a whole that truth and justice always prevail beyond the cycle of life and death.

"For every wrong he has done to anyone a man must pay the penalty in turn, ten times for each, that is to say once every hundred years, this being reckoned as the span of a man's life. He plays therefore tenfold retribution for each crime, and so for instance those...for each offence." (Line 615(b), Book X)

The vivid depiction reinforces the central argument that justice is not merely a societal construct but a fundamental aspect of the soul's well-being as soul is immortal. Socrates emphasizes on the fact that choices made during one's life time have an everlasting impact. He compels individuals to consider the weight of their actions and the moral implications of their choices and decisions, indirectly asserting to strive for virtue and justice.

The myth clearly introduces the idea of the soul' immortality as Er's death was not the end of his journey but was the beginning of another on the path of judgement in another realm. This notion of immortality serves to elevate the importance of philosophical inquiry, ethical living, and pursuit of virtue, knowledge and justice. Socrates describes the journey of Er in detail of encountering souls after death in the realm of souls.

"He then saw the souls, whose judgement had been passed on them departing some by one of the heavenly and some by the one of the earthly chasms; while by the other...clean." (Line 614(c) Book X)

Further in the myth, the opportunity for souls to choose their next Lives emphasizes on the theme of free will and personal choice. In the myth souls are given a chance to select their future existence based on their previous to undergo transformation.

"And to see the souls choosing their lives was indeed a sight, Er said, a sight to move pity and laughter and wonder. For the most part they followed the habits of the former life..." (Line 620, Book X)

This suggests that individuals have the capacity to reflect on their past choices and through wisdom make better decision in the future. The cyclical process of learning through experiences and past choices aligns with Plato's philosophical discourse of acknowledging how education is a transformative tool for the construction and existence of an ideal society.

In the text, both the myths: the myth of metals and the allegory of the cave appear at crucial junctions in the discourse. As former introduces the idea of society with distinct classes comprising of rules, guardians and producers each being represented through the metaphor of a metal to signify their inherent qualities and roles; the latter, allegory of the cave stands as the metaphor for human perception and journey to enlightenment. Through both the extended metaphors the importance of education to construct an ideal society is presented by Plato, through the dialogues. Similarly, the myth of Er that appears in concluding section of the text builds on the ideas developed in the former allegories of how an individual's conduct is the result of the education received by the respective individual.

The myth of Er serves as a philosophical closure to the text bringing together its core themes of justice, knowledge, enlightenment and the nature of the souk.

Plato with this conclusion encapsulates all the arguments that were discussed within the discourse regarding the various subjects. He through the myth tries to entrust the individuals with their respective roles to constitute the "ideal" society.

Critics like Richard Kraut interpret the myth of Er in the narrative as a demonstration of Plato's commitment to a just society. He points out that the math's portrayal of moral accountability and the consequences of one's actions serves to motivate individuals to strive for justice in their lives.

The myth of Er narrated by Socrates in the concluding section of the text 'The Republic', thus recounts on all the ideals and virtues that were discussed throughout the text, and invites a through reflection on all the themes that are essential to love a just and ideal life.

5. References and suggested readings:

i.   Plato: The Republic,
     (Penguin Classics)
ii. Raphael Foshay: Mimesis in 'The Republic'
     Dialectic and Poetics
iii. Sfeteu, Nicolae: 'Plato: The Republic'
     In Telework. DOI (2022)
iv. Taylor, C.C.W. 2009: 'Plato's Epistemology'
     The Oxford Handbook of Plato.
v.   Harry Blamires: A History of Literary
     Criticism
vi. Allott. Phillip.2011: 'On First Understanding
     Plato's Republic

UNIT- 1

ARISTOTLE: POETICS

1. **About the Author**

2. **Poetics**

    a. Introduction

    b. Synopsis

    c. Analysis

3. **Probable Questions:**

    a. Evaluate on the key concept of mimesis as outlined by Aristotle in the "Poetics".

    b. Evaluate on Aristotle's assessment of plot in Tragedy.

    c. Analyse Aristotle's view on Tragedy and essentials of tragedy how does Aristotle differentiate between tragedy and epic? Elaborate. Access Aristotle's assessment of epic poetry.

    d. Evaluate Aristotle's treatment of Diction

    e. Analyze Aristotle views on comedy and its essentials.

    f. Short notes – (a) Hamartia (b) Peripeteia (c) catharsis

4. **References and Suggested readings**

1. About Aristotle

Aristotle (334-322 BCE) was a prominent Greek Philosopher and Polymath whose ideas have significantly shaped various fields, including philosophy, Science, politics, ethics and arts. He was the student of Plato and later became the tutor of Alexander the Great. Aristotle is considered as one of the greatest philosophers in western history whose contributions span across various fields.

Aristotle was born in 384 BCE in Stagira in Northern Greece. His father, Nicomachus was a physician to the King of Macedon, which likely influenced Aristotle's interest in Biology and the natural sciences. His intellectual journey began at the age of 17 when he moved to Athens to study at Plato's Academy where he remained for almost two decades developing a close intellectual bond with Plato. During his time at the academy, he acquired Plato's ideas particularly regarding forms and nature of reality.

After Plato's death, Aristotle left the academy, and travelled to Lesbos where he conducted significant biological research. He met and married his wife Pythias and had a daughter. With time his reputation grew as a learned man as he continued with his philosophical and empirical researches.

In 343 BCE, King Philip of Macedon invited Aristotle to tutor his son Alexander at the court of Pella. This opportunity not only shaped his views on leadership and governance but also forged his connections that would influence his works. Aristotle's influence on young Alexander was immense according to historians. Aristotle remained the tutor of Alexander, until the young prince reached the age of fifteen. When Alexander began to serve as commander for his father, Aristotle slowly retired from his service. Historians say that Aristotle was also commissioned by King Philip to oversee the restoration of the city of Stagira. After completion of the work, Aristotle returned to Athens and founded his own school, Lyceum, where he dedicated himself to teaching and composing his philosophical ideas. Unlike Plato's Academy where Aristotle studied, which is mostly favored by aristocracy, Aristotle's Lyceum drew students largely from the middle-class sections of Athenian society.

There he taught Mathematics, politics, metaphysics, botany, medicine among various other subjects. He produced several prominent students including Ptolemya and others. After the death of his first wife Pythias, he married his second wife Herpyllis. His later wife was mostly dedicated towards his study of subjects like philosophy, poetry, politics etc. His exploration of natural challenges philosophy laid the groundwork for scientific inquiry. His works in physics addressed questions of motion and causation. In his work 'Polities' he examines various political systems advocating for a constitutional government that balances the interests of all the sections of the society. He categorizes government into three true forms - monarchy, aristocracy and polity.

Aristotle's life was marked by intellectual rigor and a commitment to inquiry but he also faces particularly during the political turmoil, following Alexander's death. His philosophical ideas sometimes faced rigorous backlash due to the odds of the prevailing society. By 323 BCE he left Athens and settled in Euboca.

He died at the age of 62 in 322 BCE leaving behind his legacy of contributions to philosophy, ethics, politics, literature, science etc. which were unparalleled. In the centuries following his death, particularly in the age of Renaissance there was a revival of Aristotelian thought, which greatly influenced the scholars and scientists of the period. His discourses had a profound impact in shaping of the western philosophy so much so that he is often referred as the Father of Western Philosophy.

His notable works:

Aristotle is believed to have written about 200 treatises and other works covering a wide range of subjects. While many were lost in the flow of time, some of them managed to survive.

1. *"Politics"*

   In this Aristotle explores various forms of government and their purposes. He also explores the subject of justice, citizenship etc.

2. *"Poetics"*

In poetics he analyses the principles of art and poetry, tragedy, emphasizing plot, characters and catharsis as essential components in a drama.

3. *"Physics"*

    Aristotle explores the nature of the physical world focusing on causes, motion, time and change through his underlying principles.

4. *"Nicomachean Ethics"*

    Aristotle here deals with human happiness through moral and intellectual virtues, and gives the argument that virtue is achieved through habit and practical wisdom.

---

2. Poetics

- **Introduction**

Aristotle's "Poetics" composed around 330 BCE, in the 4th century BCE is one of the earliest works of literary criticism and theory which significantly shaped the foundation of western literature. In "Poetics" Aristotle provides his philosophical ideas regarding poetry and its various forms; tragedy, plot, tragic hero, comedy among the others.

The term "Poetics" generally refers to the study of the principles and forms of poetry and literature. It encompasses the analysis of artistic creation and expression, exploring how various elements combines to evoke emotions and convey meaning. Aristotle's "Poetics" specifically examines the nature of poetry and drama, focusing on their structure, function and their significance.

Aristotle's "Poetics" delves into the concept of mimesis or imitation. The word Mimesis in Greek means "imitation". The text provides a thorough examination of various forms of poetry, particularly tragedy and epic poetry. This notion suggests that poets and playwrights do not merely replicate reality; rather they distil and represent the essence of human experience through their craft. Aristotle's understanding of "mimesis" is particularly significant because it separates arts from mere representation. He defines poetry as "an imitation "of action which suggests that art reflects human experiences and emotions. He asserts that art imitates not the show of things, but the 'ideal reality' embodied in the very object of the real world.

Aristotle categories poetry into different genres as - epic, tragedy and comedy; each characterized by unique forms and purposes, thereby laying the groundwork for the study of literary genres. Among the various forms of poetry, Aristotle elevates tragedy as the highest expression of artistic endeavor. He elaborates on the six components of tragedy: plot, character, thought, diction, melody and spectacle; among these he considers plot to be the most critical of tragedy. He asserts that a well-constructed plot must possess unity, coherence and a sense of inevitability where in each event must be inconsistent to one another leading to a coherent and inevitable conclusion. The other components are discussed vividly within the discourse of the text.

Aristotle further delves into the element of use of diction in a literary framework. He explains that the poet should use the proper words stressing that language should enhance the emotional and intellectual resonance of the narrative. He also acknowledges the importance and role of spectacle in drama. The visual elements of performance conclude his analysis of tragedy.

The impact of "Poetics" extends beyond the immediate contexts of Aristotle's time, reaching into the resonance, enlightenment and modern literary criticism. The revival of classics during the Renaissance witnessed a renowned interest in Aristotle's literary theory regarding tragedy, plot and characterization. The distinctions laid by him have guided literary classification and interpretation of the different genres. Its influence spread across genres, influencing playwrights and poets for centuries.

Aristotle's "Poetics" serves as both a response to and a development of the ideas presented in Plato's 'Republic'. While Plato advocates for caution and censorship regarding the arts due to their potential to mislead, Aristotle one the other hand, recognizes the inherent value of poetry in exploring and expressing the complexities of human experience.

In conclusion, Aristotle's 'Poetics' provides profound insights on the art of poetry and drama establishing key concepts that are central to literary discourse.

- **Synopsis**

Aristotle sets the agenda of his discourse in the beginning itself i.e. to discuss the art of poetry and its species. He sets the ideas to discuss the nature of poetry, the way it should be constructed and how it can be effective. He begins with the first i.e. the nature of all artists' works, mimesis.

Aristotle emphasizes the importance of understanding the principles of imitation (mimesis) and catharsis as the process that is evoked by art in the audiences. He considers that every form of art including poetry as a species of imitation. He differentiates imitation into three respects medium, object and mode.

Aristotle regards imitation and the universal pleasure in imitations i.e. catharsis as the origin of poetry. He takes both of these causes as natural. He categorizes poetry into several distinct genres, focusing primarily on tragedy and epic poetry and also other forms as comedy. His classifications are based on the characteristics of each genre based on their subject matter, style and emotional impact on the audience. Each of these genres he considers to serve a distinct purpose, appealing different emotions and engaging the audience in different ways.

He then provides a detailed analysis of the genre of tragedy as a classification of poetry. He defines tragedy as the imitation of an action that is complete, serious, that invokes the language of pleasure which is performed by the actors not through narration but by performance that awakens a process of catharsis in the audience. He lays down six essential components of tragedy as - plot, character, diction, reasoning, spectacle and lyric poetry. He put plot at the top of the hierarchy of the six components and terms it as the soul of the tragedy.

Aristotle dives deeper into each of the six components of tragedy starting with plot. He insists that there must be a clear beginning, middle and end for a plot to be considered as whole. The plot must have magnitude and unity to achieve the success for the characters. Aristotle provides a vivid sketch of the tragic hero with tragic flow. In the process of defining the components, he constantly credits poets like Homer for his works 'The Iliad', 'The Odyssey'. He clarifies his understanding of good tragic plot, the one that is complex rather than simple.

Aristotle provides four kinds of tragedies- complex, suffering, character and simple. He also sheds light on the importance of the other elements like astonishments, spectacle, chorus and most importantly diction. Diction he defines as a whole has many elements like phoneme, syllables, connective, noun, verb, conjunction, inflection, utterance. He defines each of these elements vividly.

Epic poetry he recognizes to have the same characteristics as that of a tragedy, except it is more descriptive in length written in verse form. He acknowledges length as an important distinctive resource for epic poetry. Heroic verse is praised to be most adequate for the genre. He credits Homer for aligning all the components properly in his works - 'The Iliad' and 'The Odyssey'.

Aristotle describes the poet like a painter to be engaged in imitation. In addition, he recognizes two errors in poetry that might occur in the process - while one is intrinsic, the other is incidental. He defines both of these errors with instances in which they occur.

In the final segment of "Poetics", Aristotle examines the question of whether epic poetry or tragedy is greater and superior. He concludes with tragedy being the superior as it contains all the elements of epic poetry within a concrete structure and provides more pleasure without breaking the concentration that too within a limited time.

- **Analysis**

Poetics is organized into several sections that address different aspects of poetry and drama with a primary emphasis on "Tragedy", which Aristotle regards as the highest form of artistic expression.

Aristotle begins by exploring different forms of artistic expression and categorizing them as modes of "imitation" or mimesis. By "imitation," Aristotle refers to the artist's endeavor to represent reality, emotions, or human actions through various art forms.

"Epic poetry and tragedy, as also comedy, dithyrambic poetry and most flute playing and lyre- playing are all viewed as a whole, mode of imitation……" (2. Poetics)

Aristotle lists epic poetry, tragedy, comedy, dithyrambic poetry, and music like flute and lyre-playing as art forms that imitate life, though each differs in its manner and mode of representation. Aristotle's through these examples asserts that "imitation" reflects the essence of human experience in different forms.

Aristotle argues that mimesis is deeply ingrained in human nature. From initial stages i.e. childhood, humans learn and find pleasure in imitation, particularly when it reflects human actions and emotions.

"Imitation comes naturally to human beings from childhood...so does the universal pleasure in imitations.' (Line 48(b) - 3.1 'Poetics')

Aristotle's observation here emphasizes that the instinct to imitate is fundamental to human nature and forms the basis of artistic creation. Aristotle traces imitation and the pleasure derived through it to be the reasons for development of poetry as an art form of expression.

Aristotle divides the object how imitation into superior action and inferior action. Comedy he attributes to be *"an imitation of inferior people"(49(a)- 3.4 Poetics)* and *"identifies it as the laughable species of what is disgraceful"(49(a)-3.4 Poetics)*. The proper object of comic imitation is however not *"every sort of fault"*, but *"the ridiculous which is a series of the ugly and distorted but does not involve pain"(49(a)-3.4 Poetics)*.

Aristotle credits Sicily and Crates among the Athenian poets who were responsible for plot construction for comedy. he credits Crates who abandoned the trivial forms and constructed plots which were universally acceptable and suited the genre.

"..it is not known who introduced masks prologues number of actors and so forth.But plot construction came originally from Sicily; among Athenian poets it was Crates who first abandoned the form of lampoon and began to construct universalised stories and plots."(3.4- 49(b) Poetics)

Aristotle defines tragedy by breaking down its essential characteristics and its purpose.

"Tragedy is an imitation of an action that is admirable, complete and possess magnitude; in language made pleasurable, each of its species separated in different parts; performed by actions, not through narration; effecting through pity and fear, the purification of such emotions." (49(b) - 4.1 'Poetics')

Each part of the definition reflects a key aspect of how tragedy functions to create meaning and emotional impact on the audience. Aristotle defines "Tragedy" as the imitation of an action that is serious, complete and possesses magnitude. These actions he asserts are performed by actions, rather than narrated and aims to evoke pity and fear to accomplish catharsis. The primary function of tragedy according to the definition is that the action being imitated must be 'serious' meaning that it deals with important and meaningful human experiences. Aristotle makes it clear through the definition that tragedy doesn't concern itself with trivial matters, but with the realities of life, such as suffering loss and moral dilemmas. Moreover, the action depicted must be 'complete' in the sense that it possesses a clear harmony.

Since tragedy as an art form, is an imitation of an action, it is embodied by specific agents, or characters, who perform it. These agents or characters are not simply passive figures but are rather acting participants in the unfolding drama and imitate the actions of reality in the narrative. As the characters enact their roles their moral dilemmas and tragic flows become visible and tangible, enhancing the cathartic effect of pity and fear.

"Tragedy as a whole necessarily has six component parts which determine the tragedy quality i.e. plots, character, diction, reasoning, spectacle and lyric poetry."

(50(a) - 4.2 'Poetics')

These six components he regards are essential for a well-constructed tragedy to evoke pity and fear, ultimately leading to the cathartic experience for the audience.

Among the six components, he considers "plot" at the top of the hierarchy.

"Plot is the imitation of the action" (50(a) - 4.2 'Poetics')

Aristotle states that plot is "the imitation of the action." By this, he means that the plot is the essence of a tragedy, the structured arrangement through which the series of events and incidents is presented to the audience. The plot is the framework that organizes this action coherently and purposefully, with a clear beginning, middle, and end. Through the plot, the tragedy imitates life's complexities, including moral choices, reversals of fortune, and the consequences of actions. The events in the plot should be interconnected, with each action or event leading naturally to the next. He insists of the consistency in a plot that must occur.

"A whole is that which has a beginning, a middle and an end" (50(b) - 5.1 'Poetics')

Aristotle describes the fundamental structure of a unified and complete tragedy, emphasizing that it must have a beginning, middle, and end. This structured approach ensures that the events are logically connected, guiding the audience smoothly from one point to the other.

The character's actions should reflect a moral purpose and must have conduct consistently, in ways that are true to their established traits and nature. Aristotle draws a sketch of characteristics that define the characters in a tragedy, particularly focusing on the tragic hero. The characters must meet certain criteria to make the tragedy compelling. They must possess effectively to evoke emotions of pity and catharsis. He defines four features that the characters must have: goodness, appropriateness, likeness, consistency. (53(b) - 8.1 'Poetics').

A well-constructed tragedy, according to Aristotle, involves the depiction of a significant reversal of fortune; a shift from good to bad fortune or vice versa or from bad to worse, which would affect the protagonist. Magnitude according to him is not merely about length but of appropriate scale, ensuring that the plot has sufficient scope to encompass significant events, moral depth and emotional resonance.

Aristotle next defines diction as the medium through which ideas, thoughts and emotions are expressed in language. It is not merely about the choice of words, but how those words function within the overall artistic expression

"Diction as a whole has the following elements: Phoneme, syllable, connective, noun, verb, conjunction, inflection, utterance." (56(b) - 9.2 'Poetics')

Aristotle defines diction to have numerous elements like phoneme, syllables, connective, noun etc. each of them having their role in the whole. Diction must serve both clarity and expressiveness, contributing to the audience's understanding and emotional engagement with the play.

Epic poetry, Aristotle provides that like tragedy imitates noble actions and elevated subjects but it differs in it's method of presentation, relying on narrative rather than direct enactment.

"Epic is differentiated in the length of its plot structure and in it's verse form." (59(b) - 10.3 'Poetics')

Aristotle distinguishes epic poetry from tragedy based on two key characteristics: the length of its plot structure and its verse form. These distinctions help to clarify the unique qualities of epic poetry as a genre and how it functions differently from tragedy. Unlike tragedy that Aristotle asserts to be bound by limitations of time focusing on single action, the epic is not bound by such. It can cover long periods of time and a wide array of events.

In the concluding section, Aristotle examines upon the question of whether epic or tragedy is superior, since both have almost the same components. He comes to the conclusion that tragedy is superior in all terms as it generates more pleasure as in the form of catharsis that too in a limited period of time without breaking the concentration which is less in case of epic.

"Tragedy has everything that epic does (it can even make use of it's verse form) and additionally it has a major component part music and spectacle; this is a source of intense pleasure." (62 (b) - 12.2 'Poetics')

Although Aristotle acknowledges the grandeur structure of narrative of epic, to advocate for tragedy as there is no scope for digression and subplots. Since it is performed on stage for a limited time it maintains the curiosity and enthusiasm of the audience.

Aristotle concludes his discussion with these views on the two genres.

> *Important terms to remember*
>
> ❖ *Mimesis: Imitation*
> ❖ *Mythos: Plot-story-fiction*
> ❖ *Hamartia: Tragic flaw*
> ❖ *Hubris: Pride*
> ❖ *Peripeteia: The sudden reversal in fortune*
> ❖ *Anagnorisis: The discovery of truth in the house of the plot*

3. Probable questions:

1. Evaluate the key concepts of mimesis as outlined by Aristotle in the 'Poetics'.

Answer:

Aristotle's theory of mimesis in his critical assessment 'Poetics' refers to the nature of art and poetry being imitative. But it is different from the one by his predecessor Plato. He begins the 'Poetics' with his theory of mimesis; the word 'Mimesis' that he takes up from Plato.

Aristotle defines mimesis or imitation as the key concept to his understanding of art as all creative art forms are imitative in nature.

"Epic poetry and tragedy, as also comedy, dithyrambic poetry and most flute playing and lyre- playing are al viewed as a whole, mode of imitation……" (47(a)-2. Poetics)

Aristotle considers imitation as the common basis of all fine arts. He refers to painting and all other visual arts in order to make a point about poetry. He considers these analogies as valid as all these are forms of mimesis.

Aristotle argues that mimesis is deeply ingrained in human nature. From initial stages human learn and find pleasure in imitation, particularly when it reflects human actions and emotions. For Aristotle mimesis is more than copying the external world - more about imitating actions, emotions and life itself, focusing on universal truths. He tracks the origin and evolution of poetry in mimesis. Rather than viewing it as a necessary derogative activity, he treats it as a basic human instinct and allows it as a way towards truth and knowledge. Imitation is treated as both as a mode of learning and also as a source of pleasure.

"Imitation comes naturally to human beings from childhood' (Line 48(b) - 3.1 'Poetics')

Aristotle further differentiates imitation into three aspects- medium, object and mode. These categories explain how various forms of art differ in the way they represent reality and human actions.

"...imitation can be differentiated in these three respects as we said at the outset, medium, object and mode." (Line 48(a) - 2.2 'Poetics')

By 'Medium' he refers to the materials or tools used to convey the imitation. Different art forms use different medium to represent their subjects. For instance, Poetry uses language to imitate actions and events, while "music uses melody and rhythm only." (Line 47(a) - 2.1 'Poetics'). Each art form relies on its medium to projects it's imitation of reality and the medium determines the nature of the artistic representation. Similarly, the object refers to what is being imitated in the artwork. He provides the instance of characters in a drama can be portrayed as better than or worse than or the same as they are in real life. He hereby provides the differences between comedy and tragedy as in the former the agents imitate noble and serious action while the latter is about imitating actions and persons who are inferior or ridiculous. The object just varies based on what the art form seeks to portray. Likewise, mode refers to the manner in which the imitation is presented or the way the imitation is presented.

While Plato in "The Republic" rejected poetry and tragedians and glorified the philosophers, Aristotle on the other hand deals with poetry and art from an aesthetic perspective rather than moral. It deals with the art of poetry and the essential qualities of it. Aristotle's stance is defensive in 'Poetics', as he asserts that a poet uses imaginative reconstruction of the reality to present in the form of poetry or dramatic poetry. Plato on the contrary condemned poetry and dramatic poetry as poor imitation of imitation that simply exerts "Likeness" rather than reality.

Aristotle treats poetry as an essential form of mimetic art, emphasizing its ability to imitate life and evoke profound emotional responses unlike Plato who criticized mimesis for leading people away from truth. Plato argues in 'The Republic' that art as imitation, is a copy of the material world, which is itself a flawed representation of the higher world of forms which is why he characterizes it to be thrice away from reality. He goes to the extent of asserting that it corrupts the soul by stirring irrational emotions. On the other hand, Aristotle's treatment of mimesis is a natural human activity that is essential learning and pleasure. He treats it as a process that starts from childhood itself. Aristotle views mimetic art form to evoke Catharsis into people which provides them with both emotional relief and moral insight. While Plato is concerned in his discourse about mimesis to promote and encourage irrationality and desires for censorship of certain forms of imitative art; Aristotle argues in 'Poetics' that forms of mimetic art like tragedy can provide moral reflections and promote virtues - considers tragedy as the highest form of mimetic art.

In conclusion, Aristotle's concept of mimesis is crucial to understand because it lays the foundation for western theories of art, literature and drama. His defense of imitation as a natural human process and its being as a reflection of reality allows for the appreciation of art and other creative forms. It provides a framework for appreciating the transformative power of arts, it's emotional and educational significance.

2.Evaluate on Aristotle's assessment of plot in Tragedy.

OR

Analyze Aristotle's view on Tragedy and essentials of tragedy.

Answer:

Tragedy as a genre in literature focuses on serious and often tragic themes that typically involve human suffering, moral dilemmas, downfall of the main character etc. In essence it delves into the complex aspects of human life and fate along with moral conflicts.

Aristotle's theory of tragedy is rooted in his broader philosophical system which seeks to explain the nature of reality, human improvisation and evolution over time through the contributions of Aeschylus, Sophocles, and others into its natural form. Aristotle views imitation as a means of engaging with universal truths. He regards in tragedy; the imitation takes the form of depicting human action in a way that reveals deeper morals and existential truths. He defines tragedy as:

"Tragedy is an imitation of an action that is admirable, complete and possess magnitude; in language made pleasurable, each of its species separated in different parts; performed by actions, not through narration; effecting through pity and fear, the purification of such emotions." (49(b) - 4.1 'Poetics')

In other terms, Aristotle defines Tragedy as the imitation of an action that is serious, complete and possesses magnitude. These actions he asserts are performed by actions, rather than narrated and aims to evoke pity and fear to accomplish catharsis. The primary function of tragedy according to the definition is that the action being imitated must be 'serious' meaning that it deals with important and meaningful human experiences. Aristotle makes it clear through the definition that tragedy doesn't concern itself with trivial matters, but with the realities of life, such as suffering loss and moral dilemmas. Moreover, the action depicted must be 'complete' in the sense that it possesses a clear harmony.

Aristotle after defining tragedy as a form of imitation or 'mimesis', moves on to the role of agents i.e. the characters in the narrative of a tragedy.

He emphasizes on the active role of the agents who must actively embody the central themes of the play reflecting human experiences of reality.

"Tragedy is an imitation of an action, and the action is performed by certain agents."(49(b) - 4.1 'Poetics')

These agents or characters are not simply passive figures but are rather acting participants in the unfolding drama and imitate the actions of reality in the narrative. As the characters enact their roles their moral dilemmas and tragic flows become visible and tangible, enhancing the cathartic effect of pity and fear. Aristotle's focus on tragedy also highlights his broader theory of mimesis. Mimesis in tragedy as he asserts is not a mere replication of life, but an imitation of significant human actions.

Aristotle establishes an elaborate framework for a precise understanding of the structure and functions of tragedy. He identifies six essential elements for tragedy.

"Tragedy as a whole necessarily has six component parts which determine the tragedy quality i.e. plots, character, diction, reasoning, spectacle and lyric poetry."(50(a) - 4.2 'Poetics')

These six components he regards are essential for a well-constructed tragedy to evoke pity and fear, ultimately leading to the cathartic experience for the audience. Among the six, he places plot at the top of the hierarchy, defining it as:

"Plot is the imitation of the action" (50(a) - 4.2 'Poetics')

By plot here he clarifies to refer to the organization of events.

Plot or 'Mythos', Aristotle regards it as the 'soul' of tragedy for:

"Tragedy is not imitation of persons, but of actions and of life." (50(a) - 4.3 'Poetics')

He further terms it as the 'source' of tragedy. He defines a structure for the organization of the events. For him, a tragedy must have a unified plot, meaning that the events must exist in consistent to each other linked in a coherent structure with a clear 'beginning', 'middle' and 'an end':

"A whole is that which has a beginning, a middle and an end" (50(b) - 5.1 'Poetics')

Aristotle clearly insists that plot must be complete i.e. it should have the clear beginning, middle and end to culminate the action of imitation. The beginning doesn't necessarily follow from anything else but rather introduces the characters and the situation of action; the middle likewise involves a series of events that follow the former, while the end at last should bring the narrative to a resolution and leaves nothing else after it. Aristotle believes that structural coherence is essential for achieving the catholic effect which he considers as the purpose of tragedy. Without a clear and logical progression, the tragedy would lose its essence of serious action. Aristotle credits Homer for his excellence in the aspect of setting the plot in 'The Iliad' and 'The Odyssey'.

 The unity of action like plot is also essential so that it can evoke the emotions of the audience. The unity of action, Aristotle asserts that the tragedy is not fragmented.

"...as the imitation of an action should imitate a single, unified action and one that is also a whole." (51(a) - 5.4 'Poetics')

The notion of action is central to Aristotle's views of tragedy as it unifies the other components and features including plot, character, diction, thought, spectacle and song. Aristotle defines this unity in terms of both space and time. He also introduces magnitude as an essential component in his discourse. Magnitude according to him is not merely about length but of appropriate scale, ensuring that the plot has sufficient scope to encompass significant events, moral depth and emotional resonance.

A well-constructed tragedy, according to Aristotle, involves the depiction of a significant reversal of fortune; a shift from good to bad fortune or vice versa or from bad to worse, which would affect the protagonist.

"The magnitude in which a series of events occurring sequentially in accordance with probability or necessity gives rise to a change from good fortune to bad fortune, or from bad fortune to good fortune is an adequate definition of magnitude." (51(a) - 5.2 'Poetics')

The magnitude of this reversal is essential for eliciting the audience's emotions of pity and fear, ultimately leading to catharsis. He argues that the best tragic plots are those that include a significant change in fortune, typically from state of happiness or success to one of suffering or downfall.

Aristotle draws a sketch of characteristics that define the characters in a tragedy, particularly focusing on the tragic hero. The characters must meet certain criteria to make the tragedy compelling. They must possess effectively to evoke emotions of pity and catharsis. He defines four features that the characters must have: goodness, appropriateness, likeness, consistency. (53(b) - 8.1 'Poetics'). He provides example of the character of Odysseus as consistent in the plot. Aristotle provides that the characters in a tragedy must act consistently. Their actions and decisions should align with the personality traits they exhibit throughout the play. Inconsistencies in character's behavior disrupt the audience's engagement which distracts the effectiveness of the tragic experience.

The next element diction, Aristotle defines it as the medium through which ideas, thoughts and emotions are expressed in language. It is not merely about the choice of words, but how those words function within the overall artistic expression. It plays a crucial role upon how the plot and characters are communicated. While the first element 'Plot' serves as the spirit and soul of a tragedy it is through diction that the nuances of the character's thoughts, motivations and emotions are revealed. Aristotle defines diction to have numerous elements like phoneme, syllables, connective, noun etc. each of them having their role in the whole.

The reasoning and lyric poetry among the other components form the integral parts. While reasoning refers to the intellectual content or thought in the tragedy; lyric poetry refers to the poetic and musical elements of the tragedy which are mostly expressed through the chorus.

Aristotle views reasoning as crucial since it conveys the themes and ideas of the play. Through valid and complex themes, the audience can be kept engaged into the plot. It allows the characters to express their motivations, beliefs and values which helps the audience to understand the underlying themes the tragedy seeks to convey. It is particularly evident when characters engage in dialogues or discuss to reflect on ethical dilemmas, justice, fates and other. Aristotle considers it essential in terms of plot construction. He insists that every tragedy consists of a complication and a resolution.

In the case of Lyric poetry, Aristotle acknowledges its importance for its emotional and aesthetic appeal. It contributes to the overall rhythm and mood of the tragedy. He defines it to serve as a bridge between the action and the audience.

"It should be part of the whole and should contribute to the performance."(Line 56(a) - 8.9 'Poetics')

He draws a difference between chorus and interludes and stays critical of poets and tragedians whose chorus have less to do with the action of the plot. He credits Sophocles for the appropriate portrayal of the chorus in his plays.

The final element i.e. Spectacle refers to the visual and auditory elements that can enhance the emotional resonance with the action on the stage.

"In reversals and in simple actions poets use astonishments to achieve their chosen aims."(Line 56(a) - 8.8 'Poetics')

The spectacle and astonishments as Aristotle asserts must complement the tragedy but it should not dominate the plot and character developments.

Aristotle further provides that there are four kinds of tragedy which can be distinguished through his analysis of tragic elements, plot structures and other elements.

"There are four kinds of tragedy: Complex Tragedy, depending entirely on reversal and recognition; Tragedy of suffering (e.g. Plays about Ajax or Ixion); Tragedy of character (e.g. Woman of Phthia and Peleus); and fourth, simply Tragedy (e.g. Daughters of Phoreys,

Prometheus, and plays set in the world)."(56(a) - 8.6 'Poetics')

He insists about four kinds - complex tragedy, tragedy of suffering, tragedy of character and simple tragedy. The categorization he insists can be done only by comparing and contrasting the plots and proper examination of whether the complication and resolution are the same. Each of the kind he mentions reflects different mechanisms for achieving the tragic effect of pity, fear and ultimately catharsis.

Aristotle's analysis of tragedy as form of mimesis thus, provides a systematic framework for understanding tragedy which has influenced the development of dramatic theory throughout western literature. His concepts of plot, character, diction, spectacle, reasoning, chorus together enhance the catharsis which he recognizes as the intent of mimetic works.

4. How does Aristotle differentiate between tragedy and epic? Elaborate.

OR

5. Access Aristotle's assessment of epic poetry.

Answer:

[Include a brief assessment of Aristotle's views regarding tragedy]

Aristotle draws a clear distinction between two major forms - epic poetry and tragedy. He insists that both these forms are the result of imitation of human experiences and actions. He agrees that both the genres represent serious and morally significant subjects, usually involving heroic figures or characters who embody universal human qualities.

"Epic must also have the same kind of tragedy; it is either simple or complex, or based on character or on suffering." (59(b) - 10.2 'Poetics')

Aristotle recognizes that except lyric poetry in epic, all the other components are the same like tragedy. He credits Homer as the first epic poet to have excelled in using all the components in his epics - 'The Iliad' and 'The Odyssey'.

Epic poetry like tragedy imitates noble actions and elevated subjects but it differs in its method of presentation, relying on narrative rather than direct enactment.

"Epic is differentiated in the length of its plot structure and in it's verse form." (59(b) - 10.3 'Poetics')

Unlike tragedy that Aristotle asserts to be bound by limitations of time focusing on single action, the epic is not bound by such. It can cover long periods of time and a wide array of events.

"Epic has an important distinctive resource for extending its length. In tragedy it is not possible .... may cause tragedy to fail."

For Aristotle this larger scope is a distinctive strength of the epic form. It provides space for detailed description, multiple incidents and various subplots, all of which contribute to the narrative for being effective. While epic poetry allows for episodic structure, tragedy must maintain a tight structure, ensuring that every element contributes to the inevitable resolution of the central conflict.

Aristotle addresses the verse form of epic poetry and regards its suitability for the grandeur of the epic form. He praises the Heroic verse to uplift the impact of the narrative in epic.

"Heroic verse is the most stately and grandiose form of verse."

The Heroic verse aligns with the length and scope of epic narratives allowing for more elaborate descriptions and extended storytelling which is central to the epic tradition. The heroic verse refers to the dactylic hexameter, a meter made up of six metrical feet, which was traditionally used in Greek epic poetry, including works of Homer - 'The Iliad', 'The Odyssey'.

Aristotle in the concluding section of the discourse examines the question of whether epic imitation or tragic is superior as both have the almost same components. He through his agreements provides the answer that the tragedy is superior in comparison. While he acknowledges the grandeur and flexibility of the epic form, he still considers tragedy to have a higher artistic impact.

"Tragedy has everything that epic does (it can even make use of its verse form) and additionally it has a major component part music and spectacle; this is a source of intense pleasure." (62 (b) - 12.2 'Poetics')

Tragedy is recognized by him to allow for greater complexity and evoke greater emotional expression. It can generate more pleasure in comparison to epic through its additional components like music, and spectacle within a limited period of time without breaking the concentration. The tight structure of tragedy contributes to the intensity of the emotional experience although Aristotle recognizes that epic can maintain unity of action, its broader scope allows for more digression and subplots which breaks the contraction in the narrative.

"......the epic poet's imitation is less unified." (62(b) - 12.2 'Poetics')

Aristotle believes that concentrated forms of tragedy heighten the emotional intensity, making the experience more powerful than the more extended narratives of epic poetry. By witnessing the dramatic action unfold, the audience of a tragedy experiences a deeper emotional response which Aristotle regards as central to its artistic value. Tragedy due its concentrated format is preferable both in reading as well in performance.

"It has vividness in reading as well as in performance." (62(b) - 12.2 'Poetics')

In Conclusion, Aristotle argues that tragedy is superior to epic poetry due to its tighter structure, greater emotional impact, and concentrated focus on the action, although he acknowledges the grandeur of epic poetry.

6. Evaluate Aristotle's treatment of Diction.

Answer:
Diction in general refers to the choice of words and style of expression that an author or speaker uses. It can

convey tone, mood, and character and can vary. In 'Poetics', Aristotle defines diction - 'Lexis' as one of the six essential elements of tragedy along with plot, character, thoughts, spectacle and melody. His examination of diction provides a detailed framework for understanding how language operates in tragedy. He describes diction to have numerous elements:

"Diction as a whole has the following elements: Phoneme, syllable, connective, noun, verb, conjunction, inflection, utterance." (56(b) - 9.2 'Poetics')

Aristotle defines diction as the medium through which ideas, thoughts and emotions are expressed in language. It refers to the choice of words, their arrangement, and the style of delivery within a tragedy. Diction is not merely the words themselves but how those words function within the overall artistic expression. Diction therefore must serve both clarity and expressiveness, contributing to the audience's understanding and emotional engagement with the play. Diction plays a crucial role as it shapes how the plot and character are communicated. While plot serves as the "soul" of tragedy, it is through diction that the nuances of the character's thoughts, motivations and emotions are revealed. For Aristotle, diction is the verbal embodiment of the dramatic action, allowing abstract ideas to take concrete form.

Aristotle dives deeper into each of the components of diction. He starts with Phoneme and defines it as -

"A Phoneme is an indivisible vocalization." (56(b) - 9.2 'Poetics')

Phoneme is an abstract representation of sounds that speakers of a language perceive as distinct. He refers to Phoneme to differ in the shape of the mouth, in the point of contact. He apprehends speech as composition of various sounds which can be thought of as components that create meaning. He further classifies Phoneme as vowels, continuant and mutes.

Syllable, the second element of diction, Aristotle approaches it as a unit of sound that is formed by the combination of one or more phonemes. He defines it as -

"A syllable is a non - signifying composite vocalization comprising a mute and phoneme which has an audible sound." (56(b) - 9.2 'Poetics')

Although Aristotle doesn't provide a clear definition of syllable, he recognizes the structural aspects of syllables and their significance in creating rhythm and musicality, which are fundamental to the aesthetic experience of Poetic works. His insight into syllables reflect an early awareness of how sound and structure contribute to meaning and expression in language.

Connective, the third element is not explicitly defined by Aristotle. However, he explores how connectives aid in persuasive speech and writing. The use of connectives helps in structuring arguments and in guiding the audience through the speaker's reasoning. He insists that the arrangement of connectives can affect the emotional impact of a speech. He in this segment focuses more on non-signifying vocalization which neither prevents nor affects the composition of a single significant vocalization from two or more vocalizations.

Now he describes it as one of the fundamental parts of speech. He defines it as "a composite significant vocalization" which doesn't express tense (57(a) - 9.2 'Poetics').

Verb, he considers to have a significant vocalization that does refer to tense. Aristotle's examination of verbs occurs within his broader discussions of language used in poetry and tragedy. While Aristotle doesn't formally categorize verbs as modern linguistics, rather he recognizes them as functions.

"The significance of 'walks' or 'walked' includes present and past tense respectively." (97(a) - 9.2 'Poetics')

Inflection, Aristotle recognizes as crucial role in the structure of language, allowing for the pre use expression of relationships between words in sentences. He defines it as the modes of expression. The inflection of a noun according to him indicates its role in the sentence, whether as a subject, direct object, or indirect object.

Lastly, Aristotle defines utterance to refer to the vocal expression of thoughts, ideas, or emotions through language. In his view utterance is a fundamental aspect of human communication. He asserts that not every utterance is a composition of a verb and a noun and even possible with no verb but not without a noun. He recognizes that effective utterance relies on clarity, style, and the speaker's ability to engage the audience and evoke catharsis.

Aristotle considers the figures of speech as an important aspect of diction. The way the characters of a tragedy speak is reflected in the choice of words and style of expression. Aristotle emphasizes that tragedy should employ elevated diction to reflect the seriousness of its themes. Elevated diction serves to enhance the aesthetic experience of the audience, allowing them to engage more deeply with the tragic events.

In Conclusion, Aristotle views diction as a fundamental element of tragedy for conveying catharsis. By effectively employing diction, playwrights can create profound and impactful tragic experiences.

7. Analyze Aristotle's view on comedy and essentials of comedy .

Answer:
Aristotle divides the object how imitation into superior action and inferior action. Comedy he attributes to be *"an imitation of inferior people"(49(a)- 3.4 Poetics)* and *"identifies it as the laughable species of what is disgraceful"(49(a)-3.4 Poetics)*. The proper object of comic imitation is however not *"every sort of fault"*, but *"the ridiculous which is a series of the ugly and distorted but does not involve pain"(49(a)-3.4 Poetics)*. Comedy imitates the subject of ridicule and human folly but it does so through a filter that excludes that tragic consequences of moral feeling. In comedy folly is revealed through ridicule and exercised not through death or destruction but through laughter and exposure. "Laughable errors" or disgraces don't involve pain, but for instance, a comedic mask may be ugly and distorted but it does not reflect pain. This indicates the philosophical tension in his theory of comedy premised on a disjunction between the aesthetic deformity of a

character and the ethical or emotional consequences typically associated with it.

From the fact that comedy is an imitation of the inferior action derives the requirement that it should represent a complete and whole action with magnitude and must have the same constitutive elements as tragedy. As in form of imitation it has to speak somehow of 'the universal'. Comic action too should likewise contain a proper 'beginning, middle and end' and should proceed in necessary or probable sequence. He asserts the comic form to be larger than the iambic poem. There is no Aristotelian equivalent to catharsis in comedy in the extent 'Poetics', but later texts such as the 'Tractatus Colslinianus' taken to be a possible synopsis of Aristotle's lost work on comedy suggests that comedy like tragedy involves the process of catharsis through laughter, joy, follies instead of pity and fear while tragedy elicits fear and pity to purge these emotions through dramatic structure, comedy presumably purges vanity, arrogance, or other tendencies by provoking laughter and the absurdities of human pretentions. Through the loss sections on comedy of Aristotle cannot confirm whether he held the same view for comedy as he did for tragedy, the extent commentary allows one to infer a differing emphasis. Comedy by its nature leans more on character types and situations on the depiction of recognizable, exaggerated figures such as the boastful hero, cunning slave or the miser merchant, etc. These characters in the plot of comedy do not undergo development or face irreversible consequences as the characters in tragedy plots do. Instead comedy reveals the notions of repetition and restoration. The plots may turn on mistaken identities, coincidences, folly incidents, to provoke laughter while reaffirming a normative order.

Aristotle affirms that comedy as a genre has not always been taken seriously, so little attention was paid to it. It took a long time for devices like the chorus to become a standard feature for the genre. It is therefore unclear which comic poets were responsible for the development of comedy and introduction of props like use of masks, the number of actors, and presence of prologues at the beginning. Aristotle credits Sicily and Crates among the Athenian poets who were responsible for plot construction for comedy. he credits Crates who abandoned the trivial forms and constructed plots which were universally acceptable and suited the genre.

"..it is not known who introduced masks prologues number of actors and so forth.But plot construction came originally from Sicily; among Athenian poets it was Crates who first abandoned the form of lampoon and began to construct universalised stories and plots."(3.4- 49(b) Poetics)

The disdain for the comic is less overt in case of Aristotle but more insidious than Plato's outright censure. In "The Republic", Plato banishes the comic poets' from encouraging irrationality, disorder and mockery of the respectable. Aristotle on the other hand allows for the existence of comedy but confines it to the realm of the ridiculous and inferior. Comedy in this framework, is the art of containment that isolates the ridiculous, contains it's threat through ridicule and neutralizes its transgressive potential through laughter. In Aristotelian terms the comic character is exposed for its preventions his ignorance or his vice. While Aristotle attempts closely to diction, thought and plot devices and construction in case of tragedy he offers no analysis of such techniques, no taxonomy of comic figures, no meditation on irony or parody in 'Poetics'.

In conclusion, Aristotle's views on comedy in 'Poetics' through limited and often evasive offer a complex and valiant foundation for thinking about the genre. Though it is fragmented and incomplete, it is not devoid of historical theoretical substance; reaffirms the vitality of human nature, being imitation of life.

7. Short notes:

a) Hamartia

Answer:

Hamartia refers to describing a tragic flaw or error in judgment that leads to the downfall of the protagonist, particularly in classical tragedy. The concept of hamartia is considered essential to creating a character in a tragedy who is relatable yet flawed, evoking pity and fear in the audience.

Aristotle in "Poetics" defines hamartia in Poetics as the "error" or "mistake" that leads to the tragic hero's downfall. According to Aristotle, the tragic hero should be a man who is not, however, pre-eminently "virtuous and just", whose misfortune, however, is brought upon him not by vice and depravity but by some "error" or "tragic flaw". In simple words, the tragic hero is neither purely good nor entirely wicked but rather stumbles into disaster by a misstep that is, perhaps, born of ignorance, pride, or rash judgment which he terms as the tragic fall.

Aristotle implies that the tragic flaw is not superficial in a tragedy but instead is a reflection of imperfections of human nature and experience. In this context he considers the "error" to add to the element of 'catharsis', as the audience can relate to the imperfections depicted in the tragic character. Aristotle further adds to the cathartic nature of 'hamartia' through anagnorisis (recognition) and peripeteia (reversal). While anagnorisis marks the moment when the hero discovers their truth for the first time; peripeteia refers to the sudden turn of fortune that brings them down from grace to despair. He cites "Oedipus Rex", where this dual blow lands when Oedipus, realizing the full horror of his actions, is stripped of his royal dignity, cast down from a life of respect into shame and ruin. Here, hamartia unravels not only Oedipus's life but the very fabric of the world he believed he knew, bringing the audience face to face with the tragic irony of human nature. Hamartia in this sense is crucial to the structure of the tragedy since it transforms the hero's fate from an act of mere "misfortune" into a compelling, instructive downfall. The tragic flaw thereby creates catharsis, allowing the audience to experience and release emotions of pity and fear.

Thus, hamartia is not simply a character flaw but a pivotal element that gives tragedy its depth, portraying the tension between human choices and the forces beyond our control.

b) Peripeteia

Answer:
Aristotle while drawing a framework for tragedy recognizes six essential elements. He introduces magnitude as an essential component in his discourse that falls under "action". Magnitude according to him is not merely about length but of appropriate scale, ensuring that the plot has sufficient scope to encompass significant events, moral depth and emotional resonance.

A well-constructed tragedy, according to Aristotle, involves the depiction of a significant reversal of fortune. The shift from good to bad fortune or vice versa or from bad to worse, which would affect the protagonist. "Peripeteia" he refers to as a "reversal of fortune" or a sudden change in a character's circumstances, often shifting from prosperity to disaster in tragedy. This reversal is a pivotal moment in the plot, where actions produce an outcome opposite to what was intended or expected.

"The magnitude in which a series of events occurring sequentially in accordance with probability or necessity gives rise to a change from good fortune to bad fortune, or from bad fortune to good fortune is an adequate definition of magnitude." (51(a) - 5.2 'Poetics')

The magnitude or depth of this reversal is essential for eliciting the audience's emotions of pity and fear, ultimately leading to catharsis. Peripeteia signifies the dramatic shift in direction for the main character's fortunes, often moving from prosperity to catastrophe. Aristotle's concept of peripeteia revolves around his view of tragedy as a reflection of human life, where events can change dramatically due to forces beyond an individual's control. He argues that the best tragic plots are those that include a significant change in fortune, typically from state of happiness or success to one of suffering or downfall. Aristotle explains that the best tragedies combine the elements of "peripeteia" with recognition so that the reversal and recognition occur simultaneously, creating an intense emotional experience and a profound sense of irony. Aristotle cites the classic example of it in 'Oedipus Rex', where the revelation of truth leads to the turn of events that carry the depth in magnitude of effecting the audience.

c) Catharsis

Answer:

Aristotle refers 'Kathersis' or 'Catharsis' as the emotional experience that audiences undergo when engaging with tragic narratives, specifically through the emotions of pity and fear. He recognizes catharsis as the ultimate goal and purpose of tragedy.

Aristotle's concept of catharsis can be derived from his definition of tragedy,

"Tragedy is an imitation of an action that is admirable, complete and possess magnitude; in language made pleasurable, each of its species separated in different parts; performed by actions, not through narration; effecting through pity and fear, the purification of such emotions." (49(b) - 4.1 'Poetics')

The "effecting through pity" and "purification" of emotions can be achieved only when all the components of a tragedy are present and consistent to each other, which takes the audience into another dimension of emotional expression. Although Aristotle does not extensively elaborate on the term 'catharsis', it is generally understood as the emotional release or purification experienced by the audience through their engagement with tragedy. The effect is both psychological and moral. By engaging with the intense emotions in an artistic form, the audience undergoes a psychological release or "cleansing" that restores emotional balance and evokes self-reflection.

Thus, 'catharsis' is regarded as the ultimate role of tragedy as it encapsulates the emotional, psychological, moral, and social functions that tragic narratives serve.

4. References and Suggested readings:

i.   Aristotle Poetics (Penguin Classics)
ii.   The poetics of Aristotle (https://www.gutenberg.org)
iii. Schaper, Eva. "Aristotle's Catharsis and Aesthetic Pleasure." The Philosophical Quarterly, Vol.18.
iv.   Dr. P. Jayalakshmi: Aristotle: Hamartia and Catharsis.
v.   The Classical Quarterly (2021): "The Beauty of Failure: Hamartia in Aristotle's Poetics."
vi.   James Kachere: Aristotle ideas of Tragedy

UNIT- 2

HORACE: ARS POETICA

1. **About the author**
    a. His early and later life
    b. His notable works

2. **Ars Poetica**
    a. Introduction
    b. Synopsis
    c. Analysis

3. **Probable Questions**
    a. Evaluate on the principles of poetic decorum as proposed by Horace.
    b. How does Horace explain the concept of decorum in relation to character and action?
    c. In what ways does Horace's concept of decorum reflect coherence and unity?
    d. How does Horace define the role of a poet.
    e. Analyze the concept of "mad poet" as provided by Horace.

4. **References and suggested readings.**

1. About Horace

Horace(65–8 BCE) was a Roman poet; a central figure in the canon of Western literature, known for his profound influence on poetry, literary criticism, and the development of poetic forms. Horace's literary output is diverse, encompassing various genres, including satire, lyric poetry, and literary theory.

Quintus Horatius Flaccus, commonly known as Horace, was born in 65 BCE, in Venusia, a town in southern Italy. He was the son of a freedman who worked as a collector of taxes, which afforded Horace a good education. He studied at Rome and later in Athens, where he became acquainted with Greek philosophy and literature, influences that would permeate his later works.

His life unfolded during a period of significant upheaval in Roman history i.e. during the turbulent period following the assassination of Julius Caesar in 44 BCE. Horace was initially aligned with the Republican cause. He served in the army under Brutus, one of Caesar's assassins, but after Brutus's defeat at the Battle of Philippi in 42 BCE, Horace returned to Rome. He faced a period of uncertainty, having lost his family estate and fortune.

Upon his return, Horace began to establish his literary career. He was fortunate to gain the patronage of Maecenas, a close advisor to Emperor Augustus, who recognized Horace's talent and offered him financial support. This relationship significantly impacted Horace's career and allowed him to focus on poetry.

Horace's works include various genres, but he is best known for his "Odes," "Satires," and "Epodes." His Odes are a collection of lyric poems that express a range of themes, including love, philosophy, and the beauty of nature. His Satires provide a humorous and critical commentary on social issues and human behavior, while the Epodes consist of shorter, often more personal poems. Horace's poetry is characterized by its wit, emotional depth, and philosophical insights.

Horace died in 8 BCE, in Rome, leaving behind a legacy that would greatly influence Western literature. His work has inspired countless poets and writers throughout history, shaping the development of lyric poetry and literary criticism. His principles of poetic form and expression continue to resonate in literary discussions to this day.

His notable works:

1. *"Epistles"*

   Published around 20 BCE it comprises of a series of letters written in poetic form, these 20 epistles discuss topics like happiness, personal ethics, and friendship. They are reflective and philosophical, with Horace considering what it means to live a good life. He focuses on inner contentment, wisdom, and the avoidance of excess. Horace composed a second part at around 14 BCE. It contains only two epistles, with the second one, known as Ars Poetica (The Art of Poetry), being particularly influential. In Ars Poetica, Horace sets out principles of poetic composition and taste, discussing unity, decorum, character consistency, and the purpose of poetry.

2. *"Satires" (Sermones)*

The first book of Satires consists of ten poems published around 35 BCE that address human vices and societal issues. Horace comments on topics like wealth, ambition, and hypocrisy, using a conversational and self-mocking style. He presents himself as an observer of human folly, often highlighting his own flaws. In the second book it comprises of eight poems, Horace continues his reflections but adopts a more philosophical tone, delving into questions of human nature and morality.

3. *"Odes" (Carmina)*

Books I-III said to be written and published around 23 BCE. The first three books of Odes consist of 88 poems, where Horace addresses themes like the joy of simple pleasures, friendship, love, nature, political stability, and philosophical acceptance of fate. The next part Book IV was written and published around 13 BCE.It contains of about 15 poems that celebrate the virtues of Roman life and the emperor's achievements.

----

2. ARS POETICA

• Introduction

"*Ars Poetica*," often referred to as "The Art of Poetry", composed by Horace in 19 BCE, is a Latin verse-epistle that offers advice to aspiring poets on the principles of good poetry and drama. It examines various elements of poetic composition, including the significance of decorum, the need to balance emotion with reason, and the dual role of the poet as both a creator and an instructor. Written in the form of verses, it is structured as a series of reflections, maxims, and insights that convey Horace's views on the craft of writing, the responsibilities of poets, and the relationship between poetry and life.

"Ars Poetica" is composed in the form of a didactic poem, which means it is intended to teach and instruct. The text is written in hexameter and pentameter lines, a common meter in Latin poetry that lends a rhythmic quality to the work. The poem consists of 476 lines and nearly 30 maxims for young poets. It can be divided into several sections, each addressing different aspects of poetic creation. "Ars Poetica" offers a comprehensive exploration of the principles of poetry, highlighting the responsibilities of poets and the philosophical implications of their art.

Unlike his predecessors, Horace takes a more practical and prescriptive approach, focusing on the craft of poetry itself rather than delving into metaphysical concerns. His work is grounded in the realities of poetic composition and the responsibilities of poets to their audiences. He emphasizes on decorum, unity, and emotional resonance, making it more about the art and technique of writing poetry than about philosophical aspects. Horace presents the poet as a craftsman with specific responsibilities. He insists on the need for poets to consider their audience, maintain coherence, and balance emotion and reason. His view highlights the idea that poetry should serve both an artistic and a moral function. While he sets certain standards, Horace allows for creativity within those parameters, promoting a balance between technical skill and individual expression.

In conclusion, Horace's "Ars Poetica" has profoundly influenced the development of poetry by establishing foundational principles that guide poetic practice and criticism. One of its most significant contributions is the emphasis on decorum and the importance of unity and coherence in poetic works. The notion that poetry should engage with moral and ethical dimensions has also resonated through literary history. This idea became especially significant during the Renaissance and Neoclassical periods, where the ethical implications of art were debated extensively. Through its exploration of the craft and moral implications of poetry, "Ars Poetica" has played an essential role in shaping the development of poetic traditions and continues to inspire poets and critics alike.

- **Synopsis**

Horace advices on how the writers should approach their craft, emphasizing the importance of choosing appropriate subjects, exercising self-awareness, and using language with precision and creativity. Horace believes that good writing requires discipline, thoughtful selection, and an understanding of one's own capabilities.

Horace discusses the evolution of language, emphasizing that language should grow and adapt over time to meet new needs and reflect changing societies. He encourages Roman poets and writers to enrich the Latin language, drawing inspiration from Greek and creating new expressions as needed, as long as they do so thoughtfully and sparingly.

Horace advises poets on the importance of consistency, originality, and focus in their work. He emphasizes that if a writer chooses to create new characters or reinterpret traditional ones, they must maintain consistency in character portrayal and narrative structure. He warns against ambitious yet misguided attempts that lack coherence, urging writers to present their ideas clearly and with well-crafted unity.

Horace advises writers and dramatists on the art of characterization and appropriate portrayal on stage. He begins by stating that if playwrights want the audience to remain engaged until the final applause, they must accurately depict the traits and behaviors appropriate to each stage of life. He addresses the style and tone appropriate for Satyr plays, a genre that blends elements of tragedy with light-hearted, often coarse humor.

Horace contrasts the evolution of Greek and Roman theatre, recognizing the innovations and discipline of Greek playwrights while lamenting the lack of revision and polish in Roman works.

Horace discusses the dual purpose of poetry: to instruct and to entertain. He argues that poets should aim to both benefit and delight their audience, as the most memorable and valuable works are those that combine practical wisdom with enjoyment.

Horace explores the relationship between innate talent and learned skill in creating exceptional poetry, cautioning against the pitfalls of flattery, emphasizing that both natural ability and rigorous training are crucial for success, likening it to the dedicated practice of athletes and musicians, and criticizing those who rely on wealth or status rather than craftsmanship.

- **Analysis**

Horace's 'Ars Poetica' can be classified as a verse-letter with directions for a poet. The poem is divided into various sections each focusing on a different aspect of poetry.

Ars Poetica: 1- 37 On unity and Harmony

"If a painter had chosen to set a human head
On a horse's neck, covered a melding olimbs.
Everywhere, with multi-coloured plumage, so.
That what was a lovely woman, at the top,
Ended repulsively in the tail of a black fish:
Asked to a viewing, could you sniffle laughter, my
friends?"
(Ars Poetica)

In these opening lines of 'Ars Poetica', Horace presents a vivid and absurd image to illustrate the importance of coherence and unity in art. He illustrates a painter who creates a deformed creature by combining unrelated parts: a human head attached to a horse's neck, limbs covered in bird feathers, and a woman's upper body ending in the tail of a black fish. This bizarre combination of elements, although individually familiar, results in a repulsive and laughable whole. By painting this picture, Horace warns against the arbitrary mixing of unrelated elements in any form of artistic creation, including poetry. Just as the disjointed parts make the painting absurd rather than beautiful, a poem that constitutes unrelated images or ideas loses its aesthetic value and becomes incoherent. For Horace, each element of an artwork should be chosen carefully to serve a unified vision, rather than existing as isolated or deformed parts. This warning is not merely about visual harmony but about maintaining thematic and conceptual unity, so that the audience can appreciate the work as a complete, harmonious entity rather than a confusing or laughable mess.

"To a unified form. 'But painters and poets
Have always shared the right to dare anything.'"
(Ars Poetica)

He acknowledges poetic liberty but is critical of its abusive use by poets. Horace's views on decorum is rooted in the idea that poetry should be a unified whole, with every part contributing to a cohesive and harmonious effect. He insists that art requires discipline and careful structuring. He continues with examples, such as contrasting "wild and tame" animals or "snakes" and "birds," to reinforce that certain elements simply do not belong together, even in creative work. Horace uses the example of a wine-jar transforming into a pitcher to highlight how the integrity of form should be maintained through artistic processes.

"In despair? It started out as a wine-jar: then why,
As the wheel turns round does it end up a pitcher?"
(Ars Poetica)

Through this imagery he insists that works should remain true to their original nature, avoiding changes that distort their intended form. Horace again provides an example of a painter who might depict a dolphin in a forest or a boar in the ocean, highlighting the absurdity of creating art that disregards natural order and context.

"But the man who wants to distirt something unnaturally
Paints a dolphin among trees, a boar in the waves."
(Ars Poetica)

Horace through this metaphor reinforces his advice that, while creativity is essential, it should not defy basic principles of coherence and appropriateness of nature.

"The humblest craftsman, down by Aemilius' School,
Who moulds finger-nails in bronze, imitates wavy hair,
Isunhappy with the result, because he's unable
To create a whole…"
(Ars Poetica)

Horace then introduces the figure of the "humblest craftsman", referring to "Aemilius' School," who focuses passionately on minor details, such as imitating wavy hair or intricate fingernails in bronze. Such craftsman represents artists who become so focused on specific details that they lose sight of the broader composition and unity of their work. Horace remarks on the importance of embracing natural flaws rather than striving for unnatural perfection. He asserts that he would rather live "with a crooked nose", than attempting to reshape his identity into something inauthentic. He gives the notion that art should strive for naturalness and integrity over contrived flawlessness.

ArsPoetica: 38-72 The writer's aim

In this section of Horace provides advice on how writers should approach their craft, emphasizing the importance of choosing appropriate subjects, exercising self-awareness, and using language with precision.

"You who write, choose a subject that's matched by
Your powers, consider deeply what your shoulders
Can and cannot bear. Whoever chooses rightly"
(ArsPoetica)

Horace begins by advising writers to choose a subject that matches their abilities. He encourages self-assessment, reminding poets to consider what they "can and cannot bear." The writers should select topics they are equipped to handle both intellectually and emotionally, as choosing topics beyond one's skill can result in weak or ineffective writing. Horace suggests that writing should be direct and relevant, expressing "what's to be said here and now" as it encourages writers to stay focused on the present purpose of their work rather than becoming distracted by irrelevant details.

Horace insists on the importance of selection and refinement, encouraging writers to carefully decide what to include and omit in their writing. He advises writers to be "cautious and precise," implying that the quality of a piece often depends on the careful choice of words and ideas. Through this process, a writer weaves words together in a way that brings new life to common expressions, enhancing their charm and effectiveness.

"If you need to indicate abstruse things by novel terms.
It's your chance to invent ones the kilted Cethegi
Never heard: licence will be given you if wisely used:
Indeed, new-minted words will gain acceptance"
(ArsPoetica)

Horace acknowledges that sometimes writers may need to create new words if necessary, so long as they do so with wisdom and restraint. Horace asserts that newly coined words can gain acceptance if they serve a clear purpose and are used judiciously. His approach to poetic innovation is balanced; while he values tradition, he also allows for linguistic creativity, as long as it enhances the work rather than detracts from its clarity.

Horace argues that if Greek poets like Virgil and Varius are allowed to be innovating, the Roman poets too should likewise afford the same liberty. He questions why Romans would deny themselves the right to expand their language, as earlier poets like Caecilius, Plautus, Cato, and Ennius did. Horace argues that these earlier figures enhanced Latin with new terms and expressions, showing that language change have long been an accepted and celebrated tradition.

"Enriched our mother-tongue,? It's been our right, ever
Will be our right, to issue words that are fresh-stamped.
As the forests shed their leaves, as the year declines,
And the oldest fall, so perish those former generations"
(ArsPoetica)

He asserts that it is the right of each generation to introduce "fresh-stamped" words into the language. By comparing the aging and renewal of language to the natural cycle of forests shedding their leaves, Horace illustrates how older words fall out of use while new ones are born and thrive, much like the natural life cycle of living beings.

"And learnt better ways: our mortal works will vanish.
The beauty and charm of speech no more like to live.
Many words that are now unused will be rekindled.

Many fade now well-regarded, if Usage wills it so,"
(ArsPoetica)

Horace insists that no matter how grand or enduring a human endeavor may seem, whether it's a project to guard ships from the north winds, drain marshes, or control rivers, eventually all things including human language, will fade. He uses this to highlight the idea that language, like human achievements, is impermanent and must be refreshed and adapted over time to remain relevant. Horace asserts that it is "Usage" that ultimately governs language. Words fall in and out of favor according to how they are used and accepted by society. This personification of "Usage" suggests that language change is a natural and democratic process, directed by the preferences of its speakers rather than rigid rules.

Ars Poetica:73-118 What the tradition dictates

Horace regards the ancient traditions that dictated how certain subjects and styles should be handled.

"Homer's shown the metre in which the deeds of captains
And kings, and the sorrows of war, may be written.
First, lament was captured in elegiac couplets,"
(ArsPoetica)

He cites Homer, who is credited with establishing the meter for epics that recount the deeds of "captains and kings" and the sorrows of war. Couplets were the chosen form for expressing lamentation and gratitude, even though there remains scholarly debate on who first composed these elegies. He refers to Archilochus , suggesting the significance of the iambic meter for more direct, often satirical expressions, suited to the dual genres of comedy and tragedy. It emphasizes how specific poetic forms carry different expressive capacities, aligning with the intended mood and setting of the narrative.

"Suited to dialogue, able to overcome the noise
Of the pit, and naturally appropriate to action."
(Ars Poetica)

Horace emphasizes the importance of using appropriate styles for each genre. For instance, comedy should not adopt a tragic tone, nor should tragic events be reduced to the simplicity of comedic language. He cites Thyestes' gruesome feast, for instance, is unfit for comic treatment, as the weight of the subject demands a more solemn tone. However, there is some flexibility, as comedy can elevate its voice in moments of high emotion, and tragedy can also employ a straightforward, prose-like quality when characters express deep personal grief. This reflects Horace's belief that poetry requires not only technical skill but also sensitivity to the nuances of each emotion and scenario.

Herefers to the power of emotional authenticity in poetry, suggesting that poets must feel genuine emotion to evoke it in their audience. He suggests listeners are more likely to be moved if they perceive that the speaker genuinely feels the sorrow or joy being conveyed. This expectation of alignment between internal emotion and external expression is the key to an effective performance, as mismatched tones lead to a failure in communication and can provoke unintended laughter.

"Jests suit the playful, serious speech the solemn.

Nature first alters us within, to respond to each
Situation: brings delight or goads us to anger,
Or weighs us to the ground, tormented by grief:
Then, with tongue interpreting, shows heart's emotion."
(Ars Poetica)

Horace further asserts that the appropriateness of language varies depending on the identity of the speaker whether a god, an elder, a youth, or a person of a specific cultural background. This aspect in character voice helps reinforce the narrative's realism, as audiences expect different expressions from various types of individuals.

Ars Poetica:119-152 Be consistent if you are original

Either follow tradition, or invent consistently.
If you happen to portray Achilles, honoured,
Pen him as energetic, irascible, ruthless,
Fierce, above the law, never downing weapons."
(Ars Poetica)

Horace begins by advising writers to either adhere to established tradition or be consistent in their innovations. He insists that if a poet chooses to portray great characters like Achilles, Medea, or Orestes, they must remain true to the character traits that audiences expect. For instance, Achilles should always be depicted as "energetic, irascible, ruthless," while Medea should be "wild" and "untamable". By keeping characters consistent, Horace suggests that poets maintain believability and honour the essence of these figures from myth and legend.

"If you're staging something untried, and dare

*To attempt fresh characters, keep them as first
Introduced, from start to end self-consistent."*
(Ars Poetica)

However, if a poet ventures to create original characters, they should ensure that these characters are consistently portrayed from beginning to end. Horace believes that maintaining consistency in character traits is essential, as it helps readers or audiences follow the narrative more easily and trust the characters' authenticity.

Horace also points out the challenge of presenting universal themes in specific, fresh ways. He encourages writers to weave stories from familiar material, like the "poem of Troy" because these themes already resonate with audiences. Yet, he also cautions against framing stories in a predictable or overly literal manner.

*"Don't keep slowly circling the broad beaten track,
Or, pedantic translator, render them word for word,"*
(Ars Poetica)

Instead of translating or copying renowned stories, he advises writers to bring their own perspective and creativity, avoiding the "broad beaten track" and refraining from becoming "pedantic translators"

He criticizes those who make grand promises at the beginning of their works without fulfilling them. To illustrate this, he references an old epic writer who starts with "Of Priam's fate I'll sing, and the greatest of Wars" but fails to deliver on the grandeur expected from such an opening. This results in an underwhelming outcome, symbolized by a "ridiculous mouse" emerging from "mountains" that "will labour". Horace stresses the importance of making reasonable promises in the introduction and fulfilling them throughout the narrative.

Horace advises writers to start the narrative in media res, or "in the midst of the action". He suggests that the beginning should smoothly connect to the middle, and the middle to the end, creating a cohesive and logical progression.

"He always hastens the outcome, and snatches the reader
Into the midst of the action, as if all were known,
Leaves what he despairs of improving by handling,"
(Ars Poetica)

Writers should not attempt to explain every background detail, but instead focus on drawing readers into the core of the story and maintaining a consistent tone and direction.

Ars Poetica:153-188 On characterization

Horace advises writers and dramatists on the art of characterization and appropriate portrayal on stage.

"You're to note the behaviour of every age-group,
Give grace to the variation in character and years."
(Ars Poetica)

Horace first outlines the characteristics associated with youth. Young boys are playful, quick-tempered, and easily distracted but equally quick to forgive and forget.

"The lad who can answer now, and set a firm foot
To the ground, likes to play with his peers, loses but
Quickly regains his temper, and alters with the hour.
The beardless youth, free of tutors at last, delights"
(Ars Poetica)

Horace suggests that teenagers or young men, who have recently gained some independence, are passionate and impulsive. They are drawn to activities such as sports and adventure, are malleable and susceptible to vice, and often dismiss advice from their elders. They lack foresight, spend freely, and are easily swayed by new interest.

"Slow in making provision, lavish with money.
Spirited, passionate, and swift to change his whim."
(Ars Poetica)

Men in their prime are more practical, seeking wealth, friendships, and social standing. They become cautious, aware of the consequences of their actions, and careful about making decisions they might later regret.

"Manhood's years and thoughts, with altering interests,
Seek wealth and friendship, devoted to preferment,
Wary of doing what they may soon labour to change."
(Ars Poetica)

Horace highlights that middle-aged men are devoted to advancing their careers and forming meaningful relationships but remain wary of committing to actions they may wish to reverse later.

Horace describes the elderly as generally more frugal, timid, and less active. They tend to avoid risks, are cautious about spending their savings, and often have a pessimistic outlook. The elderly are described as nostalgic, frequently reminiscing about their youth and criticizing the younger generation.

"The advancing years bring many blessings with them,
Many, departing, they take away. So lest we chance

To assign youth's part to age, or a boy's to a man,
Always adopt what suits and belongs to a given age."
(Ars Poetica)

Horace notes that with age comes both gains and losses, and playwrights should be careful to assign actions and dialogue that are suitable for each character's age, ensuring that the portrayal is consistent and believable. Horace hereby suggests to be cautious while engaging in characterization.

Horace then addresses the issue of whether events should be depicted on stage or merely reported.

"Events are either acted on stage, or reported.
The mind is stirred less vividly by what's heard"
(Ars Poetica)

He argues that the audience is more emotionally affected by what they see than by what they hear. However, he warns against depicting certain shocking or supernatural acts directly on stage, suggesting they be narrated instead to preserve credibility and avoid alienating the audience. For instance, he believes that scenes such as Medea murdering her children, Atreus cooking human flesh, and the mythical transformations of Procne and Cadmus should not be staged.

"Folk shouldn't see Medea slaughter her children,
Impious Atreus mustn't openly cook human flesh.
Nor Procne turn into a bird, or Cadmus a snake.
Any such scenes you show me, I disbelieve, and hate"
(Ars Poetica)

Such events, if shown visually, would appear unbelievable or grotesque, making it difficult for the audience to remain engaged with the story.

Ars Poetica:189-219 On the gods, chorus and music

Horace insists that a play should ideally be five acts long, as this structure has become a standard that satisfies audience expectations.

"No play should be longer or shorter than five acts,
If you hope that, once seen, it'll be requested, revived."
(ArsPoetica)

He suggests that this length helps ensure the play's success and makes it more likely to be requested and revived. He also cautions against the overuse of divine intervention in the plot. Gods should only appear to resolve situations that truly require a supernatural solution.

"And no god should intervene unless there's a problem
That needs that solution, nor should a fourth person
speak."
(Ars Poetica)

The supernatural element should be used sparingly to maintain the believability of the narrative.

Horace further advises limiting the dialogue to three main speakers per scene, keeping the narrative focused and the stage uncluttered.

"That needs that solution, nor should a fourth person
speak."
(Ars Poetica)

Horace elaborates on the role of the chorus. Rather than simply singing between acts, the chorus should actively contribute to the plot, rather than becoming like another actor on stage. Its actions and commentary should be relevant to the plot, to move it forward.

"The Chorus should play an actor's part., energetically,
And not sing between the acts unless it advances,
And is also closely related to the plot.
It should favour the good, and give friendly advice,"
(Ars Poetica)

The chorus is tasked with upholding moral values by supporting virtuous characters, offering advice to those who are angry or fearful, and promoting ideals such as humility, justice, and peace. In such manner, the chorus serves as a moral compass for the play, reminding the audience of ethical importance.

Horace suggests that the chorus should keep certain secrets and appeal to the gods to balance the fortunes of the proud and the wretched.

"It should hide secrets, and pray and entreat the gods
That the proud lose their luck, and the wretched regain
it."
(Ars Poetica)

The chorus should function as a force of moderation, desiring that the arrogant are humbled and the unfortunate find relief.

Horace shifts his discourse towards the evolution of the flute and the lyre in theatre. He traced how the flute was a simple instrument with limited stops, used to support the chorus without overpowering it.

"The flute, once, not bound with brass as now to rival
The trumpet, but simple and slender with few stops,
Was used to lead and support the Chorus, and to fill"
(Ars Poetica)

Horace asserts that in the early days ,the audience was small, innocent, and modest, and so the music was correspondingly simple and unadorned. However, as Rome expanded, Horace observes its citizens became more indulgent and less restrained, leading to a shift in musical tastes. He provides the instance of the flute's design which became more elaborate, and its sound more robust to keep up with the growing crowds and changing tastes. The lyre's range expanded as well, bringing more energy and expressiveness to theatrical performances.

Horace describes how the transformation in music reflects a broader cultural shift. The theatre adapted to accommodate the interests of a larger, more diverse, and less educated audience, who sought greater spectacle and entertainment. Musical instruments, once restrained, grew in complexity, and performances became more dynamic. This change marked a departure from the gravity and wisdom of early performances, which often conveyed philosophical or prophetic themes.

Ars Poetica:220-250 On style

"The man who once competed for a lowly he-goat
With tragic verse, soon stripped the wild Satyrs,
And tried coarse jests without loss of seriousness,
Since only the attractions and charms of novelty
Held the spectator, drunken and lawless, after the rites."
(Ars Poetica)

Horace begins by recounting the origin of Satyr plays, which started as a form of entertainment where poets competed for small prizes, such as a goat. These plays traditionally featured Satyrs as wild, drunken creatures associated with revelry and included a mix of serious and humorous content. This genre emerged as a way to entertain an unruly audience, drawn in by the novelty of these performances. Satyr plays often followed tragic plays, providing a lighter contrast to relieve the tension. Despite the comedic elements, Horace argues that Satyr plays require a delicate balance between serious and light tones. Writers must transition smoothly from tragedy to humour, ensuring the style doesn't undermine the dignity of the gods and heroes previously depicted in tragic scenes. He warns against portraying these noble characters in overly vulgar settings or using crude language, as this would conflict with their regal and dignified roles. The gods and heroes, previously shown in royal attire, should not appear in degraded or ridiculous situations that clash with their established personas.

Horace uses the analogy of a noble lady who is forced to dance at a festival to emphasize the awkwardness of mixing low humour with a traditionally serious form. Just as it would be unseemly for a dignified woman to act in a way that compromises her status, so too would it be inappropriate for a tragic style to adopt language or settings that are overly base when transitioning into a Satyr play.

"Tragedy, to whom spouting low verse is unworthy,
Like a lady forced to dance at a festival,
Will join the insolent Satyrs with no small shame."
(Ars Poetica)

The poet advises that while writing Satyr plays, one should avoid using overly simple or colloquial language, as this would diminish the artistic quality of the work. Instead, the language should retain some sophistication, blending lightness with the elevated style of tragedy.

Horace specifically mentions the characters like Davus, a slave, and Pythias, a scheming woman, as examples of figures who could speak plainly in comedies but would be out of place in a Satyr play if portrayed too crudely. Likewise, Silenus, the drunken companion of the god Dionysus, should retain a certain poetic dignity even in his humour. He stresses that crafting effective Satyr plays requires a high level of skill, as it involves arranging familiar words and ideas in a way that feels fresh and compelling. The poet should aim to please a more discerning audience, including the upper class, who may not appreciate lowbrow content.

Ars Poetica: 251-274 On Meter

Horace begins by examining the iambic meter, specifically the iambic trimeter, which consists of six syllables in each line (three pairs). Traditionally, an iambic foot is composed of a short syllable followed by a long one, creating a rhythmic, quick-paced meter. This meter is known for its swiftness and energy, qualities that make it suitable for certain types of dramatic verse.

Horace then notes that Roman poets have adapted this classical form.

"Not every critic can detect unmusical verse,
So Roman poets have been granted unearned licence."
(Ars Poetica)

While this practice adds variety, it also risks disrupting the rhythm, which Horace criticizes as potentially careless. He specifically mentions that poets like Ennius often used this substitution in a way that could make their work feel heavy or less precise, suggesting it reflected either a disregard for the art or a lack of skill.

The reference to Accius also implies that even notable Roman poets were not immune to such criticism. Horace points out that Roman audience have historically been lenient with such variations, showing "unearned license" to poets who might not strictly follow the ideal meter. He questions whether he himself should write more freely, as Roman poets have been allowed to do, or remain cautious, aware of criticism. Ultimately, he advises aspiring poets to study Greek models rigorously, which provide a disciplined standard of metrical and poetic excellence.

"...As for yourselves, have Greek models
In your hands at night, and in your hands each day."
He suggests that adherence to these classical forms brings more artistic integrity than mere novelty or easy praise.
(Ars Poetica)

Ars Poetica:275-294 Greeks and Romans

"Thespis, they say, discovered the Tragic Muse,
An unknown form, presenting his plays from carts."
(Ars Poetica)

He credits Thespis, the founder of Greek tragedy, who introduced the genre by performing on carts with actors whose faces were painted with "wine lees". Thespis's invention laid the groundwork for a new art form, making way for Aeschylus, who enhanced the dignity and spectacle of tragedy by adding masks, elaborate costumes, and staging techniques. Aeschylus emphasized powerful, dramatic speeches and the use of "buskins" (high-heeled shoes) to increase the presence of his actors.

"Aeschylus, after him, introduced masks, fine robes,

Had a modest stage made of planks, and demanded
Sonorous speech, and the effort of wearing buskins."
(Ars Poetica)

These advancements brought a sense of grandeur and formality to the art.

Horace then addresses the rise of Old Comedy, which gained popularity for its daring, often unrestrained satire. However, the freedom it enjoyed ultimately led to excess, prompting legal intervention to restrict its abuses.

"But its freedoms led to excess, to unruliness
Needing legal curb: the law was obeyed, the chorus,"
(Ars Poetica)

As a result, the chorus -the voice of public and moral critique in the plays was silenced and lost its role as a commentator on society. This historical shift Horace observes that it serves as a cautionary reminder about the balance between artistic freedom and responsibility.

Turning to Roman poets, Horace praises their creativity and willingness to explore a diverse range of subjects, including themes unique to Rome. Roman playwrights had begun to diverge from Greek influences to celebrate distinctly Roman characters and stories.

"Our own poets have left nothing unexplored,
And have not won least honour by daring to leave
The paths of the Greeks and celebrate things at home,
Whether in Roman tragedies or domestic comedies."
(Ars Poetica)

Horace suggests that Rome could achieve literary greatness comparable to its military and political power if its writers were more diligent in revising their work. He implies that many Roman poets avoid the rigorous editing required to refine their craft, preferring immediate success over the labour of improvement.

Ars Poetica:295-332 How to be a good poet

Horace refers to the philosopher Democritus, who claimed that raw talent outweighed technique, and that true poets must be eccentric or mad to excel. This belief leads some would-be poets to embrace unfurnished appearances and avoid grooming.

"Or beards, haunting secluded spots, shunning the baths.
Surely a man will win the honour and name of poet"
(Ars Poetica)

Horace mocks this notion, questioning if eccentricity alone is enough to be called a poet and suggesting that even excessive madness couldn't inspire some individuals to produce great poetry. Horace reflects on his own methods, humorously claiming he only "purges" his madness in the spring though he doesn't actually write poetry. Instead, he takes on the role of a "grindstone," offering guidance and sharpening others' skills without creating original works himself.

"Ah. fool that I am, taking purges for madness each spring!
Though no one composes better poetry: it's really
Not worth it. Instead let me play the grindstone's role,"
(Ars Poetica)

This analogy highlights his preference for teaching the craft and sharing his insights into what forms a great poet, focusing on wisdom, technique, and understanding over mere eccentricity.

Horace argues that a poet should first acquire wisdom, which is "the source and fount of excellent writing." He believes that reading the works of Socrates and other philosophers will provide a rich content base, enabling poets to convey meaningful messages.

"The works of the Socratics provide you with content,
And when content's available words will quickly follow."
(Ars Poetica)

Knowledge of societal roles and relationships is essential for portraying characters authentically, as poets must understand the duties of citizens, senators, judges, and generals to depict them convincingly.

"he Muse gave the Greeks talent, rounded eloquence
In their speech, they were only greedy for glory.
Roman lads learn long division, and how to split
A pound weight into a hundred parts..."
(Ars Poetica)

Horace contrasts poetry with practical education in Rome, pointing out that Greeks, driven by a desire for fame, excelled naturally in eloquence and expression. In contrast, Roman youths are primarily trained in arithmetic, focusing on wealth management rather than the arts. This approach, Horace argues, "stains the spirit" and stifles creativity, making it difficult to produce works worthy of preservation.

Ars Poetica:333-365 Combine instruction with pleasure

Horace explores the dual purpose of poetry: to instruct and to delight. He explains that when providing instruction, poets should be concise.

"Poets wish to benefit or to please, or to speak
What is both enjoyable and helpful to living.
When you give instruction, be brief, what's quickly
Said the spirit grasps easily, faithfully retains:
Everything superfluous flows out of a full mind."
(Ar sPoetica)

He believes that the human mind absorbs and remembers simple, direct ideas better than lengthy explanations, while excessive details can overwhelm and lead to forgetfulness. He suggests that fictional elements in poetry should also feel realistic i.e. readers should not be asked to believe anything which is entirely unbelievable or absurd, like a child surviving in the belly of the Lamia (a mythical creature). Grounding the plots in believability keeps the audience engaged and enhances the impact of the message.

"So your play shouldn't ask for belief in whatever
It chooses: no living child from the Lamia's full belly!"
(ArsPoetica)

The ideal poet, according to Horace, is one who blends usefulness with pleasure, achieving a balance that captivates and instructs. Such a work appeals to a broad audience and gains lasting popularity. Such type of poetry earns fame for its author, and stands the test of time.

"A few blots won't offend me, those carelessly spilt,

Or that human frailty can scarcely help. So what?
As a copyist has no excuse if he always
Makes the same mistake, no matter how often he's told.
As a harpist is mocked who always fluff's the one note:
So to me one who often errs is a Choerilus,
Whose one or two fine lines prompt startled smiles:
And yet I'm displeased too when great Homer nods,
Somnolence may steal over a long work it's true."
(Ars Poetica)

Horace acknowledges that even great poems will have minor flaws. Mistakes in rhythm, phrasing, or aimsuch as a 'bass' note unexpectedly coming out as a treble which he considers to be forgivable if the work contains enough merit to outweigh them. Occasional slips are natural and don't necessarily ruin the poem, but consistent mistakes from the poet suggest a lack of skill. While even Homer, the revered poet, might "nod" or grow "drowsy" in long works, these rare lapses are overlooked because of his overall greatness.

Horace compares poetry to visual art, noting that just as some paintings are best appreciated up close while others look better from a distance, poetry has varied strengths. Some poems withstand detailed analysis, while others may be better appreciated for their overall effect. This comparison emphasizes that different works of poetry have unique qualities that appeal to readers in distinct ways, and that truly great poetry has a timeless appeal, enduring even the closest scrutiny.

Ars Poetica:366-407 No mediocrity: recall the tradition!

Horace asserts that some professions can tolerate mediocrity and ignorance. However, in poetry, mediocrity is intolerable, it is rejected by everyone, from common readers to gods and even booksellers, who won't profit from selling subpar works.

"Is only properly allowed in certain fields. A lawyer,
A mediocre pleader of causes, may fall short
Of Messalla's eloquence, know less than Aulus
Cascellius, yet have value: but mediocrity
In poets, no man, god or bookseller will accept."
(Ars Poetica)

Horace illustrates that just as certain unpleasant elements can ruin a fine "meal", orlike an out-of-tune instrument or perfume; a poorly written poem disrupts the pleasure that poetry should ideally bring.He observes that people are more cautious in other fields: those unskilled in sports avoid embarrassing themselves in public, for fear of becoming the subject of ridicule. Yet, he insists that, many who lack knowledge or skill in verse feel free to write poetry, seeing themselves as entitled to this creative endeavour because of their social status, wealth, or other external qualifications.

"Scribble, let it enter Tarpa the critic's ears,
Your father's and my own, then put your manuscript
Away til the ninth year: you can always destroy
What you haven't published: once out there's no recall."
(Ars Poetica)

Horace suggests that his young listener, however, is wise enough to avoid this mistake, guided by the wisdom of Minerva (the goddess of wisdom). But if he does write poetry, Horace advises him to submit it to trusted critics, and to keep the work unpublished for nine years, allowing time for reflection and revision. Since once the poem gets published, there's no undoing it, and thus, it should be perfected before release.

Horace cites ancient examples to illustrate the elevated role of poets in society. He recalls Orpheus, the mythical poet and musician, who was believed to civilize humanity with his songs, taming even wild animals. Amphion, another legendary musician, used his lyre to move stones and build Thebes, symbolizing how poetry and music shape civilization. Poets who once taught society moral distinctions, upheld marriage laws, built cities, and set down laws; they were honored for their wisdom and their role in guiding humanity. Figures like Homer gained lasting fame for their contributions, while Tyrtaeus inspired soldiers through his verses. Horace recalls that poetry was also the medium for oracles and moral teachings, and kings rewarded poets for their work.Through these examples, Horace reminds Piso's son of poetry's legacy as a sacred art. Rather than dismissing poetry as a trivial pursuit, he argues that poets should strive to meet the high standards set by their predecessors. The skill required in poetry is as worthy of respect as that of any other discipline; it is a discipline where one should aspire to the same excellence as the classical poets who shaped culture and inspired societies.

Ars Poetica:408-437 Nature plus training: but see through flattery

"Whethera praiseworthy poem is due to nature
Or art is the question: I've never seen the benefit
Of study lacking a wealth of talent, or of untrained
Ability: each needs the other's friendly assistance."
(Ars Poetica)

In these lines, Horace discusses the interplay between natural talent and training for the creation of great poetry, while also warning against the dangers of flattery. Horace opens with the question of whether a praiseworthy poem arises more from nature that is innate talent or from learned skill. He argues that both of these are essential as natural talent without training is useless, just as skill gained through study alone is insufficient without inherent ability. Horace suggests that poetry, like any other challenging pursuit, demands dedication, sacrifice, and discipline, comparing it to the rigorous training of an athlete or a musician. For instance, a flautist who performs at the prestigious Pythian Games would have spent years mastering his craft under strict instruction.

Horace criticizes poets who write without having learned or practiced enough, relying on the assumption that their wealth or status is enough to make their work respectable. Some poets are more interested in impressing others than in honing their skills. This is often further worsened by the company of flatterers who offer insincere praise, seeking to benefit from the poet's wealth and generosity rather than offering honest feedback. Wealthy poets who attract such people, he says, risk being surrounded by false admirers who will praise their work excessively without genuine appreciation.

"Like an auctioneer drawing a crowd to the sale,
So a poet whose rich in land, with large investments,
Is bidding flatterers come to him, and profit."
(Ars Poetica)

Horace warns against the deception of these flatterers by comparing them to professional mourners at funerals, who express exaggerated emotions that surpass those of the genuinely grieving. Similarly, these false admirers may display excessive enthusiasm, even to the point of tears, pretending to be moved by the poetry they hear.

They may cry out, "Lovely! Fine! Grand!" and engage in exaggerated gestures of admiration, but this is mere pretence.

"As those hired to mourn at funerals do and say
Almost more than those who are grieving deeply,
The hypocrite's more 'moved' than the true admirer."
(Ars Poetica)

Horace advises that poets should be cautious of such flattery, which can mislead them into believing their work is better than it is.

"They say kings anxious to test someone, to see if
He's worthy of friendship, urge on him many a glass,
Ply him with wine: so, if you should fashion verses,
Don't be deceived by the fox's hidden intent."
(Ars Poetica)

He compares the situation to kings who test a person's loyalty by offering them many drinks; a poet should likewise test those who praise him to see if they are sincere. In this way, Horace encourages poets to seek honest and discerning critics rather than relying on the false praise of those who may have hidden motives, or "the fox's hidden intent."

Ars Poetica:438-476 Know your faults and keep your wits

"If you ever read Quintilius anything, he'd say:
Oh do change this, and this.' If, after two or three
Vain attempts, you could do no better, he'd order
Deletion: 'return the ill-made verse to the anvil'."
(Ars Poetica)

Horace eludes Quintilius, as an ideal critic and to the kind of criticism he would offer. Horace insists that if a poet showed him a flawed piece, Quintilius would urge them to change it. If the repeated attempts failed to improve the work, he would advise to revise the verses altogether, suggesting that sometimes, a line is so flawed and inconsistent to the entire piece that it should better be removed from the work and revised again. If the poet stubbornly clings to these errors, Horace insists that Quintilius would cease to argue, understanding that further effort would be futile against the poet's pride and self-indulgence.

Through this illustration, Horace explains that an honest critic should point out flaws in a straightforward manner, even though it is against the poet's feelings.

"An honest, sensible man will condemn lifeless verse,
Fault the harsh, smear the inelegant with a black
Stroke of the pen, cut out pretentious adornment,
Force you to elucidate where it's not clear enough,
Denounce the ambiguous phrase, mark amendments,"
(Ars Poetica)

The ideal critic according to Horace, would condemn lifeless and overly complex lines, eliminate unnecessary ornamentation, demand clarity where needed, and figure out any confusing or ambiguous passages. Horace compares such a critic to Aristarchus, a famous Alexandrian scholar who is known for his strict and discerning approach to evaluating literature.

Horace warns against the danger of a poet who becomes overly attached to his work and loses his grip on reality. He insists that such obsessive poet, who ignores the sound advice and honest criticism, becomes a figure of mockery.

"He, inspired, goes wandering off, spouting his verses,
And if like a fowler intent on blackbirds, he falls
Into a well, or a pit, however much he cries:
Help me, citizens! none will bother to pull him out.
If anyone did choose to help, and let down a rope,
I'd say: Who knows if he didn't do that on purpose,"
(Ars Poetica)

Horace illustrates such self obsessed poet to like someone who is sickened with madness or an "evil itch," as they wander around, reciting their own verses to anyone who will listen. Horace describes themas' mad poets' who falls into a well or pit as he remains fixated on his poetry. No one is inclined to rescue him, and if someone does let down a rope, they might question whether he intentionally fell to gain attention or to be considered as martyrdom. Horace ironically suggests that poets should have the freedom to "kill themselves" through the illustration of the story of Empedocles. For Horace, this reflects the danger of ego-driven obsession, which blinds poets to constructive criticism and traps them in a self-destructive pursuit of fame.

In the concluding lines,

"He's mad: like a bear, that's broken the bars of its cage
The pest puts all to flight, learned or not, with reciting:
Whom he takes tight hold of, he grips, and reads to
death,
A leech that never looses the skin, till gorged with
blood."
(Ars Poetica)

Horace describes how such a poet becomes a "leech," clinging to anyone who will listen, reciting his work compulsively, and draining their patience. The poetic obsession of such a poet is like a parasite that feeds on attention, unable to stop until he's "gorged with blood." Through these images, Horace warns poets to avoid becoming too attached to their work or ego, emphasizing the importance of knowing one's limitations, seeking honest critique, and staying grounded. In Horace's view, a good poet not only seeks excellence but also remains aware of their own faults and flattery; and obsessive self-promotion.

3. Probable Questions

1. Evaluate on the principles of poetic decorum as proposed by Horace.

OR

2. How does Horace explain the concept of decorum in relation to character and action?

OR

3. In what ways does Horace's concept of decorum reflect coherence and unity?

Answer:

Horace in his literary discourse 'Ars poetica' presents his theory on the concept of decorum, which is a foundational principle of classical poetics. Decorum is general sense refers to the rules and notions that defines dictates the appropriateness of style, content, and expression in literary works. Horace's treatment of decorum emphasizes on the importance of harmony between a work's subject matter and its style, which he insists that poets must exercise while writing. His reflections on decorum span various aspects of poetry, including genre conventions, character representation, language, and emotional tone, revealing his belief that adherence to decorum is essential for creating a coherent and relevant literary work.

Horace's exploration of decorum in "Ars Poetica" begins with the notion that style must be appropriate to the subject matter being depicted. He insists that only through this adherence, poets can create a harmonious and unified work that avoids the pitfalls of excessive poetic liberty, which can lead to a loss of coherence and artistic integrity. Horace states that poets must respect the internal logic of their work, preserving its aesthetic unity while balancing artistic freedom with responsibility of not alternating the rules of nature. He illustrates this vividly in the very first two lines of the poem:

"If a painter had chosen to set a human head
On a horse's neck, covered a melding of limbs, "
(Ars Poetica)

He illustrates the idea of coherence and unity with the metaphor of a painter who attaches a horse's neck to a human head, and adds feathers to the body. The outcome of this imagery would be a monstrous- one that no one would admire. Horace at the very beginning itself warns the poets against mixing incompatible elements in their poetry. Just as a painting must have consistency in its parts, a poem should maintain a unified structure. Throughout the first section of Ars Poetica, Horace illustrates with numerous instances of inconsistency in a work of art that result in chaos. He acknowledges poetic liberty but is critical of its abusive use by poets:

"To a unified form. 'But painters and poets
Have always shared the right to dare anything.' "
(Ars Poetica)

Horace's idea on decorum stems from the idea that poetry should be a unified whole, with every part contributing to a cohesive and harmonious effect. In his view, a poem is like a carefully constructed piece of art in which the relationship between its elements style, tone, character, and plot. Each of these elements must work together to serve the central theme or message. The presence of inconsistent elements can disrupt and shatter this unity, resulting in a poem that feels chaotic or unbalanced. He warns against the abuse of poetic liberty, cautioning poets to avoid introducing absurd, disjointed, or illogical elements that might disrupt the coherence of their work. He advises that the aspiring poets should study and mimic the works of the great Greek and roman poets of the past.

Horace stresses that characters must speak and act in ways that align with their age, social status, gender and personality. For instance, he advises that a young man should not deliver overly philosophical or mature reflections; as such speech would clash with the expected behavior of youth. This principle ensures that the audience's expectations are met, lending credibility and authenticity to the work. By aligning characters with their natural or conventional attributes, the poet creates a more immersive and relatable narrative.

Horace provides advice on how writers should approach their craft, emphasizing the importance of choosing appropriate subjects, exercising self-awareness, and using language with precision.

"You who write, choose a subject that's matched by
Your powers, consider deeply what your shoulders
Can and cannot bear. Whoever chooses rightly"
(Ars Poetica)

Horace begins by advising writers to choose a subject that matches according to their abilities. He encourages self-assessment, reminding poets to consider what they "can and cannot bear." The writers should select topics they are equipped to handle both intellectually and emotionally, as choosing topics beyond one's skill can result in weak or ineffective writing. Horace suggests that writing should be direct and relevant, expressing "what's to be said here and now" as it encourages writers to stay focused on the present purpose of their work rather than becoming distracted by irrelevant details.

Horace acknowledges that sometimes writers may need to create new words if necessary, so long as they do so with wisdom and restraint. Horace asserts that newly coined words can gain acceptance if they serve a clear purpose and are used judiciously. His approach to poetic innovation is balanced; while he values tradition, he also allows for linguistic creativity, as long as it enhances the work rather than detracts from its clarity.
Horace argues that if Greek poets like Virgil and Varius are allowed to be innovating, the Roman poets too should likewise afford the same liberty. He questions why Romans would deny themselves the right to expand their language, as earlier poets like Caecilius, Plautus, Cato, and Ennius did. Horace argues that these earlier figures enhanced Latin with new terms and expressions, showing that language change have long been an accepted and celebrated tradition.

Horace also applies decorum to the use of language and style, advocating for simplicity and clarity over unnecessary ornamentation. He criticizes those who prioritize ornate phrasing or obscure diction at the expense of effective communication. Poets, he asserts, must tailor their language to suit the subject matter and the audience. For instance, a tragic epic demands lofty and elevated language, while a comedy calls for a lighter and more conversational tone. Any mismatch between the style and the genre undermines the work's impact, distracting the audience from its intended effect. Horace's advice to "choose words suited to the matter" reinforces the idea that language must serve the work's purpose, enhancing rather than obscuring its meaning.

In addition to language, Horace addresses the element of emotional tone and its relationship to decorum. He asserts that a poet must evoke emotions in a manner that feels genuine and appropriate to the scene. A character's grief, joy, or anger must be portrayed with a natural intensity that resonates with the audience. This requires not only an understanding of human psychology but also sensitivity to the context of the narrative. He famously advises that "if you wish me to weep, you must first feel grief yourself," highlighting the poet's role in authentically channeling emotion to create a compelling experience.

Horace's doctrine of decorum extends beyond individual works to the broader conventions of genre. He emphasizes that each genre has its own rules and expectations, and the poet must respect these boundaries to avoid confusing the audience. For example, a tragedy should not include humor or frivolous language, just as a satire must not adopt the grandeur of an epic. While innovation is permissible, it must operate within the confines of the genre's established framework. By adhering to these conventions, poets ensure that their work aligns with the audience's understanding and appreciation of the genre.

Horace insists on the practical implications of decorum for poets, linking it to their broader responsibilities as artists. He stresses that poets must be both skilled and disciplined, balancing creative inspiration with rigorous self-critique. He warns against the temptation to prioritize novelty over coherence or personal ambition over audience engagement. For Horace, the ideal poet is one who combines technical mastery with an awareness of cultural and artistic traditions, crafting works that are both innovative and grounded in established principles.

Horace compares poetry to visual art, noting that just as some paintings are best appreciated up close while others look better from a distance, poetry has varied strengths. Similarly some poems withstand detailed analysis, while others may be better appreciated for their overall effect. This comparison emphasizes that different works of poetry have unique qualities that appeal to readers in distinct ways, and that truly great poetry has a timeless appeal, enduring even the closest scrutiny.

"Ah. fool that I am, taking purges for madness each spring!
Though no one composes better poetry: it's really
Not worth it. Instead let me play the grindstone's role,"
(Ars Poetica)

This analogy highlights his preference for teaching the craft and sharing his insights into what forms a great poet, focusing on wisdom, technique, and understanding over mere eccentricity. Horace argues that a poet should first acquire wisdom, which is "the source and fount of excellent writing." He believes that reading the works of Socrates and other philosophers will provide a rich content base, enabling poets to convey meaningful messages.

"The works of the Socratics provide you with content,
And when content's available words will quickly follow."
(Ars Poetica)

In conclusion, Horace's principle of decorum in ArsPoetica underscores the importance of unity and coherence in poetry. By maintaining a consistent style, ensuring that characters behave in ways appropriate to their roles, and adhering to the conventions of the chosen genre, poets can create works that are harmonious and unified.

4. How does Horace define the role of a poet?

OR

5. Analyse the concept of "mad poet" as provided by Horace.

Answer:
According to Horace, in 'Ars Poetica' poetry should not only merely entertain but also should offer profound moral and philosophical insights, which appeal to both the intellect and emotions of its audience. With this view regarding poetry, Horace in his critical discourse emphasizes on the dual role of a poet.

A poet according to him is assigned with the dual role to entertain by providing pleasure as well as to teach and promote morality through his artistic creativity. To achieve this, mastery over the literary craft is essential. Horace emphasizes the importance of technical skill, and decorum set for different genres; urges poets to pay attention to language, structure, and style. He insists that a poem must possess unity and coherence, with every element serving the overall purpose. For instance, he cautions against mixing incompatible tones or styles, likening such failures to a painter who places a horse's head on a human body. A poet with true sensibility will tailor their language, tone, and style to suit the subject and audience, adhering to the principle of decorum. He advises the poets to have a thorough study of the classics and the works of great ancient poets.

Horace views the poets as a moral instructor whose work shapes and refines the character of the audience. He advocates for the truthful portrayal of human nature, believing that such authenticity fosters deeper understanding and self-reflection. The poet should also be mindful of their audience, adapting their work to resonate with diverse groups. For example, Horace advises tailoring themes to suit the maturity and tastes of different ages, illustrating his awareness of poetry's social impact. He advises on the art of characterization and language that should be employed in the literary works according to the respective genre and scenario of the contemporary time.

Emotional engagement is another critical element of Horace's vision. He famously asserts that a poet must "feel deeply" in order to instigate genuine emotions in their audience, highlighting the importance of pathos in creating a lasting impression. This ability to evoke emotion, combined with moral guidance and technical excellence, elevates the poet's work from mere craftsmanship to an enduring art form.

Horace acknowledges that strong emotion and inspiration are vital to poetry, but he emphasizes that they must be tempered by reason and an awareness of artistic principles. A poet with refined sensibility knows how to channel their emotions into coherent and impactful work, striking the delicate balance between natural talent and technical skill. By contrast, the mad poet is overwhelmed by unchecked inspiration, mistaking passion alone for artistic merit. Their work often becomes erratic, marked by excessive ornamentation, incoherence, or misplaced ambition, as they lack the discernment to shape their ideas into a unified and polished whole.

"Or beards, haunting secluded spots, shunning the baths.
Surely a man will win the honour and name of poet"
(Ars Poetica)

Horace mocks this notion, questioning if eccentricity alone is enough to be called a poet and suggesting that even excessive madness couldn't inspire some individuals to produce great poetry. Horace reflects on his own methods, humorously claiming he only "purges" his madness in the spring though he doesn't actually write poetry. Instead, he takes on the role of a "grindstone," offering guidance and sharpening others' skills without creating original works himself.

A poet with refined sensibility is one who can harmonize inspiration and technique, producing work that resonates deeply and endures over time. Horace also connects poetic sensibility to the ability to connect with an audience. He argues that poets must understand human nature, portraying characters and situations with authenticity and emotional depth. A poet with true sensibility will tailor their language, tone, and style to suit the subject and audience, adhering to the principle of decorum.

In Ars Poetica, Horace's concept of the "mad poet" is intricately tied to his reflections on poetic sensibility, which he sees as a balance between passion, reason, and craftsmanship. Poetic sensibility, in Horace's view, is the ability of a poet to perceive and express the essence of human experience in a way that is both emotionally compelling and intellectually sound. The "mad poet," however, represents the reverse of this ideal, as their unrestrained obsession with their own ideas undermines the harmony and discipline necessary for great art.

"He's mad: like a bear, that's broken the bars of its cage
The pest puts all to flight, learned or not, with reciting:
Whom he takes tight hold of, he grips, and reads to death,
A leech that never loses the skin, till gorged with blood."

Horace describes how such a poet becomes a "leech," clinging to anyone who will listen, reciting his work compulsively, and draining their patience. The poetic obsession of such a poet is like a parasite that feeds on attention, unable to stop until he's "gorged with blood." Through these images, Horace warns poets to avoid becoming too attached to their work or ego, emphasizing the importance of knowing one's limitations, seeking honest critique, and staying grounded. He humorously critiques the mad poet's social behavior as well, portraying them as oblivious to the reactions of others. Their inflated self-perception blinds them to constructive criticism, isolating them from their peers and society. He suggests that if someone were to take one of these poets to a physician, the poet would insanely deny of help, insisting on their own brilliance even as they subjected to artistic failure.

Through this concept, Horace underscores the importance of balance in poetry. While creativity and passion are essential, they must be guided by reason, technique, and a clear understanding of the audience. The mad poet serves as a warning against the dangers of excess and self-delusion, highlighting the necessity of humility and the willingness to learn from others. The critique of the mad poet is not merely a condemnation but a reminder of the responsibility that comes with artistic ambition. By presenting this archetype, Horace encourages poets to strive for excellence through a combination of inspiration, discipline, and critical self-awareness, ensuring their work is both meaningful and enduring.

In broad sense, Horace presents the "mad poet" can also be apprehended as the reflection of the broader tension in his work between maintaining decorum and exploration of new ideas and styles. While he acknowledges the importance of inspiration and passion in the creative process, Horace warns that these qualities must be treated with discipline, study, and critical assessment. Poets who only rely on raw talent or emotional intensity, without honing their craft are prone to the risk of producing work that lacks coherence and resonance.

In conclusion, Horace uses the concept of the mad poet as a cautionary figure to underscore the importance of cultivating poetic sensibility and understanding of artistic decorum emphasizing the fact that while creativity and passion are essential to poetry, they must be balanced with discipline, critical judgment, and a respect for the audience and tradition. . Horace thus presents the poet as a multifaceted figure whose creations are not only aesthetically pleasing but also meaningful, impactful, and timeless.

4. References and Suggested readings:

i.   Horace: Ars Poetica
ii.   Horace: Ars Poetica, The Poetry Foundation (https://www.poetryfoundation.org)
iii.   The Satires of Horace, Niall Rudd
iv.   The Cambridge Companion to Horace, ed., Stephen Harison
v.   Epistula and Pisoners and the poetry of antiquity", the times Literary Supplement
vi.   Harry Blamires: A History of Literary Criticism

UNIT – 2

LONGINUS: ON THE SUBLIME

1. **About the author**

2. **On the Sublime**

    a.   Introduction

    b.   Synopsis

    c.   Analysis

3. **Probable Questions:**

    a.   Theorize the concepts of sublimity and it's five principal sources.

    b.   Analyze how Longinus' text on sublimity is a digression front the thinkers like Plato and Horace.

4. **References and suggested readings**

1. About the author

Longinus is a somewhat enigmatic figure in ancient literary criticism best known for his influential work "On the Sublime". The identity of Longinus is not known. The author was certainly not the third century rhetorician Cassius Longinus to whom the work was often attributed as per the historians and the critics.

Modern readers encounter in Longinus, as a writer who is far more akin to them than to Plato, Aristotle or Horace. Though his identity remains uncertain and scholars have long debated who he was, the work under this name has left a significant impact on literary and aesthetic thought, particularly on the idea of the 'sublime'.

Although Longinus may not be as widely known as Aristotle or Plato, his work has had a profound effect on literary theory, particularly in understanding the emotional and transcendent qualities of art.

2. On the Sublime

• Introduction

On the Sublime written in the 1st century CE is attributed to the Greek philosopher Longinus, whose real identity remains a mystery. This influential work explores the concept of sublimity in literature, focusing on what elevates certain texts to greatness and evokes profound emotional responses in readers. Longinus addresses the need for authenticity and passion in writing, arguing that true sublimity arises from the writer's powerful soul and genuine emotional experiences rather than from mere technical skill or rigid adherence to form. He identifies several sources of sublimity, including nature, emotion, the use of rhetorical figures, the greatness of thought, and dignified language. By emphasizing the importance of emotional engagement and the organic flow of ideas, Longinus critiques the formalism seen in the works of his contemporaries. This work not only seeks to define the essence of sublime literature but also serves as a guide for writers, encouraging them to tap into universal emotions and lofty themes that resonate deeply with audiences.

The ideas presented in 'On the Sublime' have significantly influenced literary criticism throughout history, shaping discussions around the nature of art, aesthetics, and the emotional power of language, making it a seminal text in the field of rhetoric and literary theory. This influential work explores the concept of sublimity in literature, focusing on what elevates certain texts to greatness and evokes profound emotional responses in readers. Longinus addresses the need for authenticity and passion in writing, arguing that true sublimity arises from the writer's powerful soul and genuine emotional experiences rather than from mere technical skill or rigid adherence to form. He identifies several sources of sublimity, including nature, emotion, the use of rhetorical figures, the greatness of thought, and dignified language. By emphasizing the importance of emotional engagement and the organic flow of ideas, Longinus critiques the formalism seen in the works of his contemporaries, particularly in the teachings of Horace, who favored structure and decorum. This work not only seeks to define the essence of sublime literature but also serves as a guide for writers, encouraging them to tap into universal emotions and lofty themes that resonate deeply with audiences.

The ideas presented in 'On the Sublime' thus, have significantly influenced literary criticism throughout history, shaping discussions around the nature of art, aesthetics, and the emotional power of language, making it a seminal text in the field of rhetoric and literary theory.

- **Synopsis**

Longinus explores the essence of greatness in literature, particularly focusing on the concept of sublimity. He defines sublimity as a quality of writing that elevates the audience's emotional and intellectual experience, inducing feelings of awe and grandeur. Unlike mere artistry or technical skill, sublimity goes beyond the ordinary expression, providing readers with profound insights into the human condition. At the heart of

Longinus' argument is the intrinsic quality of the writer's spirit; he posits that a powerful and passionate soul is essential for producing sublime literature. This innate sense of greatness enables writers to tap into and express universal emotions that resonate across time and culture. Longinus emphasizes that writers who possess a deep connection to the complexities and beauties of the world around them can channel these insights into their writing, thereby capturing the essence of the sublime.

Longinus identifies several key sources from which sublimity can arise. First, he discusses nature, asserting that a writer's natural disposition and inner strength are fundamental to achieving sublimity. This power within the writer allows them to perceive the world in a profound way and communicate these insights effectively. He emphasizes on emotion, arguing that the intensity of feeling whether drawn from personal experiences or universal themes greatly influences the sublime nature of a text. Longinus believes that emotional depth not only engages the audience but also connects them to the narrative on a visceral level, allowing for a shared experience that heightens the text's impact.

Longinus highlights the use of figurative and rhetoric language, asserting the importance of rhetorical devices such as metaphors, hyperbole, and rhetorical questions in enhancing the grandeur of a text. He illustrates how effective imagery and well-crafted metaphors can evoke powerful emotional responses, drawing readers into the narrative. Longinus asserts of the greatness of thought, arguing that profound ideas contribute significantly to the perception of sublimity in literature. Themes that explore human existence, morality, and the divine resonate deeply with readers, prompting them to reflect on their own lives. Longinus also addresses the necessity of dignified language in creating sublime literature, arguing that the choice of words and their arrangement must reflect the grandeur of the ideas being expressed. While emphasizing the importance of elevated language, Longinus warns against excessive ornamentation and exaggerated style that can detract from the core message. He asks for a balance that preserves the authenticity of the expression.

Sublime literature he acknowledges has the power to transport readers beyond their ordinary experiences, allowing them to grasp higher truths and experience moments of clarity and insight. This transformative quality of literature is what makes it significant and enduring; it engages both the heart and mind of the reader, leaving a lasting impression. He articulates that sublimity is not a mere artistic technique but a dynamic force that resonates with readers through the authentic expression of emotion, the exploration of universal themes, and the effective use of rhetorical devices. By positioning sublimity as an essential quality of great literature, Longinus invites writers to embrace the raw power of authentic emotion and the potential of their art to elevate the human spirit, making his work a seminal reference in the study of literature, rhetoric, and the enduring quest for greatness in artistic expression.

[120]

- **Analysis**

Longinus begins with his critique of the treatise on the sublime written by Caecilius, which he and his friend Terentianus previously examined. He feels Caecilius's work lacks depth and fails to address the core elements necessary in a discussion of the sublime. Longinus points out that Caecilius's treatise does not fulfill two essential tasks for such a work. First, Caecilius does not define the subject clearly. Second, and more importantly, he does not offer guidance on how readers might elevate their own abilities to achieve sublimity in their writing. Instead, he observes that Caecilius focuses too much on examples, as if readers were unfamiliar with the concept of the sublime. Longinus implies that merely illustrating the sublime is insufficient; the real value of a treatise lies in teaching the reader how to attain it themselves. Despite these shortcomings, Longinus acknowledges that Caecilius's efforts are commendable in intention, even if they lack a complete treatment of the subject. Longinus acknowledges Terentianus who asked Longinus to write his own reflections on the sublime, which Longinus now undertakes with a view toward providing insights that might benefit those engaged in public life or "men of affairs."Longinus expresses confidence in Terentianus's ability to understand and appreciate his ideas, showing trust that his friend will offer honest and constructive criticism.

Longinus defines the sublime as a form of "loftiness and excellence of language" that elevates a work and grants it enduring greatness.

"...the Sublime, wherever it occurs, consists in a certain loftiness and excellence of language, and that it is by this and this only, that the greatest poets and prose-writers have gained eminence..."

He explains that the sublime goes beyond merely convincing the reader rationally; it is so powerful that it "takes him out of himself" by stirring awe and emotional engagement. This effect, Longinus argues, is what has given the greatest poets and prose writers their lasting fame.

Longinus contrasts the sublime with other literary qualities such as skilled invention and clear organization that build appreciation gradually as one reads. The sublime, on the other hand, has a sudden and overwhelming effect, like a "lightning-flash" that reveals the full power of an orator or writer in an instant.

"...but a sublime thought, if happily timed, illumines an entire subject with the vividness of a lightning-flash, and exhibits the whole power of the orator in a moment of time."

He suggests that sublime moments in literature do not merely appeal to reason or agreement; they compel readers to feel admiration, overriding mere judgment.

Longinus addresses a critical question: can the quality of sublimity in writing be taught, or is it purely a natural gift.

"The first question which presents itself for solution is whether there is any art which can teach sublimity or loftiness in writing."

Some critics argue that sublime writing cannot be reduced to rules or can be taught through art; they believe it springs directly from the genius, which is prone to getting diminished when imposed by technical rules on it. According to this view, attempting to teach sublimity risks of stripping away its natural essence and replacing it with lifeless formulas. However, Longinus counters this claim by asserting that while the sublime originates from nature and passion, it can indeed be refined through the guidance of art. He explains that true greatness in writing requires not just natural talent but also the discipline and structure provided by technique. Using the metaphor of a ship, he compares unrestrained passion to a vessel adrift without ballast, which may lose direction and purpose. He asserts that just as great passions need both encouragement and restraint, a writer's genius, if ungoverned by technique, risks becoming uncontrolled and ineffective.

Longinus further references Demosthenes's insight that fortune is invaluable, yet it needs the "good counsel" of reason to reach its full potential.

"...for good fortune is utterly ruined by the absence of good counsel, may be applied to literature, if we substitute genius for fortune, and art for counsel."

He applies this to writing, suggesting that while natural genius like fortune is essential, it requires the discipline of art to be truly effective. Art, in Longinus's view, enables a writer to know when to follow raw inspiration and when to temper it with skill. He urges critics to reconsider their dismissal of art's role in achieving sublimity, suggesting that these insights may lead them to value the balance between genius and method in creating enduring literature.

Longinus critiques a common flaw in writing i.e. the pursuit of superficial qualities like brilliancy, polish, and attractiveness. He observes that some writers, in their attempt to appear refined or captivating, end up producing work that seems trivial, insincere and superficial.

"Such expressions, and such images, produce an effect of confusion and obscurity, not of energy; and if each separately be examined under the light of criticism, what seemed terrible gradually sinks into absurdity."

This issue, as Longinus notes, often arises when an author is swept away by personal feelings that don't align with the subject, resulting in displays of emotion that may feel forced or disconnected. It results with the failure to resonate with the readers.

Longinus critiques three major flaws in writing that undermine the pursuit of sublimity- bombast, puerility, and false sentiment. Each of these vices arises when the writers fail to balance authenticity, restraint, and grandeur, leading their work to appear exaggerated, trivial, or emotionally hollow. Longinus notes that writers often fall into the misconception when they fear their style might otherwise seem weak or lacking. To avoid "feebleness and poverty of language," they try too hard to elevate their writing, creating a style that becomes hollow and unnatural. Puerility, according to Longinus, stems from an overly pedantic, meticulous style that lacks emotional depth or naturalness. Writers who fall into puerility focus excessively on polish, refinement, and intellectual cleverness, over elaborating details in a way that leads to "frigidity," or a cold, detached effect.

"By puerility we mean a pedantic habit of mind, which by over elaboration ends in frigidity."

The third flaw i.e. false sentiment, involves a misuse of emotion in writing. Longinus explains that, as described by Theodorus.

"...Theodorus used to call false sentiment, meaning by that an ill-timed and empty display of emotion, where no emotion is called for, or of greater emotion than the situation warrants."

False sentiment is the display of emotion that is either inappropriate for the situation or overly exaggerated. It often occurs when an author is carried away by personal feelings that do not fit with the subject matter, resulting in expressions of emotion that seem misplaced or irrelevant.

Longinus critiques the writing of Timaeus, who, according to him, exemplifies the poor judgment often associated with plagiarists. He suggests that Timaeus lacks originality and insight, even appropriating a particularly ineffective phrase from Xenophon, which he describes as "frigidity." Longinus uses a specific example from Timaeus's narrative about Agathocles, who abducted his cousin from a festival. Timaeus's question "Who could have done such a deed, unless he had harlots instead of maidens in his eyes?", is seen as lacking depth and creativity by Longinus, as he finds the phrasing to be an ineffectual attempt that fails to convey the seriousness of the action being described. Longinus also turns his attention to Plato, a figure he otherwise regards as a "supreme master of style." He points out two passages in which Plato's choice of words lacks the eloquence expected of such a distinguished philosopher. For instance, in discussing recording tablets, Plato writes,

"They shall write, and deposit in the temples memorials of cypress wood."

Longinus implies that this description lacks the vividness and weight that would befit a philosophical discourse. Here, he seems to find Plato's metaphors inadequate and lacking in the sublime quality that characterizes his best work.

Longinus extends his criticism to Herodotus, noting that when he describes beautiful women as "tortures to the eye". While Longinus acknowledges that this comment may have been made in the context of drunken barbarians, he still argues that such errors in taste are unacceptable in great literature. The portrayal of beauty in this manner is seen as inappropriate, detracting from the overall dignity and impact of the narrative.Longinus emphasizes that even revered authors like Plato and Herodotus can lapse into mediocrity through poor choices in language and imagery.

Longinus suggests that the pursuit of novelty can lead to the creation of sublime and captivating images that enhance a text's appeal, but at the same time it can also result in significant failures of style that diminish a writer's work. Longinus emphasizes that the very elements that can elevate a piece of writing such as stylistic ornaments, figures of speech, and vivid imagery are also the sources of potential failure. For instance, he mentions various literary devices like transitions and hyperboles, suggesting that while they can enhance a text's dynamism and expressiveness, they also carry inherent risks if are used improperly. Overly ambitious attempts at expressions can lead to confusion or a lack of cohesion in a piece, as writers may lose sight of their original intent or the clarity of their message. He mentions the using plurals for singulars indicating a possible inclination toward excessive ornamentation, which can further detract from the intended meaning and effectiveness of the writing.

Longinus elaborates on the characteristics of true sublimity in literature, emphasizing the importance of depth and lasting impact in writing. He posits that a passage qualifies as sublime when it is so compelling that it captures and holds the reader's attention to the extent that it becomes hard, and impossible, to distract the attention from it:

"...when a passage is pregnant in suggestion, when it is hard, nay impossible, to distract the attention from it, and when it takes a strong and lasting hold on the memory, then we may be sure that we have lighted on the true Sublime..."

This suggests that the language, ideas, or emotions presented in such passages is so engaging that they command the reader's focus, creating an immersive experience. For Longinus, true sublimity is marked by its ability to "take a strong and lasting hold on the memory." This implies that sublime writing is memorable; it leaves a profound impression that persists long after the reader has finished engaging with the text. Such a lasting effect indicates that the writing resonates deeply, provoking thought and reflection beyond the immediate act of reading.

Longinus further asserts that words deemed to be truly noble and sublime possess a universal appeal, meaning they have the capacity to please and engage all readers, regardless of their individual differences. He emphasizes that when a single book consistently elicits the same positive response from diverse audiences regardless of their pursuits, lifestyles, aspirations, ages, or languages it exemplifies a remarkable "harmony of opposites." This concept suggests that despite the varied backgrounds and perspectives of its readers, the work achieves a consensus of appreciation and admiration. This harmony lends the text an "irresistible authority," meaning that the collective positive reception reinforces the work's value and significance.

"For when the same book always produces the same impression on all who read it, whatever be the difference in their pursuits, their manner of life, their aspirations, their ages, or their language, such a harmony of opposites gives irresistible authority to their favourable verdict."

Longinus implies that such universal acclaim not only speaks of the quality of the writing but also elevates the work to a status of enduring relevance and respect within the literary canon.

Longinus outlines five essential sources of sublimity in writing and oration, emphasizing that mastery of language is a prerequisite for achieving true sublimity. Each of these sources contributes to the overall impact and effectiveness of a text, and Longinus is keen to differentiate between different aspects of writing that can lead to sublime expression

"enumerate the five principal sources, as we may call them, from which almost all sublimity is derived, assuming, of course, the preliminary gift on which all these five sources depend, namely, command of language. The first and the most important is (1) grandeur of thought, as I have pointed out elsewhere in my work on Xenophon. The second is (2) a vigorous and spirited treatment of the passions. These two conditions of sublimity depend mainly on natural endowments, whereas those which follow derive assistance from Art. The third is (3) a certain artifice in the employment of figures, which are of two kinds, figures of thought and figures of speech. The fourth is (4) dignified expression, which is sub-divided into (a) the proper choice of words, and (b) the use of metaphors and other ornaments of diction. The fifth cause of sublimity, which embraces all those preceding, is (5) majesty and elevation of structure."

The first and foremost source is grandeur of thought, which refers to the depth and significance of the ideas presented. Longinus argues that profound insights and themes are essential for resonating with readers and creating a lasting impact. He draws on his previous work on Xenophon to illustrate how great thoughts contribute to the sublimity of a text. The second source is the vigorous treatment of the passions. Longinus posits that engaging with human emotions in a spirited and intense manner elevates writing to a sublime level. This involves not merely evoking emotional responses but doing so with genuine vigor and passion, making the writing powerful and memorable. The third source pertains to artifice in the employment of figures, which includes both figures of thought and figures of speech. Longinus emphasizes the importance of skillfully using rhetorical devices to enhance the text's expressiveness and engagement. The effective manipulation of these figures enriches the narrative and contributes significantly to its sublimity. The fourth source focuses on dignified expression, which Longinus subdivides into the proper choice of words and the use of metaphors and other linguistic ornaments. He highlights that selecting appropriate language is crucial for conveying the subject matter effectively and that figurative language can add layers of meaning, enhancing the aesthetic quality of the writing. This dignified expression is essential for achieving sublimity. The fifth source encompasses majesty and elevation of structure, which refers to the overall organization and integrity of the work. Longinus argues that a well-structured text, with a seamless arrangement of ideas, reinforces the grandeur of the writing. An elevated structure ensures that the writing flows smoothly and maintains a sense of magnificence, contributing to the reader's experience of the sublime.

Longinus critiques the earlier writer Caecilius for omitting some of these essential sources, particularly the treatment of emotions. He suggests that Caecilius may have mistakenly equated sublimity with pathos, believing that they are always interdependent. He critiques Caecilius's perspective, suggesting that if Caecilius believes that pathos does not contribute to sublimity, he is mistaken. Longinus asserts that genuine passion can significantly enhance sublimity. He describes this passion as an "appropriate display" that possesses a sort of "fine madness" and "divine inspiration". Longinus emphasizes that the use of plurals to amplify a subject should be judicious. He cautions against excessive ornamentation, warning that "to overlay every sentence with ornament is very pedantic."

Longinus underscores the necessity of precision in language, particularly when addressing monumental events such as shipwrecks or historical conquests. The focus on the artistry involved in crafting vivid descriptions that convey deep emotional resonance and gravitas. The core idea presented is that sublime writing depends on the selection of essential details that contribute to the overall emotional landscape of the narrative. Longinus emphasizes that authors who master these crafts such as those who depict a shipwreck or Demosthenes recounting the news of Elatea, are capable at distilling their narratives to only the most impactful elements. This approach not only enhances clarity but also fosters a sense of immediacy and urgency.

Longinus asserts that nothing amplifies the energy of a speech quite like the combination of different figures of speech. This multi-purpose approach allows orators to engage their audience on multiple levels, enhancing the vigor, cogency, and beauty of their arguments. The collaborative effect of various rhetorical strategies creates a dynamic presentation that can stir the emotions of the audience. Longinus highlights that the orator's shift in direction and structure serves to avoid monotony in the speech. He notes that stillness in language produces rest, which can detract from the passionate nature of the subject matter. Instead, the "disorder of language" reflects the agitation and turmoil of the human soul, mirroring the emotional intensity of the situation being described. He cites Demosthenes as a prime example of how effective use of repetition, varied structure, and emotive language can create a powerful oratorical effect that resonates deeply with the audience.

Longinus examines the rhetorical power of plural forms in language, emphasizing their ability to convey a sense of magnitude and emotional weight. He specifically points out how the use of plurals can create an impression of multiplied calamity or significance, thereby enhancing the impact of the narrative.

Longinus highlights how the use of singular forms to represent collective entities can imbue a statement with dignity and grandeur. He cites Demosthenes's phrase, "Thereupon all Peloponnesus was divided," where the contraction of a plural concept (the region of Peloponnesus) into a singular expression elevates the significance of the event. By referring to the whole region as a singular entity, Demosthenes bestows a sense of importance and unity upon the event, suggesting a collective impact rather than mere individual actions.

",,,their betokening emotion, by giving a sudden change of complexion to the circumstances,—whether a word which is strictly singular is unexpectedly changed into a plural,—or whether a number of isolated units are combined by the use of a single sonorous word under one head."

The unexpected the unification of multiple entities creates a striking change in tone, deepening the emotional resonance of the narrative.

Longinus then shifts to another technique: presenting past events in a manner that evokes immediacy, transforming the narrative into a dramatic action. He uses an example from Xenophon, where the description of a man who strikes the belly of Cyrus's horse as it tramples him transforms a static account into a vivid scene. By framing past actions as if they are occurring in the present, the narrative gains a dynamic quality, drawing the audience into the action as though they are witnessing it firsthand.

"When past events are introduced as happening in present time the narrative form is changed into 51a dramatic action. Such is that description in Xenophon: "A man who has fallen, and is being trampled under foot by Cyrus's horse, strikes the belly of the animal with his scimitar; the horse starts aside and unseats Cyrus, and he falls." Similarly in many passages of Thucydides."

This technique is effective in capturing the intensity of the moment, making the audience feel the urgency and drama of the situation. Longinus notes that Thucydides employs similar strategies throughout his works, indicating that this method is not just a stylistic choice but a fundamental aspect of effective narrative that heightens emotional engagement.

Longinus examines the effectiveness of changing perspectives and emotional expressions in enhancing the sublimity of literary works. Longinus argues that such stylistic devices can evoke profound feelings and captivate audiences, drawing attention to specific emotions and ideas. He refers to Hector in the narrative of 'Iliad' which provides a rich example of how shifts in emotional tone and perspective contribute to the grandeur of literary expression.

"To have interposed any such words as "Hector said so and so" would have had a frigid effect. As the lines stand the writer is left behind by his own words, and the transition is 53effected while he is preparing for it. 2Accordingly the proper use of this figure is in dealing with some urgent crisis which will not allow the writer to linger, but compels him to make a rapid change from one person to another…".

He begins by noting that the poet assumes the narrative voice, which is essential for storytelling, but then immediately attributes an "abrupt threat" to Hector, the Trojan chief, without any prior indication. This method is effective because it immerses the reader in the immediate emotional state of the character without the distancing effect of a formal introduction, such as stating, "Hector said so and so." By omitting this framing, the poet allows the intensity of Hector's anger to unfold naturally; creating a sense of urgency that propels the narrative forward.

Longinus illustrates this technique further with the example from Hecataeus, where Ceyx speaks directly and urgently to the children of Heracles, commanding them to leave to avoid harm. The directness of Ceyx's speech, marked by the imperative "get ye forth into some other land," exemplifies how rapid transitions can reflect the gravity of the situation, effectively conveying the emotional stakes involved. Longinus acknowledges the importance of abrupt transitions and shifts in perspective as powerful tools for enhancing emotional depth and urgency in literature. By effectively employing these techniques, writers can create moments of sublime intensity that resonate with readers and convey the profound emotions experienced by the characters.

He highlights on the role of periphrasis or the use of circumlocution that is the use of many words where fewer would do; in enhancing the sublimity of language. Longinus draws a parallel between music and languages, asserting that just as simple melodies are enriched by harmony, so too can straightforward expressions gain beauty and depth when expressed through periphrasis. This technique allows for a more elegant and elevated presentation of ideas, provided that it avoids becoming inflated or harsh.

Longinus supports his argument with examples from notable literary figures. He cites Plato's Funeral Oration, where the phrase "destined journey" elegantly encapsulates the concept of death. By using periphrasis to describe death in this way, Plato imbues the notion of mortality with dignity, transforming a stark reality into a more profound and respectful representation. The phrase "sped on your way" further elevates the language, highlighting the ceremonial nature of death and burial, which aligns with the honor and respect owed to the deceased. Longinus points out that these expressions are akin to musical harmonization they take simple, raw ideas and infuse them with a melodic quality that resonates more deeply with the audience. He also references Xenophon, who uses periphrasis to express the idea of labor as "the guide to a pleasant life." By expanding the language in this way, Xenophon enhances the significance of labor, transforming a straightforward statement into a reflection on virtue and the soldierly spirit. This elevation of language adds a layer of complexity and nobility to the sentiment being expressed.

Longinus argues that the use of appropriate and striking words is crucial for all orators and writers, as it imbues their works with an inherent beauty and grandeur comparable to the finest sculptures. This concept aligns with his broader thesis on sublimity, where he asserts that the elevation of thought and feeling in literature is achieved through the mastery of language. He emphasizes on that the appropriate language not only enhances the aesthetic appeal of a text but also grants it a "vocal soul," bringing the facts and ideas to life for the reader. This metaphor suggests that the choice of words can animate and energize ideas, making them resonate on a deeper emotional level. He compares beautiful language to light, indicating that it illuminates thought and enhances the reader's understanding and appreciation of the subject matter. However, Longinus also cautions against the indiscriminate use of grandiose language. He notes that using imposing language for trivial subjects can lead to absurdity, comparing it to placing a large tragic mask on a child. This illustrates the idea that while elevated language can elevate thought, it must be appropriately matched to the subject matter. The elegance of language should not overshadow or misrepresent the essence of the topic being addressed. This balance is critical in achieving sublimity in writing. Longinus's emphasis on the appropriateness of language underscores his belief that true greatness in literature is not merely about the use of lofty or elaborate expressions but about their effectiveness in conveying deeper meaning and emotion.

He emphasizes on the significant impact of figurative language, particularly metaphors, on the elevation of literary expression. Longinus argues that the effective use of figurative language can significantly enhance the sublimity of a text, especially in impassioned and descriptive passages.

"...that the choice of appropriate and striking words has a marvellous power and an enthralling charm for the reader, that this is the main object of pursuit with all orators and writers, that it is this, and this alone, which causes the works of literature to exhibit the glowing perfections of the finest statues, their grandeur, 57their beauty, their mellowness, their dignity, their energy, their power, and all their other graces, and that it is this which endows the facts with a vocal soul;"

He acknowledges that, while metaphors can elevate language, they also carry the risk of excess, which can detract from clarity and effectiveness. Longinus critiques Plato for his tendency to indulge in overly extravagant metaphors and allegories, suggesting that such "frenzies of language" can lead to a lack of sobriety in writing. For instance, he references Plato's metaphor of a city blended like wine in a bowl, illustrating how Plato's lofty comparisons, while imaginative, can veer into the realm of the absurd. This tendency to employ excessive metaphorical language can make an otherwise profound idea seem trivial or overly complex.

The criticisms from contemporaries, like Caecilius, serve to highlight a broader tension between different styles of rhetoric. Caecilius's praise of Lysias as a more faultless writer contrasts with his disparagement of Plato, indicating a preference for clarity and simplicity over the passionate expressiveness.

"Caecilius made his ground of attack, when he had the boldness in his essay "On the Beauties of Lysias" to pronounce that writer superior in every respect to Plato…"
Longinus defends Plato, asserting that the latter's occasional lapses into metaphorical excess are outweighed by the grandeur and depth of his insights.

Longinus reflects on the extraordinary qualities of a great orator, presumably referring to figures such as Demosthenes, who are celebrated for their exceptional rhetorical skills. He explores the distinctions between two prominent figures in the light of oration: Plato and Lysias. He highlights that while Lysias although is an accomplished writer, falls short of Plato not only in the degree of his merits but also in their quantity.

"But in the case of Plato and Lysias there is, as I said, a further difference. Not only is Lysias vastly inferior to

Plato in the degree of his merits, but in their number as well; and at the same time he is as far ahead of Plato in the number of his faults as he is behind in that of his merits."

In other words, Lysias possesses less strength as a rhetorician compared to Plato and, conversely, has more significant faults. This comparison sets the stage for a broader philosophical discussion about the nature of human aspiration, creativity, and the inherent drive toward greatness.

Longinus reflects on the interplay between nature and art, particularly in the context of literature and sculpture. He begins with a poetic reference to the enduring beauty of nature, using the imagery of lofty trees and restless waters to evoke a sense of the sublime through elements that are grand and timeless. Longinus addresses a debate about the merits of two types of sculptures: the "Colossus," which is a massive and disproportionate statue, and the "Doryphorus" created by Polycletus, known for its ideal proportions and human likeness. He acknowledges that some critics argue against preferring the Colossus due to its lack of proportionality.

"...we should not prefer the huge disproportioned Colossus to the Doryphorus of Polycletus."

Longinus counters this argument by emphasizing that in art, precision and exactness must be appreciated, in respect of nature. He suggests that while visual arts focus on human resemblance, literature seeks to evoke emotions and ideas that surpass human experience essentially, it aims for the sublime. He further explains that the faculty of speech and expression in literature is derived from the inspiration of nature. This connection underscores his belief that literature should aspire to capture the grandeur of the natural world, aspiring for something beyond mere human representation.

Longinus discusses the use of hyperbole in literature, particularly on how it can be most effective when it arises naturally from the context of a dramatic or emotional situation.

"Hence it is necessary to know where to draw the line; for if ever it is overstepped the effect of the hyperbole is spoilt, being in such cases relaxed by overstraining, and producing the very opposite to the effect desired."

He emphasizes that the power of hyperbole is amplified when it is not overly obvious or forced; rather, it should emerge organically from the circumstances being described. Longinus asserts that hyperbole, an exaggerated statement not meant to be taken literally can be impactful when it appears subtle or disguised within a larger narrative. This effectiveness is particularly evident when an author conveys strong emotions or describes intense events.

"...the hyperbole is then most effective when it appears in disguise. And this effect is produced when a writer, impelled by strong feeling, speaks in the accents of some tremendous crisis; as Thucydides does in describing the massacre in Sicily..."

He cites Thucydides as an example, specifically referencing his account of the massacre in Sicily. Longinus observes that in this passage, Thucydides illustrates the horrors of war by describing how the

Syracusans not only pursued their enemies but also continued to drink from a river that was polluted with mud and blood. The shocking nature of this scene makes the hyperbole credible; the reader can understand the desperation and chaos that would drive people to such extremes in the face of war and destruction. Longinus discusses how hyperbole can serve dual purposes of either it can amplify a statement to make it seem larger than life or minimize something to make it seem less significant.

Longinus examines the relationship between language, rhythm, and the emotional impact of rhetoric, using a specific example from Demosthenes. He highlights how the structure and arrangement of words in a phrase can greatly enhance or diminish its sublimity. Longinus quotes Demosthenes' decree and points out that the sentiment expressed is profound and significant, indicating that the decree was pivotal in informing a serious threat to the city. However, he also emphasizes that the effectiveness of this statement lies not only in its meaning but also in its rhythmic quality. The passage that is entirely in dactylic meter is characterized by a rhythmic pattern that is considered noble and majestic, contributing to the overall gravitas of the statement. Longinus argues that if this phrase were moved to the beginning or if even one syllable were cut off, the impact of the passage would be significantly weakened.

Longinus highlights the importance of arrangement and diction in achieving sublimity in writing, particularly in poetry. He begins by citing a common phrase, "I'm full of woes, I have no room for more," illustrating how even ordinary words can attain a sublime quality through careful selection of words and their arrangement. This asserts his point that it is not solely the ideas or thoughts expressed in a work that contribute to its greatness, but also how those ideas are presented. Longinus uses the example of Euripides' lines about Dirce being dragged by a bull to illustrate this concept further.

"The circumstance is noble in itself, but it gains in vigour because the language is disposed so as not to hurry the movement, not running, as it were, on wheels, because there is a distinct stress on each word, and the time is delayed, advancing slowly to a pitch of stately sublimity".

He notes that while the event described is inherently noble and significant, it is the arrangement of the words that evokes its emotional impact and grandeur. By emphasizing on the deliberate pacing and the distinct stress placed on each word, Longinus argues that the movement of the language plays a critical role in creating a sense of "stately sublimity". Such careful structuring not only enhances the visual aspect of the scene but also allows the audience to fully absorb the gravity of what is being depicted.

Longinus critiques the use of certain rhythmic patterns in writing that detract from the overall tone and dignity of a style. He identifies an "effeminate and hurried movement" in language that arises from the overuse of specific metrical feet like the pyrrhics, trochees, and dichorees that can create a rhythmic effect akin to a "regular dance measure."

"Nothing so much degrades the tone of a style as an effeminate and hurried movement in the language, such as is produced by pyrrhics and trochees and dichorees..."

This type of rhythm is viewed as inappropriate and detrimental to the gravitas expected in sublime writing. Longinus argues that such rhythmic excess leads to a sense of coxcombry (excessive self-conceit) and petty affectation, making the writing tiresome due to its monotonous and repetitive nature. He emphasizes that the primary concern of sublime writing should be its meaning and emotional impact rather than the cadence of the words. When passages become overly rhythmic, they can distract the audience from the content of the message. Just as listeners to a ballad might focus more on the melody than the lyrics readers or listeners of over-rhythmical passages can become preoccupied with the rhythm itself rather than the meaning conveyed in the verses. Furthermore, Longinus warns against reducing sentences to overly simplistic structures filled with short words and syllables that crowd too closely together. This fragmentation can lead to a loss of coherence and fluidity in the writing, making it feel artificial or forced. Such construction, while technically sound, lacks the elegance and grace needed for effective and powerful communication.

Longinus emphasizes on the balance that is needed in diction to achieve sublimity in writing, emphasizing that both excessive brevity and excessive length can detract from the quality of expression. He argues that when diction is overly confined or compressed, it leads to a diminishment of sublimity, resulting in a lack of grandeur in the writing. This compression does not refer to the effective use of compact phrases that convey meaning efficiently but instead refers to a style that is so strained that it loses its effect and depth. Longinus warns that cutting words too short can lead to a loss of meaning, similar to pruning a tree to the point where it can no longer thrive.

"To cut your words too short is to prune away their sense, but to be concise is to be direct. On the other hand, we know that a style becomes lifeless by over-extension, I mean by being relaxed to an unseasonable length.
The use of mean words has also a strong tendency to degrade a lofty passage."

It indicates that while conciseness is a valuable trait in writing, it must not come at the expense of clarity or richness of expression. Conciseness should be about being direct and to the point, ensuring that the message remains impactful and resonates with the audience. On the contrary, he notes that a style can become "lifeless" when it is excessively extended.

Longinus elaborates on the ideal qualities of sublime writing, reinforcing the need for nobility and dignity in literary expression. He begins with the idea that when aiming for sublimity, writers should avoid descending into base or trivial subjects unless absolutely necessary. This reflects a commitment to maintaining a high standard in writing that aligns with the elevated themes being discussed. Heinsists that he does not need to enumerate the specific faults that can diminish a literary style. Instead, he emphasizes the importance of understanding and implementing the qualities that bestow nobility and loftiness on writing. By doing so, he implies that writers should inherently recognize that anything contrary to these principles will inevitably degrade and deform their work.

"It is clear, then, that whatever is contrary to these will generally degrade and deform it."

In the concluding section, Longinus offers a scathing critique of the moral and ethical decay present in contemporary society and its impact on the quality of literary criticism and artistic creation. He begins by drawing an analogy between a corrupt judge who accepts bribes and the broader societal conditions that undermine integrity and excellence.

"If a judge who passes sentence for a bribe can never more give a free and sound decision on a point of justice or honor..."

Just as a bribed judge is incapable of making fair judgments about justice and honor because his decisions are influenced by self-interest, Longinus argues that contemporary critics and creators of literature are similarly compromised by greed and moral decay. He expresses doubt that, amidst rampant corruption and avarice, any critic can render an unbiased judgment of literary works, as they are influenced by their own selfish desires. Longinus paints a tainted picture of his contemporaries, suggesting that the pervasive culture of bribery and self-serving behavior has rendered the pursuit of genuine artistic merit nearly impossible. He reflects on how people are driven by a "slavish greed," actively seeking personal gain at the expense of moral principles. The lamentation continues as Longinus remarks on the wasted potential of contemporary genius. He notes that the prevailing indifference that characterizes society endangers true creativity and intellectual engagement. When individuals do choose to act, their motivations are often shallow, driven by the desire for pleasure or public acclaim rather than a deeper, more meaningful pursuit of knowledge or virtue.

3. Probable Questions:

1.   Theorize the concepts of sublimity and its five principal sources.

Answer:

In 'On the Sublime', Longinus explores the concept of sublimity as a quality in writing that elevates it beyond ordinary expression, capturing the reader's imagination and stirring profound emotions. He identifies sublimity as a crucial element of great literature and rhetoric, discussing its sources, characteristics, and effects.

The concept of the sublime refers to an aesthetic quality that transcends or takes beyond ordinary beauty, evoking a profound emotional response characterized by feelings of awe, wonder, and sometimes terror. It represents a state or experience that exceeds the limits of human understanding and expression, often associated with grandeur, vastness, and the overwhelming power of nature or art. In the context of literature, the sublime refers to a quality or effect in writing that evokes deep emotional responses, often characterized by awe, wonder, and a sense of grandeur. It transcends mere beauty and engages the reader on a profound level, stirring feelings that can be both uplifting and overwhelming. Although Longinus doesn't clearly define the term, it can be observed based on his discourse that "Sublimity" according to him is an elevation of thought and expression that evokes profound emotions and inspires admiration in the audience, transcending ordinary language to touch on the universal truths of human experience. He identifies several key sources of sublimity, the first being the writer's innate genius or "natural temperament." This inherent passion and depth of feeling are crucial, as they allow the writer to connect deeply with the emotions of the audience. Longinus argues that sublime writing must arise from genuine emotional experiences, whether personal or shared, as it is this intensity of feeling that communicates significance and resonates with readers on a visceral level.

The authenticity of emotional experience plays a critical role in crafting sublime literature. Longinus asserts that, whether stemming from personal experiences or tapping into collective sentiments, genuine emotional engagement is vital for creating literature that resonates deeply with readers. He asserts that writers who are deeply passionate about their subjects can infuse their work with an intensity that resonates with readers. The intensity of feeling be it joy, sorrow, love, or despair infuses the text with significance, transforming it from mere words into a powerful emotional journey that captures the audience's emotional state.

Longinus addresses the stylistic qualities that enhance sublimity. He believes that a varied and dynamic style is essential for maintaining the audience's interest and evoking emotional responses. He cautions against excessive ornamentation, which can detract from the intended effect, advocating instead for a balance that allows for natural expression of thought and feeling. Longinus praises authors who master this balance, enabling their works to convey both emotional power and intellectual depth. Longinus discusses the role of figures of speech in achieving sublimity. He identifies the effective use of metaphors, hyperbole, and rhetorical questions as essential tools for enhancing the grandeur of a text. For instance, he highlights the ability of vivid imagery to create mental pictures that immerse readers in the narrative, making the experience more impactful.

Longinus highlights the importance of arrangement and diction in achieving sublimity in writing, particularly in poetry. By emphasizing the deliberate pacing and the distinct stress placed on each word, Longinus argues that the movement of the language plays a critical role in creating a sense of "stately sublimity". This careful structuring not only enhances the visual aspect of the scene but also allows the audience to fully absorb the gravity of what is being depicted in the work. Longinus argues that the use of appropriate and striking words is crucial for all orators and writers, as it uplifts their works with an inherent beauty and grandeur comparable to the finest sculptures. This concept aligns with his broader thesis on sublimity, where he asserts that the elevation of thought and feeling in literature is achieved through the mastery of language. Longinus highlights that appropriate language not only enhances the aesthetic appeal of a text but also grants it a "vocal soul," bringing the facts and ideas to life for the reader. He suggests that the choice of words can animate and energize ideas, making them resonate on a deeper emotional level. Longinus examines the effectiveness of changing perspectives and emotional expressions in enhancing the sublimity of literary works. Longinus argues that such stylistic devices can evoke profound feelings and captivate audiences, drawing attention to specific emotions and ideas. He refers to Hector in the narrative of 'Iliad' which provides a rich example of how shifts in emotional tone and perspective contribute to the grandeur of literary expression. Longinus provides further such examples from classical literature, illustrating how great authors managed to achieve sublimity through a careful selection of words and a genuine passion for their subjects.

Longinus defines five essential sources of sublimity in literature and oratory, emphasizing that a strong command of language is essential for achieving true sublimity. The five sources are: grandeur of thought; vigorous treatment of the passions; artifice in the employment of figures; dignified expression; majesty and elevation of structure.

He begins with grandeur of thought, which he considers the most crucial source. This concept involves the depth, significance, and magnitude of the ideas conveyed in a piece of writing. Longinus asserts that works rich with profound insights those that tackle universal themes or convey important truths resonate deeply with readers and elevate the discourse.

The second source is the vigorous treatment of the passions, which involves the passionate engagement with emotions such as love, anger, and admiration. Longinus asserts that effectively channeling and expressing these emotions can significantly enhance a text's impact. This requires an authentic intensity that captures the reader's attention and stirs their feelings. He believes that a writer's ability to evoke a powerful emotional response is integral to creating a sublime experience, as it allows the audience to connect on a deeper level with the material.

The third source pertains to artifice in the employment of figures, which Longinus categorizes into two types: figures of thought (conceptual frameworks that deeper meaning) and figures of speech (stylistic devices that enhance expression). He emphasizes that the skillful use of rhetorical devices such as metaphors, similes, and hyperbole that enriches the text, making it more engaging and memorable. These figures should be employed judiciously to create vivid imagery and elaborate on complex ideas, thereby adding layers of meaning and enhancing the text's overall aesthetic appeal.

The fourth source focuses on dignified expression, which Longinus breaks down into two components: the proper choice of words and the use of metaphors and other linguistic ornaments. He stresses that selecting precise and appropriate language is crucial for effectively conveying the intended message. The use of well-crafted metaphors and similes can evoke strong images and feelings in the reader, enhancing the text's emotional resonance and contributing to its sublimity.

The dignity of expression is crucial because it sets the tone for the piece and aligns with the elevated thoughts being presented.

The fifth source involves majesty and elevation of structure, encompassing the overall organization and coherence of the work. Longinus argues that a sublime text must have a well-structured narrative that unfolds logically and gracefully. This structure includes the arrangement of ideas and the flow of arguments, which should build upon each other to create a powerful cumulative effect. An elevated structure not only supports the grandeur of thought but also enhances the reader's experience, ensuring that the writing maintains a sense of magnificence and clarity.

At the same time, Longinus also cautions that while eloquence and figurative language can enhance a text, an overemphasis on ornamental elements can lead to what he terms "pedantry" making the work seem superficial. This occurs when writers become more focused on displaying their linguistic prowess than on conveying genuine emotion or thought. In such cases, the writing can become overly ornate, detracting from the message and ultimately alienating the reader. Longinus advocates for a balance between the use of rhetorical devices and the authenticity of the writer's expression. He asserts that true sublimity should not be the product of superficial use of language and style but should rather arise from the writer's deep engagement with the respective subject matter.

Thus, Longinus's concept of sublimity encompasses various essential elements, including the writer's genius, emotional engagement, and effective use of figures of speech, profound subject matter, and dynamic style. By emphasizing these components, he draws a framework through which sublime literature can be understood and appreciated.

2. Analyze how Longinus' text on sublimity is a digression front the thinkers like Plato and Horace.

Answer:

Longinus' treatise "On the Sublime" represents a significant digression from the philosophical frameworks established by thinkers like Plato and Horace, particularly in its approach to the nature and purpose of literary excellence. While both Plato and Horace emphasize the importance of morality and decorum in writing, Longinus shifts the focus towards the emotional and transcendent qualities of language that elevate it to the sublime.

Plato, in works such as "The Republic," primarily views literature through the lens of its moral and ethical implications. For him, poetry and such forms of artistic expression can manipulate emotions and distort truth, often leading to societal decay if not grounded in rational thought. He goes to the extent of employing censorship and putting a ban on poetry and art in his "ideal state" as such forms according to him lead to moral decay. The only form of poetry that he allowed were those which sang praises of the divine and the heroes. Poetry and such forms were put within the framework of promoting morals and virtues. Plato's ideal writer is one who seeks to promote virtue and wisdom, using language as a means to cultivate the soul. This utilitarian approach prioritizes ethical considerations over artistic expression, asserting that literature should serve the greater good and contribute to the moral fabric of society.

In stark contrast, Longinus opts for the emotional and transcendent qualities of literature, proposing that the sublime transcends ethical constraints. He posits that literature should evoke a sense of awe and elevate the reader's consciousness, a view that privileges the emotional experience over moral instruction. Longinus asserts that true sublimity arises from a writer's authentic passion, allowing them to tap into universal emotions that resonate deeply with readers. This shift in focus marks a significant departure from Plato's ideals, suggesting that the ultimate purpose of literature is not merely to instruct but also to provoke profound emotional and intellectual experiences that lead to personal transformation.

Horace, another pivotal figure in the development of literary theory, articulates a vision of poetry grounded in a structured approach to artistic creation, through in his principle of that painting is similar to poetry. This analogy underscores the notion that both forms of art require careful deliberation and a balanced composition to achieve their intended effects. For Horace, poetry is not merely a vehicle for self-expression rather it is an art form that demands discipline, precision, and adherence to established conventions. He advocates for a harmonious blend of form and content, believing that a successful poem must adhere to aesthetic ideals and rhetorical effectiveness. This perspective promotes a standard of elegance that aligns closely with societal norms and cultural values, thereby elevating poetry to a status that reflects the refined tastes of its audience. In Horace's view, the poet is similar to a skilled craftsman, meticulously shaping their work to evoke particular responses from readers. He places significant emphasis on techniques such as meter, diction, and rhetorical devices, asserting that these elements are essential for creating a resonant and impactful poem. Horace's commitment to decorum further reflects a desire to maintain moral and ethical considerations in poetic expression, suggesting that poetry should serve as a moral guide while also providing aesthetic pleasure.

In stark contrast, Longinus offers a critique of Horace's methodical approach, stating that true literary power resides not in strict adherence to form but in the ability to convey unrestrained emotion and passion. For Longinus, the sublime transcends mere technical proficiency; it arises from the writer's capacity to tap into universal feelings that resonate deeply with the audience. He cites writers such as Homer, whose works demonstrate an extraordinary ability to evoke intense emotions and grand ideas. Longinus argues that sublimity emerges when writers allow their passions to flow freely, creating a dynamic and engaging narrative that connects with readers on an emotional level. This perspective challenges Horace's emphasis on form, suggesting that rigid structures can stifle the organic expression of ideas and feelings. Longinus suggests the idea that the true greatness of a literary work lies in its emotional authenticity. He asserts that when writers embrace their innate passion and allow it to shape their narratives, they infuse their texts with vitality and authenticity that resonate far more powerfully than any calculated stylistic choice. While Horace's vision prioritizes aesthetic control and moral guidance, Longinus embraces the chaotic yet vital nature of human emotion.

Thus, Longinus' "On the Sublime" represents a significant departure from the moralistic and formal constraints of Plato and Horace. By prioritizing emotional authenticity, the capacity for language to evoke awe, and the inherent greatness of ideas, Longinus challenges the traditional frameworks of literary criticism that sought to regulate literature within ethical and aesthetic boundary.

4. References and Suggested readings:

i. Longinus: On The Sublime,
Project Gutenberg(https://www.gutenberg.org)
ii. Longinus: On The Sublime,
Poetry foundation
(https://www.poetryfoundation.org)
iii. Longinus' theory of the Sublime, Niharika Dugar
iv. Health, M (2012). Longinus and the Ancient Sublime.
v. Harry Blamires: A History of Literary Criticism

UNIT – 3

PHILLIP SIDNEY: AN APOLOGY FOR POETRY

1. **About the Author**

2. **An Apology for poetry**

   a. Introduction

   b. Synopsis

   c. Analysis

3. **Probable Questions:**

   a. Examine Phillip Sidney's defense of poetry against the attacks of Stephen Gosson.

   b. Analyze how Sidney argues for the superiority of poetry against other branches of knowledge?

   c. Explore Sidney's views on purpose of poetry including its role to teach and delight?

   d. Evaluate on Sidney's critique of his contemporary Plays of the Elizabethan Age

4. **References and suggested readi

1. About the Author

Sir Philip Sidney (1554-1586) was a distinguished English poet, diplomat, military figure, who is known for his significant literary contributions in shaping Elizabethan literature. He is considered as the first English critic poet who represents the Renaissance England.

Sidney was born on November 30, 1554 in Penshurst, Kent, England into a well-known noble family. His father Sir Henry Sidney served as the Lord Deputy of Ireland and his mother Mary Dudley was the daughter of the Duke of Northumberland. His family belonged to the English aristocracy with strong ties to the Tudor court. Sidney's upbringing was characterized by privilege and had the exposure to an intellectual environment. He received his early formal education at Shrewsburry School, where he excelled in classical studies, languages and literature. He then later attended Christ Church, Oxford, where he developed a keen interest towards literature, art and philosophy. His education was further enriched by travel to France and Italy.

After completing his education, he returned to England and became an integral part of the Court of Queen Elizabeth I. His fame grew due to his literary talent, curtly manners, which were considered as the ideals of Renaissance gentleman. In addition to his courtly pursuits, Sidney took on military responsibilities. He became involved in politics and military conflicts of the time, particularly the struggle against Spain during the Eighty Years'War. His military career culminated with his participation at the seize of Zutphen in 1586. He died at the age of 31 due to wounds on 17 October, 1586.

Since Sidney education was marked by his exposure to Renaissance Humanism, it immensely influenced his literary career. He was drawn towards classical texts like his contemporaries. His style of writing is marked by a blend of traditional and innovative elements. He drew inspiration from classical literature and the Petrarchan tradition. His literary works often reflect themes of love, honor and the struggles of artistic soul. He employed metaphysical concepts and paradoxes, metaphors and imagery, quite effectively in his writings. His famous literary contributions include "Astrophel and Stella" and "The Defence of Poesy"

- **His notable works**:

1. *Astrophel and Stella*

   Written between 1580-82. It is a collection of 108 sonnets and 11 songs that explore the themes of love, desire and unrequited affection particularly. It is said that the title character Astrophel represents Sidney himself, while Stella is symbolic of his unrequited love for Penelope, the daughter of the Earl of Essex

2. *The Defence of Poesy*

   Also known as "An Apology for Poesy", written in the form of dialogue where he explores the purpose of poetry and defends it against criticism.

2. An Apology for Poetry

• Introduction

Sir Philip Sidney's "An Apology for Poetry" also known as "The Defence of Poesy" was written around 1579 but published posthumously in 1595. It is one of the earliest major works of literary criticism in English, composed in response to a specific set of cultural and intellectual developments in Elizabethan England. Sidney wrote it as a direct response to Stephen Gosson, who had attacked poetry and other forms of imaginative literature in his work "The Schoole of Abuse" (1579).

In the late 16th century, England experienced profound cultural, religious, and intellectual shifts. The Renaissance had introduced new perspectives on art, humanism, and literature, encouraging a growing appreciation for the classical traditions of Greece and Rome. However, alongside this flourishing of artistic expression, a strong Puritanical movement emerged, which denounced the arts—particularly poetry and drama—as trivial, immoral, and even corruptive. These Puritan critics viewed imaginative literature as a threat to moral and spiritual values, fueling an ongoing debate about the role of art in society.

Among the several critics of art, Stephen Gosson was one of the prominent voices of the Puritanical movement, who viewed the arts—especially poetry and drama—with suspicion and moral disdain. In his 1579 pamphlet "The School of Abuse", Gosson argued that these art forms were not only frivolous but actively harmful, leading people away from virtuous living and toward vice and idleness. Gosson's criticisms reflected broader Puritan concerns about the moral dangers of imaginative literature, which they believed could corrupt society by promoting immoral behavior and distracting individuals from their religious duties. Gosson's attack on poetry was part of this larger movement that sought to impose stricter moral and spiritual discipline, aligning with the Puritan ideal of a society grounded in practical and sober living. His views directly clashed with the humanist values of the Renaissance, which celebrated art, literature, and the exploration of human potential

In his pamphlet, Stephen Gosson criticized poetry, drama, and other forms of entertainment, which provoked a strong response and directly challenged the ideals of the Renaissance, which celebrated literature and the arts as tools for intellectual and moral elevation. Gosson's pamphlet was seen by Renaissance literary figures as a threat to the artistic and intellectual advancements. In response, literary figures like Philip Sidney expressed their defense of arts, emphasizing their role in moral education and societal reflection leading to the composition of "An Apology for poetry".

Sidney in his defense contends that poetry is fundamentally a means of moral education. He argues that the imaginative nature of poetry allows poets to craft idealized scenarios and virtuous characters that serve as models for readers. He treats poetry as a crucial art form that serves multiple functions like depicting morals, emotional engagement, and reflection of human nature. Sidney defends the artistic integrity of poetry, arguing that it should not be judged solely by its potential for misuse. He also explores the essence of poetry by differentiating it from other forms of literature such as history and philosophy, emphasizing on its imaginative and artistic qualities.

"An Apology for Poetry" is composed in the form of an extended argument which can be divided into several key sections like on defense of poetry, the role of the poet, the ethical value of poetry, etc.

In conclusion, Sidney's work elevated the status of poetry, defending it against moral and intellectual critiques that claimed poetry was frivolous or corrupting; argued that poetry, by combining delight with instruction, had the potential to improve the moral character of its audience. This perspective gave poetry a sense of dignity and importance that contributed to its central role in Renaissance culture

---

The Schoole of Abuse(1579)

Stephen Gosson's 'The Schoole of Abuse' written in the form of a pamphlet sharply criticizes the popular arts of Elizabethan England, with a particular focus on theater, poetry, and music. Gosson believed these forms of entertainment were socially and morally damaging. In 'The Schoole of Abuse', he argues that plays, poetry, and music distract people from religious devotion, encourage idleness, and even incite immoral behavior. He accuses playwrights of creating characters who glorify vices rather than virtues, suggesting that theatres serve as "schools of vice" that inspire audiences to imitate the questionable behaviors portrayed on stage. Gosson claims that theater and other arts waste time and foster indecency among viewers, thereby eroding public morals Gosson's pamphlet stands as one of the earliest examples of anti-theatrical criticism in English literature, capturing the ideological conflict over the role of entertainment during the Renaissance. It highlights the period's ongoing struggle between art and morality, a discussion that persisted into the 17th century. 'The Schoole of Abuse' sparked intense debate, most notably prompting a response from Sir Philip Sidney in An Apology for Poetry. Sidney countered Gosson's arguments by defending poetry and drama as vehicles for teaching virtues and offering intellectual value.

- **Synopsis**

Sidney begins his defense of poetry by recounting a conversation he once had with a man named, John Pietro Pugliano who had the view of his profession- horsemanship as superior in comparison to other forms like mastery over warfare, arts etc. The praises of his profession by Pietro Pugliano seemed to Sidney that self-love must prevail.

Sidney through this incident tries to establish his defense of poetry by setting up the parallel that if horsemanship something practical but not necessarily intellectual can be elevated so highly that too with arguments that are unconvincing, then poetry which deals with higher forms of learning and morality, surely deserves even greater defense and admiration. Sidney offers a comprehensive defense of poetry, asserting its superiority over philosophy, history, and other forms of writing. Sidney begins by celebrating poetry defining it as an art of imitation, which he defines as a representation that teaches and delights. He emphasizes that poets possess a unique ability to create, lifting their work beyond the limitations of nature. Sidney underscores the esteemed legacy of poetry in ancient civilizations, tracing its origins back to the Greeks and Romans, who regarded it as a paramount form of knowledge. He argues that poetry served as the first source of enlightenment for humanity, with ancient poets like Homer, Musaeus, Hesiod, and others recognized as moral educators.

Sidney laments at the decline in poetry's status, as it is often dismissed as mere entertainment in his time and treated as a means of abuse of knowledge. Sidney examines poetry's universal presence and historical significance enable it to refine and elevate minds, even in cultures lacking formal education. He cites examples such as the Turkish reverence for poets and the status of poets in Ireland, asserting that poetry once held an integral role in educating the masses, making it impossible for philosophers and historians to gain popularity without first appealing to the public through poetic expression. Sidney further explores the Greeks' understanding of poetry, highlighting that the term for poet translates to "maker," emphasizing the poet's unique creative power compared to other disciplines. He contrasts poetry with sciences like geometry, astronomy, and law, which are bound by specific constraints. In contrast, poetry is unrestricted and expansive, allowing poets to invent figures such as demi-gods and Cyclopes, untouched by reality. He uses the metaphor of a zodiac to illustrate this point, suggesting that while nature is governed by fixed laws, poetry operates freely within the imaginative realm of the poet. Through this comprehensive examination, Sidney defends poetry as a profound and liberating form of expression, vital to human culture and knowledge.

He asserts the elevated role of poets, establishing a hierarchy among them. He distinguishes "right poets," who harness their creative imagination to depict idealized images of virtue and truth, from mere imitators who can only replicate what they see. Sidney emphasizes that true poets can inspire moral action through their representations of virtues like courage and wisdom, thereby fulfilling a noble societal role.

Sidney critiques the arguments of moral philosophers and historians who claim superiority over poetry in teaching virtue. While he acknowledges their contributions, he finds them inadequate compared to the holistic effectiveness of poetry, which uniquely blends universal truths with specific instances of reality. He categorizes poetry into various forms like heroic, lyric, tragic, and more, highlighting that its essence lies not in rhyme or meter, but in its imaginative portrayal of moral ideals. He illustrates the limitations of other disciplines, noting that philosophers and historians may lack the depth and vividness that poetry provides.

Sidney addresses the critics of poetry, whom he labels as "poet-haters," arguing that their frivolous objections distract from poetry's true value. He contrasts these shallow critiques with the insightful works of writers like Erasmus and Agrippa, whose humor and irony reveal deeper truths. He critiques the superficiality of these critics, suggesting they fail to grasp poetry's significance.

Sidney addresses the criticisms of poetry, particularly Plato's perspective, acknowledging that Plato's opposition is not to all poetry but rather to its misuse. Sidney argues that philosophers may seek to undermine poets out of resentment, given that poets, like Homer, were celebrated figures in society, while philosophers sometimes faced exclusion. He contends that Plato's critiques stemmed from the poets' portrayal of flawed deities, reflecting the cultural beliefs of the time rather than the poets' inventions.

Sidney respects poetry's historical significance, citing influential figures who valued it throughout history, including kings and philosophers. However, he expresses concern about its declining status in England, lamenting that even the "earth laments it."Sidney critiques contemporary poets for lacking skill and dedication, urging them to engage in self-reflection and strive for improvement. He assesses the state of English theater, criticizing the shortcomings of tragedies and comedies that fail to adhere to the classical principles of unity in time and place, often confusing audiences. He praises "Gorboduc" as an exception but points out its flaws, advocating for narratives that engage audiences from the outset.

Sidney distinguishes between delight and laughter, arguing that while laughter can accompany delight, it should not be the sole aim of comedy. He emphasizes the importance of meaningful lessons in comedic works rather than mere ridicule. Furthermore, he critiques the excessive and inauthentic stylistic choices in poetry, likening them to ornate adornments that lack substance.

Sidney defends the English language, asserting its strength lies in its diverse origins and simplicity, which facilitates clear expression. He critiques contemporary poets for misusing language and offers a defense of poetry's accentual qualities compared to other languages, arguing that English poetry employs rhyme and caesura effectively.

In the concluding section, Sidney passionately defends poetry, rejecting its criticism and urging readers to appreciate its noble status. He cites esteemed thinkers to support his argument that poetry conveys wisdom and morality, hinting at the profound mysteries it contains. Sidney encourages a commitment to poetry, suggesting that those who embrace it will achieve fame and a kind of immortality through their association with great literary figures.

- **Analysis**

Sidney begins by recounting how during his travels on the continent, he desired to be taught horsemanship by John Pietro Pugliano, a master of the art of riding horses. Sidney humorously mentions how Pugliano, in his admiration for the skill of horsemanship, passionately praised horses and their virtues. Pugliano's enthusiasm was so convincing that he nearly persuaded Sidney to believe that the profession of horsemanship was the highest calling for mankind. Sidney finds it hilarious that Pugliano would have convinced him to be a horse, if had he been not a logician and rational.

"...if I had not been a piece of a logician before I came to him, I think he would have persuaded me to have wished myself a horse."

Sidney then uses this scenario to draw a parallel, just as Pugliano extolled the virtues of horsemanship and horses, so too could poets and poetry be defended with similar means. Sidney is pointing out that while horsemanship may be praised as a noble skill, it is equally or even more important to recognize the value of poetry in cultivating virtue and wisdom.

Sidney proceeds to demonstrate the legacy of poetry in ancient civilizations. He traces poetry back to the Greeks and Romans, who saw it as one of the highest forms of knowledge. Sidney argues that poetry was the first source of enlightenment for humanity. The ancient poets, he explains, were seen as wise and capable of teaching moral truths through their creative work. He cites classical figures like Homer, Musaeus, Hesiod, Livius, Andronicus, Enniusto; other notable literary figures like Dante, Boccace, and Petrarch; etc., to emphasize that great poets were once respected as educators and moral guides. Sidney laments how far poetry has fallen from this high status in his own contemporary time, where it is often viewed as frivolous entertainment or, worse, as a corrupting influence.

Sidney presents a compelling argument about the universal presence of poetry, its historical significance, and its power to soften and sharpen the minds of people, even in cultures where formal learning is either undeveloped or deliberately suppressed. Sidney aims to demonstrate the foundational role poetry has played across various civilizations, particularly in the education of those who otherwise have little exposure to formal philosophical or historical instruction.

"In Turkey, besides their lawgiving divines they have no other writers but poets. In our neighbour-country Ireland, where, too, learning goes very bare, yet are their poets held in a devout reverence."

He speaks of the esteemed status of poets across various civilizations and that there was no distinction between poetry and other forms of learning. He argues that neither philosophers nor historians could have gained the acceptance and attention of the masses without first appealing to them through the medium of poetry.

"...neither philosopher nor historiographer could, at the first, have entered into the gates of popular judgments, if they had not taken a great disport of poetry..."

Sidney explains that poetry was considered capable of revealing future events or serving as a tool for interpreting one's fate. This belief led to practices such as the 'sortes Virgilianae', where people would randomly access a work by the poet Virgil and proceed to mark a verse, and then interpreting whatever line they found as a sign or prophecy about their future. He mentions that historical figures, like Albinus, the Roman governor of Britain, used this practice. In his youth, Albinus encountered a line from Virgil:

"Armaamenscapio, nec sat rationis in armis".

Albinus later fulfilled this prophecy in his own life. To strengthen his argument, Sidney notes that the oracles of Delphi and the prophecies of the Sibyls, both central to ancient religious practices were traditionally delivered in verse. This rhythmic and structured form, combined with the imaginative freedom that poetry allowed, seemed to have an almost "divine force." Sidney ultimately argues that poetry's form and expression were seen by the ancients as profoundly powerful, almost as if it connected humanity with something greater than itself.

Sidney then defends poetry by exploring how the Greeks understood and esteemed it. He highlights the Greek word for poet that translates into English as "maker," speaks to the poet's unique creative power. This title is quite significant, Sidney suggests, especially when contrasted with other arts and sciences, which depend on observing and describing nature. Sidney then contrasts poetry with the sciences like geometry, arithmetic, astronomy, and art forms like music, etc by examining the objects and constraints of each field. He asserts that each of these sciences and art forms are characterized by their own respective restraints and limits but poetry on the other hand doesn't have any such restrictions or limits. Sidney continues by explaining that other disciplines, like law, history, and grammar, also lack poetry's creative freedom. Law codifies human decisions; history records human actions; grammar structures speech; and rhetoric and logic create frameworks for effective argumentation, each of these disciplines remains confined to and revolve around some pre-existing matter or truth. Unlike these, Sidney argues, poetry transcends nature's boundaries and expands its scope through invention. The poet is liberated from any such limits and hence can create figures like demigods, Cyclops, etc. which have less to do with the reality of nature.

"...forms such as never were in nature, as the heroes, demi-gods, Cyclops, chimeras, furies, and such like..."

These mythic figures showcase the poet's ability to invent, not constrained by what nature provides but driven by imagination's potential to conjure something new and impactful. Sidney emphasizes this freedom with a powerful metaphor, comparing the poet's imagination to a zodiac.

"...freely ranging within the zodiac of his own wit..."

This metaphor suggests that, while nature operates within fixed laws, poetry functions beyond it within the poet's creative mind.

Sidney creates a hierarchy of poets, placing the highest value on what he terms "right poets." These poets use their imagination to craft idealized images of virtue and truth, inspiring moral action in their readers. In contrast, he criticizes mere imitators, who are limited to simply reproducing what they see, lacking the creative depth of true poets. These poets, he argues, are like the best painters, who use their craft not to depict specific people but to represent universal virtues, as seen in the example of Lucretia's expression of noble suffering. Through this comparison, Sidney establishes that "right poets" employ their creative imagination to shape idealized representations of virtues like courage, wisdom, and chastity, which can inspire readers toward moral action.

Sidney directly confronts the objections raised by critics whom he labels as "poet-haters," who disparage poetry and poets.

"...poet-haters, but in all that kind of people who seek a praise by dispraising others, that they do prodigally spend a great many wandering words in quips and scoffs, carping and taunting at each thing..."

He emphasizes that while it is essential to listen to critiques of poetry, many of these objections are an outcome of a shallow understanding of the art form. Sidney notes that these critics often indulge in mockery and trivial jests, failing to engage with the deeper merits and understanding of poetry. He criticizes them for using "quips and scoffs" to distract from the subject's worthiness, arguing that such idle criticisms reveal more about the critics than the art itself. He believes that such critics lack genuine wisdom, as their mockery is born out of superficiality rather than insightful critique.

Sidney addresses Plato's critique of poetry.

"...Plato, being a philosopher, was a natural enemy of poets..."

He argues that Plato did not condemn all poetry but only its misuse. Sidney acknowledges that one might argue that Plato, as a philosopher, was naturally opposed to poets, especially since philosophers relied on the knowledge which the poets expressed in a "divine delightfulness" but then organized this knowledge into rigid systems. In doing so, Sidney suggests, philosophers sought to disregard poets, perhaps out of resentment, since poets were often celebrated by cities like Homer's seven rival cities, while philosophers were sometimes banned as unsuitable citizens. Sidney defends poets by pointing out that Plato criticized poetry only when it conveyed "wrong opinions of the gods," a view influenced by the existing beliefs of Plato's time rather than created by the poets themselves. The Greek religion at the time as Sidney observes included many gods with human-like flaws, and poets merely reflected these beliefs.

"Plato found fault that the poets of his time filled the world with wrong opinions of the gods, making light tales of that unspotted essence, and therefore would not have the youth depraved with such opinions. Herein may much be said; let this suffice: the poets did not induce such opinions, but did imitate those opinions already induced. For all the Greek stories can well testify that the very religion of that time stood upon many and many-fashioned gods; not taught so by poets, but followed according to their nature of imitation. "

He argues that poets, limited by the cultural and religious understanding before Christianity, were more honest in this reflection than philosophers, who, in discarding superstition, often leaned toward atheism.

"Christianity hath taken away all the hurtful belief, perchance as he thought nourished by then esteemed poets."

Sidney expresses both reverence for poetry and concern about its declining status in England. He begins by acknowledging the historical significance of poetry, noting that it has been cherished and practiced by some of the most esteemed figures in history: the kings, emperors, philosophers, and great military leaders. He cites notable individuals, such as King David, the Roman Emperor Hadrian, Sophocles, and Germanicus, who not only supported poets but also contributed to the art themselves. This historical context underscores the idea that poetry has long been held in high regard across different cultures and eras. Sidney contrasts this rich tradition with the contemporary landscape in England, where he perceives poetry to be unwelcome and marginalized. He laments that the "earth laments it," suggesting that even the very soil of England mourns the lack of poetic recognition, leading to fewer "laurels" than in the past.

Sidney acknowledges his own aspirations to be recognized as a poet and reflects on the reasons why contemporary poets lack esteem. He attributes this lack of respect to the absence of merit, suggesting that many writers pursue the title of "poet" without the requisite skill or dedication.

"But I that, before ever I durst aspire unto the dignity, am admitted into the company of the paper-blurrers, do find the very true cause of our wanting estimation is want of desert, taking upon us to be poets in despite of Pallas. Now, wherein we want desert, were a thankworthy labour to express. But if I knew, I should have mended myself; but as I never desired the title so have I neglected the means to come by it; only, overmastered by some thoughts, I yielded an inky tribute unto them."

He humbly admits that he does not wish to claim the title without deserving it and indicates that those who truly love poetry should strive to understand and improve their craft. He urges aspiring poets to engage in self-reflection and honest assessment of their abilities, using the metaphor of an "unflattering glass of reason" to emphasize the importance of critical self-awareness in artistic endeavors.

Sidney critiques the state of English theater and poetry, particularly focusing on the shortcomings of contemporary tragedies and comedies. He argues that these plays are justly criticized for failing to adhere to established rules of both civility and poetry. He acknowledges Gorboduc as a notable exception, praising its elevated language and moral lessons, yet he simultaneously points out that even this work suffers from significant flaws in its execution of dramatic form. Sidney emphasizes the critical importance of unity in both place and time, drawing on Aristotelian principles that dictate a play should occur in a single location and within a brief, logical timeframe—ideally confined to one day. He argues that many contemporary plays violate this rule by rapidly shifting between multiple settings and times, which confuses the audience. For instance, he criticizes scenarios where the stage is expected to represent a garden, a battlefield, and a cave in quick succession, making it difficult for spectators to maintain a coherent understanding of the action.

In addition to the confusion of places, Sidney also highlights the absurd compression of time that characterizes many contemporary works. He critiques the portrayal of events that should realistically unfold over much longer periods—such as a character falling in love, becoming pregnant, and giving birth—as occurring within the span of a two-hour performance. This distortion renders the narrative implausible and undermines the emotional impact of the story. Sidney contrasts the practices of contemporary playwrights with those of classical writers, particularly noting that ancient playwrights, such as those from Italy, adhere more faithfully to the principles of unity and coherence in their works. He acknowledges that some classical plays, such as Terence's Eunuch, may cover spans of time that seem extensive, but they do so in a manner that respects the narrative structure and temporal constraints.

Furthermore, Sidney asserts that tragedies are not bound by historical accuracy but by the conventions of poetry. He contends that poets possess the creative freedom to fabricate and construct new narratives or adapt historical stories for dramatic purposes. The essence of tragedy, he argues, lies in its ability to evoke powerful emotions rather than strictly following the historical events. Sidney critiques the narrative structure of many contemporary tragedies, arguing that they should not begin "ab ovo" (from the egg) with unnecessary background details that detract from the main action.

Instead, he advocates for starting with the principal event to immediately engage the audience. He illustrates this with the example of Polydorus, suggesting that a play should commence with the moment of finding the body rather than detailing the child's delivery or the lengthy journey leading to that moment.

Sidney critiques the approach of contemporary comedians in England, asserting that their emphasis on laughter as the primary goal of comedy is misguided.

"...But our comedians think there is no delight without laughter, which is very wrong; for though laughter may come with delight, yet cometh it not of delight..."

He argues that while laughter can coexist with delight, it should not be regarded as its cause. Delight arises from a connection to things that resonate with our nature or values, whereas laughter often stems from things that are trivial, out of place or disproportionate to our own experiences. Sidney illustrates the distinction between delight and laughter by providing examples. He notes that one may experience delight when admiring beauty, such as a fair woman, but this does not provoke laughter. He acknowledges that delight and laughter can coexist in certain situations, exemplified by artistic representations. Sidney argues that the purpose of comedy should not solely be to provoke laughter through ridicule or scornful portrayals. Instead, he advocates for the incorporation of meaningful and delightful lessons into comedic works.

Sidney critiques the use of language in poetry and prose, focusing on what he perceives as excessive and inauthentic stylistic choices. He compares the use of obscure diction to the appearance of a courtesan, suggesting that such language is often more about show than substance. Sidney expresses dissatisfaction with the use of elaborate or overly complicated words in writing. He describes this "honey-flowing matron eloquence" as disguising itself in a way that is more focused on superficial beauty rather than on genuine expression. He feels that some words seem like "monsters" or "strangers" to the average English speaker, indicating that the language is inaccessible and perhaps pretentious. Sidney criticizes writers for over-embellishing their language, likening this tendency to Indians who place jewels in inappropriate places like through their noses and lips to ensure they look fashionable.

"...like those Indians, not content to wear ear-rings at the fit and natural place of the ears, but they will thrust jewels through their nose and lips, because they will be sure to be fine."

This analogy underscores the idea that the effort to appear refined often leads to a loss of naturalness and authenticity in expression.

He cites Cicero's use of rhetorical repetition in his speeches as an example of effective expression. He observes that when Cicero was trying to expel Catiline, he employed repetition to emphasize his points powerfully, which Sidney suggests should be used sparingly and in appropriate contexts. He implies that the emotional intensity and naturalness of language are diminished when such techniques are misapplied.

Sidney humorously acknowledges that he might deserve criticism for derailing from the topic of poetry to discuss oration, yet he believes there is a significant connection between the two fields, particularly regarding language and expression. He clarifies that his intention is not to instruct poets on how to write but to recognize a shared issue among writers, a kind of "infection" of poor practices in language use. By acknowledging these flaws, he hopes to guide writers toward a more effective application of both content and style. Sidney defends the English language against criticisms that it is merely a "mingled language," suggesting that this combination of elements from various sources is actually a strength, as it allows the language of English to draw from the best features of other languages. He counters the argument that English lacks proper grammar by asserting that it doesn't require the complexities associated with traditional grammatical structures, such as cases, genders, moods, and tenses. Instead, he argues that the simplicity of English is an asset that facilitates clear communication. Reflecting on the biblical story of the Tower of Babel, Sidney implies that the necessity of learning one's native language formally is a kind of curse. He argues that the ability to express itself effectively should come naturally, without the burdens of adhering to grammatical rules.

Sidney explores the scope of rhyme in poetry, particularly distinguishing between English poetry and that of other languages such as Italian, Spanish, and French. He begins by asserting that while modern poetry does not adhere to the ancient practice of syllabic quantity, it still places great importance on the emphasis of words. This accentual or focus, according to Sidney, is something that many other languages either cannot or do not do effectively.

Sidney points out that certain poetic elements, such as the caesura (a pause or breathing space within a line of verse), is either absent or inadequately employed in Italian and Spanish poetry. He contrasts this with English poetry, which he claims regularly employs the caesura. He then discusses different types of rhyme: the masculine rhyme (ending on a stressed syllable), the feminine rhyme (ending on an unstressed syllable), and the sdrucciola (a rhyme that emphasizes the third-to-last syllable).

"That "cæsura," or breathing-place, in the midst of the verse, neither Italian nor Spanish have, the French and we never almost fail of. Lastly, even the very rhyme itself the Italian cannot put in the last syllable, by the French named the masculine rhyme, but still in the next to the last, which the French call the female; or the next before that, which the Italian calls "sdrucciola:" the example of the former is, "buono," "suono;" of the sdrucciola is, "femina," "semina." The French, of the other side, hath both the male, as "bon," "son," and the female, as "plaise," "taise;" but the "sdrucciola" he hath not; where the English hath all three, as "due," "true," "father," "rather," "motion," "potion;" with much more which might be said, but that already I find the trifling of this discourse is much too much enlarged."

He notes that while Italians can manage the feminine and sdrucciola rhymes, it cannot position rhymes in the final syllable of a line as effectively as English can. In contrast, English poetry can utilize all three rhyme forms, which he believes contributes to its richness and musicality. After establishing the superiority of English poetry in this context, Sidney shifts to a broader defense of poetry itself. He argues that poetry is inherently virtuous and delightful, filled with gifts that elevate its noble status. He rejects criticisms of poetry as misguided or weak, attributing the lack of respect for the art form in England to poorly skilled poets.

Sidney passionately implores readers not to disdain poetry or poets. He calls for recognition of the significance of poetry as an ancient and esteemed art that preserves knowledge and morality. He cites renowned thinkers and poets like Aristotle, Bembus, and Scaliger to empower his argument that poetry is a source of civility, wisdom, and even divine insight. He suggests that poetry contains profound mysteries that must be approached with reverence, as they are sometimes hidden to protect them from misinterpretation by those unworthy of understanding.

In the concluding section of the essay, Sidney makes an emphatic promise to those who will embrace poetry. He suggests that doing so will lead them to fame and fortune, elevating their names in literary circles and granting them a place among the greats of literature.

"...your names shall flourish in the printers' shops: thus doing, you shall be of kin to many a poetical preface: thus doing, you shall be most fair, most rich, most wise, most all..."

He implies that readers who engage with poetry can achieve a kind of immortality through association with poetic figures like Dante and Virgil, gaining a place in the pantheon of literary greatness.

3. Probable Questions:

1. Examine Phillip Sidney's defense of poetry against the attacks of Stephen Gosson.

Answer:

'An Apology for Poetry', written by Sir Philip Sidney in 1579, provides a passionate and eloquent defence of poetry in response to the criticisms of the Puritan moralist Stephen Gosson, author of "The School of Abuse"(1579). Sidney's work provides a profound defence against the puritan accusations regarding poetry.

Steohen Gosson in his pamphlet condemned poetry, drama, and other forms of imaginative literature, arguing that they promoted vice, distracted individuals from meaningful pursuits, and ultimately threatened public morals. Sidney considered these views and such accusations as a result of being grossly misunderstood the actual role of poetry and his response aims not only to defend poetry's merits but also to elevate its status as an essential part of human knowledge and morality. Sidney's work is not merely a literary response of Gosson but a profound exploration of poetry's purpose, function, and impact on society, grounded in classical and Renaissance theories of literature.

Sidney begins his defence by asserting the historical and universal significance of poetry, establishing its noble origins and enduring value across civilizations. He notes that the ancient Greeks, Romans, regarded poetry as one of the highest forms of knowledge. He argues that these civilizations considered the poets as wise and virtuous. They were treated as sources of divine inspiration and moral wisdom. He cites examples of classical figures like Homer, Livius, Andronicus, etc. who had the highest status of educators and moral guides. He illustrates through numerous cultures that developed through the essence of poetry as these cultures had less assess to formal learning.

Sidney puts the argument of how ancient civilizations like the Greeks termed the poets as "makers". He terms the poets as prophets whose verses had the ability to do prophesy. According to Sidney, poets hold a unique position among scholars and intellectuals, as they can communicate complex moral and philosophical ideas in ways that are accessible only to them. Sidney asserts that other forms like science, music, arithmetic, geometry, astronomy, law etc. are bound by limits. But the poet is not restrained by any such limits and hence can create figures like demigods, Cyclops, myths, etc.:

"...forms such as never were in nature, as the heroes, demi-gods, Cyclops, chimeras, furies, and such like..."

Sidney emphasizes this freedom with a powerful metaphor, comparing the poet's imagination to a zodiac.

"...freely ranging within the zodiac of his own wit..."

He suggests that, while nature operates within fixed laws, poetry functions beyond it within the poet's creative mind.

Sidney then argues for the elevated and noble role of the poet, distinguishing between different types of poets and their contributions to society. He establishes a hierarchy among poets; reserving the highest status for those he calls "right poets," who use the full freedom of their imagination to create idealized images of virtue and truth. Unlike the mere imitators, who, as Sidney puts it, are limited to reproducing what is directly in front of them.

"...with the fore-described name of poets. For these, indeed, do merely make to imitate..."

Sidney establishes that "right poets" employ their creative imagination to shape idealized representations of virtues like courage, wisdom, and chastity, which can inspire readers toward moral action.

Sidney illustrates and critiques the arguments presented by both moral philosophers and historians as they attempt to claim superiority over poetry in the teaching of virtue but he finds their claims and arguments inadequate. Sidney argues that poetry is the highest form of learning in its capacity to convey moral truth and inspire virtuous action. He rejects the argument that poetry is the source of all abuses of knowledge. He critiques both the historian and the moral philosopher, asserting that while each has some merit, both ultimately lack the holistic effectiveness of the poet in teaching and inspiring goodness. By contrasting the methods of the philosopher and historian with that of the poet, he argues that poetry uniquely blends universal truths with specific instances of reality, providing a more impactful understanding of virtue although he acknowledges that the philosopher and historian both contribute to ethical knowledge philosophers through precept and theory; historians through example and experiences from the past. However, both are incomplete in their approach, unable to reach the depth and vividness that poetry provides.

Sidney highlights the limitations of philosophy and history in contrast to poetry. He begins by categorizing poetry into different types—heroic, lyric, etc.

"These be subdivided into sundry more special denominations; the most notable be the heroic, lyric, tragic, comic, satyric, iambic, elegiac, pastoral, and certain others..."

Each of these kinds has their unique qualities. Sidney notes that while many poets choose to express themselves in verse, poetry is defined not by rhyme or meter but by its ability to create vivid images of virtues and vices. Sidney cites prose writers like Xenophon and Heliodorus to demonstrate that true poetry is about the imaginative portrayal of moral ideals, not necessarily the use of verse. On the other hand, other forms of disciplines like philosophy, history arithmetic, etc. need to within the limitations of moral direction. He uses vivid examples to emphasize these flaws like the astronomer who "might fall in a ditch" while focused on the heavens; the philosopher might become "blind in himself," losing personal insight while exploring abstract truths; and the mathematician might "draw forth a straight line with a crooked heart," symbolizing a failure to align moral integrity with intellectual thought. He gives the statement of poetry being the most adequate form of expression since the ancient times.

"...poetry is of all human learnings the most ancient, and of most fatherly antiquity..."

Sidney addresses the critics of poetry as "poet-haters" and their objectives of criticism. According to him, these critics distract the mind from fully understanding poetry's value. He describes their arguments as "wandering words", in other words, frivolous, misleading statements that lack intellectual depth or focus. This idle and uneasy manner of objection, Sidney claims, has nothing of "sacred majesty," implying that poetry possesses nobility that such critics fail to respect. He illustrates writers, like Erasmus and Agrippa, who were able to use humour and irony to reveal deeper truths, as seen in Erasmus's Praise of Folly and Agrippa's Vanity of Sciences. Sidney asserts that although these works appear critical on the surface, they are actually built on a "foundation" of thought and purpose. He compares it in contrast to the arguments of the typical poet-hater has no such foundation. Sidney criticizes these superficial critics, saying they

"Correct the verb before they understand the noun..."

This metaphor suggests that they attempt to correct others without truly understanding the subject matter. This ridicule is directed at those who attack poetry without understanding it.

Sidney responds to a major criticism against poetry, that rhyming and verse make it trivial or unserious. He acknowledges that many critics mock poetry's reliance on rhyme and meter, suggesting that they see these forms as unnecessary adornments rather than essential qualities. However, Sidney counters this view by demonstrating that the structured form of verse actually enhances poetry's effectiveness and intellectual value.

Sidney addresses the criticism that poetry is a less valuable pursuit compared to other forms of knowledge, particularly by referencing the argument that Plato banished poets from his 'ideal state'. He acknowledges this criticism, suggesting that it holds some weight but may not be as straightforward as critics suggest. He claims that no other discipline can teach and motivate toward virtue as effectively as poetry can, thus positioning it as an essential pursuit. Sidney employs the phrase "petere principium," which means "to seek the principle," to illustrate the flaw in the logic of those who dismiss poetry in favour of other disciplines. He contends that just because one form of knowledge might be seen as superior does not inherently diminish the value of poetry. He emphasizes that it is unjust to argue that "good is not good because better is better," insisting that the pursuit of poetry remains profoundly valuable. This argument falls within the context of the Renaissance, a period that saw the revaluation of classical philosophies and the role of art. By defending poetry's capacity to teach virtue, Sidney challenges the notion that it is merely entertainment or frivolity. His insistence that poetry serves a higher purpose aligns it with ethical education, positing it as a noble pursuit that enriches the human experience.

Sidney then argues against one of the significant criticisms of poetry i.e. the claim that it corrupts the minds of its readers by promoting sinful desires and lustful love. He acknowledges that this is one of the principal arguments against poetry by the critics, who particularly note how comedies, lyrics, and elegies often celebrate romantic and passionate themes. Sidney points out that these critics argue that these works either promote or fail to condemn "amorous conceits," portraying love as an indulgent and potentially harmful emotion. Sidney asserts that man's wit, or intellect, can distort the purpose of poetry. He implies that poetry's potential to elevate the mind is compromised when it is engaged with inappropriately, as when a painter chooses to focus on trivial subjects rather than noble themes. He uses the analogy of a painter who has the ability to create powerful and significant images but instead opts for less worthy representations. This argument places the responsibility on the reader rather than on the poet, suggesting that it is not the art form itself that corrupts but rather the intentions and desires of those who consume it. By shifting the blame from poetry to human interpretation, Sidney defends the integrity of poetic expression while highlighting the need for a more discerning audience.

Sidney encourages his audience to embrace poetry and to reject the mockery associated with the title of "rhymer." In his view, poets are not mere jesters but possess a sacred role in society, capable of elevating the human experience and granting a form of immortality through their verses. He paints a picture of the rewards that come with embracing poetry that is names that flourish in print, association with poetic legacies, and a life enriched by beauty, wisdom, and wealth

"Thus doing, your names shall flourish in the printers' shops: thus doing, you shall be of kin to many a poetical

preface: thus doing, you shall be most fair, most rich, most wise, most all..."

However, Sidney warns that if one is so entrenched in ignorance or disdain for poetry that they cannot appreciate its beauty, they will live a life devoid of love and favor, and their memory will fade into obscurity after death. He employs humorous yet biting imagery, suggesting that those who scorn poetry might deserve to suffer the consequences of their disdain, such as being marked by a lack of artistic legacy or even mocked in a metaphorical sense.

In conclusion, Sidney's argument for defence here reflects the Renaissance humanist belief that literature should both to instruct and provide delight, as this combination of qualities creates a more lasting impression on the human mind and spirit. By elevating poetry's origins and its timeless appeal, Sidney challenges Gosson's and the Puritan reductionist view and suggests that poetry holds an enduring role in human development.

2. Analyse how Sidney argues for the superiority of poetry against other branches of knowledge?

Answer:

In 'An Apology for Poetry', Sir Philip Sidney defends poetry by emphasizing its ancient and noble lineage, arguing that poetry has always been fundamental to human knowledge and moral education. He rejects the notion provided by Gosson and that poetry is the source of abuses.

Sidney refers to the status and role of poets in the cultural and intellectual development of Greece and other civilizations, showing that poets were the earliest sources of knowledge, predating philosophers and historians. Sidney cites poets like Musaeus, Homer, and Hesiod as the foundational figures in Greek literature, crediting them with capturing and preserving wisdom in a way that appealed to the emotions and imagination. He argues that poets were not only the first to convey knowledge but were instrumental in transforming "wild untamed wits" into lovers of knowledge through the charm and beauty of their verse. By invoking the mythical powers of figures like Amphion and Orpheus who were believed to influence even stones and beasts with their poetry Sidney suggests that poetry possesses an extraordinary power to inspire and elevate the human spirit. Sidney points out that the early Greek philosophers, such as Thales, Parmenides, and Empedocles, often wrote in verse, disguising their philosophical ideas within poetic forms. He implies that even the great philosopher Plato depended on poetry for its aesthetic and imaginative appeal, structuring his dialogues with poetic descriptions and myths, like the story of Atlantis. Through these examples, Sidney contends that poetry is not only a legitimate form of knowledge but also the most appealing and accessible, one that other forms of learning have historically borrowed from to gain appeal. The earliest philosophers and historians had to rely on poetry to reach and influence the public, making poetry a necessary precursor to philosophical and historical writing. Sidney argues that poetry's ability to delight and engage emotions has historically been critical in drawing people to knowledge, especially in societies that lack other forms of learning.

Sidney critiques the claims of moral philosophers and historians to be the best teachers of virtue, contrasting them with the unique power of poetry. Sidney first addresses moral philosophers, whom he describes as overly serious, appearing virtuous by rejecting "outward things." The philosophers argue that their approach of defining virtue and vice, analyzing human passions and outlining ethical duties provides the most direct path to teaching virtue. They believe that by logically dissecting these concepts, they offer the clearest guide for moral living, focusing on intellectual understanding. The philosopher teaches virtue by showing what virtue is and vice is by setting down in abstract argument and without clarity or beauty of style, the bare principles of morality. Sidney then brings in historians, who argue that their craft is superior for teaching virtue. Although historians are burdened with conflicting accounts, old records, and often unreliable sources, they insist that their work is more valuable than philosophy because it provides real, active examples of virtue rather than theoretical ideas. Historians argue that concrete examples from battles and important decisions, like those at Marathon and Agincourt, teach virtue more effectively than philosophical abstractions. The historian teaches virtue by showing the experience of past ages; but is bound to function within the limits of truth and what actually happened in the past. Sidney asserts that history provides the wisdom of past ages by giving guidance through example, while philosophers offer only theoretical lessons. He further explains that the historian since are bound by facts, must present characters with a mixture of virtues and flaws.

Sidney demonstrates how various fields of knowledge such as astronomy, philosophy, music, history, grammar, rhetoric, medicine, law, metaphysics, geometry and mathematics are motivated by a desire for understanding that elevates the intellectual engagement. He explores how poetry differs from other fields of knowledge by focusing on creation and imagination rather than merely reflecting the natural world. He begins by examining the Greek term for poet "maker," emphasizing on the poet's unique role in crafting something new. Sidney suggests that this elevated title sets poets apart from practitioners of other arts and sciences, all of which rely on nature as their foundation. He acknowledges that practical experience shows the limitations of these fields like for instance, astronomers may be absorbed in the stars but overlook practical matters, philosophers may seek knowledge yet fail to understand themselves, and mathematicians may pursue precision in their work but lack moral integrity. These disciplines are "serving sciences," each with its own value, yet they ultimately serve a greater knowledge that focuses on ethical and political considerations, leading to virtuous action rather than just knowledge for its own sake. He asserts that followers of other disciplines like astronomers study the order of the stars, musicians explore natural harmonies, and philosophers examine human virtues and vices, even metaphysics, though abstract, is rooted in the "depth of nature." These disciplines depend on what exists in nature and are limited by it. Poetry, on the other hand, Sidney defines it as not restricted in this manner. He argues that poets by their own creativity create a "second nature," improving upon or imagining beyond what exists in reality.

"...forms such as never were in nature, as the heroes, demi-gods, Cyclops, chimeras, furies, and such like..."

Poets are free to invent new forms like heroes, demigods, and mythical creatures that go beyond nature's scope, crafting worlds richer and more beautiful than the real one. He describes this imaginative power as delivering a "golden" world, contrasted with the "brazen" or ordinary reality of nature. By going beyond the natural limits, poets elevate the world with their creations, making it more beautiful and inspiring than nature alone. These mythical figures exemplify the poet's capacity for invention, unrestricted by the provisions of nature, but fueled by the imagination's ability to conjure something original and meaningful. Sidney underscores this freedom with a striking metaphor, likening the poet's imagination to a zodiac.

"...freely ranging within the zodiac of his own wit..."

This metaphor suggests that, while nature operates within fixed laws, poetry functions beyond it as per the poet's creative mind.

Sidney points out that poetry combines elements from various disciplines philosophy, history, and ethics making it a comprehensive art form. It draws from the knowledge of these fields while also possessing its own distinctive qualities. By embodying ideals and presenting moral dilemmas through storytelling, poetry inspires readers to aspire to higher ethical standards and understand the complexities of human nature. Sidney asserts that the ability of poetry to stir emotions and provoke thought makes it a powerful vehicle for conveying wisdom. The free nature of poetry allows the poets to convey the morals and ideals more appropriately without any restrictions.

Sidney also provides examples from various cultures, such as Turkey, Ireland, and Wales, where poetry retained a high value, even when other forms of formal learning may be absent. For instance, he mentions that in Turkey, poets are among the primary writers outside of religious figures, and in Ireland, poets hold a respected position in society. In each case, Sidney illustrates that poetry is a powerful means of shaping and maintaining cultural identity, even in societies labeled "barbarous" or "simple." Through such instances Sidney attempts to re-establish the status of poetry as an educational form like other disciplines.

In conclusion, Sidney considers poetry superior to other disciplines due to its creative power to transcend nature, its capacity to teach moral lessons effectively, and its ability to integrate knowledge from various fields into a cohesive and impactful form of expression. Through these attributes, he argues that poetry not only entertains but also enriches and elevates the human spirit.

3. Sidney's views on purpose of poetry including its role to teach and delight?

Answer:

In An Apology for Poetry, Sir Philip Sidney articulates a compelling vision of poetry, emphasizing its dual purpose that is to teach and to delight. He treats poetry as a noble art form that serves not only as a source of enjoyment but also as a powerful medium for moral and intellectual instruction.

Sidney asserts that poetry holds the unique capacity to instruct and influence character more effectively than philosophy alone. He references Aristotle, who stated that poetry can engage emotions and present ethical principles in ways that resonate with audiences. By inspiring readers with moral lessons, poets being fueled by divine insight can shape public virtue and civility, reflecting societal values and encouraging inspirational behavior. He categorizes poetry into three forms: religious poetry; philosophical poetry; instruct and delight poetry. Of the three he considers the third one as the superior. He emphasizes the responsibility of poets to portray the divine accurately, suggesting that their works should reflect the moral essence of the society while serving as a historical record that captures the virtues and vices of various eras.

Sidney argues that since poetry goes beyond nature's boundaries and expands its scope through invention unlike other disciplines such as geometry, arithmetic, astronomy, philosophy, history, law, etc. The poet is liberated from any such limits and hence can create figures like demigods, Cyclops, etc. which have less to do with the reality of nature. Sidney highlights that poetry combines and covers aspects from multiple disciplines, including philosophy, history, and ethics, rendering it as a holistic art form. It utilizes insights from these fields while also maintaining its unique characteristics. By embodying ideals and presenting moral dilemmas through narrative, poetry encourages readers to strive for elevated ethical standards and to grasp the intricacies of human nature. Sidney argues that poetry's capacity to evoke emotions and stimulate reflection makes it a formidable means of imparting wisdom. The unrestrained nature of poetry enables poets to express morals and ideals more effectively, free from limitations.

In addition to its instructive role, Sidney highlights the delight that poetry brings, asserting that aesthetic pleasure is an inherent part of its purpose. He emphasizes the beauty of poetic language, imagery, and structure, which engage the senses and evoke emotional responses. According to Sidney, true delight in poetry arises from its connection to beauty, goodness, and truth, allowing readers to experience joy through artistic expression. He argues that poetry should evoke a range of emotions, creating moments of reflection and introspection that foster empathy and understanding. By engaging with their own feelings through poetry, readers are led to a deeper appreciation of life and the human experience. He distinguishes between mere laughter and genuine delight, arguing that true delight arises from a connection to truths and experiences that resonate with human nature. Sidney contends that poetry should inspire admiration and appreciation for beauty, whether in the natural world or within human character. Sidney asserts that poetry's capacity to delight lies in its ability to intertwine beauty with meaning, making it an adequate expressive form of art.

Thus, Sidney believes that the combination of conveying knowledge and providing delights is what sets poetry apart from other forms of writing as it offers a holistic experience that engages both the intellect and the emotions.

4. References and Suggested Readings:

- Philip Sidney, 'An Apology for Poetry' (1579)
- M.A.R. Habib: 'Modern Literary Criticism and Theory', Blackwell
- Literary Explorations – A Quarterly International Referred Journal (September 2017)

UNIT-3

John Dryden: "An Essay of Dramatic Poesy"

1. **About the Author**
   a. Early and later life
   b. As a Literary figure
   c. His notable works

2. **An essay on dramatic poesy**
   a. Introduction
   b. Synopsis
   c. Analysis

3. **Probable Questions**
   a. AnalyzeDryden's comparative discussion of the merits of the classical drama (Ancient Greek and Roman) versus modern drama.
   b. Access critically Dryden's exploration of classical unities of time, place and action and his arguments for and against their observance in English Drama.

4. **References and suggested readings**

1. About John Dryden

John Dryden (1631-1700) was a prominent English poet, playwright, literary criticism and translator, who dominated the English literary life of the Restoration period. His career flourished amidst a period of significant cultural and political change in England from the Restoration of Charles II to the early years of the 18th century. His literary works span across several genres like satire, tragedy, comedy, prose, and literary criticism, so much so that the age is also often referred to as the "Age of Dryden".

> **The Poet Laureate**
>
> *The title of Poet Laureate is an official position appointed by the monarch that originated in England and dates back to the 17th century, with Ben Jonson being the first unofficial laureate. The poet is tasked with composing poems for state occasions, celebrations, or other significant events. Poet Laureates often serve as cultural representatives of poetry, using their role to promote literature and address contemporary themes.*
>
> *John Dryden, appointed as the first official Poet Laureate of England in 1668, set the standard for this role. He wasn't just a poet; he was a bridge between the monarchy and the people, using poetry to honor events like coronations and reflect the complexities of his era.*

Dryden was born in the village of Aldwinkle, Northamptonshire in 1631. He was the eldest of the fourteen children born to Erasmus Dryden and Mary Pickering. His family were prosperous people who brought him up in the strict Puritan faith and sent him to the famous Westminster school and then to Cambridge in 1650. He emerged as one of the best educated men of his age especially in the classics.

During the Protectorate, he returned to London and obtained work with Cromwell's Secretary of State, John Thurloe. In 1660, Dryden established his allegiance to the Restoration of the monarchy with the return of Charles II, through his work, 'Astraea Rudux'. After the death of Sir William Davena, Dryden was appointed as 'The Poet Laureate' in 1668 by Charles II, and between then and 1680, most of his works was for the stage. Dryden's tenure as the Laureate allowed him to influence the public sentiment and contribute to the cultural and political life of the Restoration England through his works. His role remained so till his final days.

Dryden's entry into playwriting came at a time when the English theatre was experiencing a revival after years of suspension. Dryden's early plays were "The wild Gallant", and "The Rival Ladies". His most influential play was "The Indian Queen", co-written with his brother-in-law Robert Ho. This play reflected the Restoration fascination of the folks with grandeur and classical narratives. Another of his plays include "The Conquest of Granada".

Though Dryden had his financial success in theatre, writing almost a play a year between 1663 and 1681, it is generally with poetry he is associated with.

Dryden's literary career as a poet began with his focus on poetic forms that blended classical influences with contemporary themes. His early poetic works include 'Heroic Stanzas', 'AnnusMerabills'. Dryden's satirical poetry is among his most enduring contributions, 'Absalom and Achitophel', 'The Medal' were among his political Satires. His mock epic, 'Mac Flecknoe' is a well-recognized satirical working which he satires Thomas Shadwell. The mock epic displays his extensive knowledge of the epic genre and the classical norms and figures.

As a poet, he established the 'heroic couplet' as a standard form of English poetry by composing several Satires, poems, epigrams, etc. He also introduced the alexandrine and triplet into the form.

His heroic couplet became the dominant poetic form of the 18th century which was also adopted by Alexander Pope.

Dryden as a critic was rooted in his deep engagement with the literary tradition of the past classical antiquity and his contemporary English context. His critical discourse includes 'An Essay on Dramatic Poesy', 'Preface to the Fables'. His critical writings advocate for the use of classical unities and values the dramatic traditions established by classical playwrights.

- **His notable works:**

<u>Plays</u>:
The Wild Gallant(1663)
The Rival Ladies(1664)
The Conquest of Granada(Part 1 in 1670, Part 2
in 1671)

The Indian Queen(1664)
All for Love(1677)

<u>Poems</u>:
Annual Mirabilis (1667)
Absalom and Achitophel(1681)
Mac Flecknoe(1676-1678)
The Medal(1682)

<u>Essays</u>:
An Essay on Dramatic Poesy (1668)
Preface to the Fables (1700)

The Restoration Age

The Restoration Age in English literature (1660–1700) was a transformative period following the reinstatement of the monarchy under Charles II after years of Puritan rule. Society, now rejecting Puritan austerity, embraced a culture of indulgence, wit, and pleasure. This shift was evident in the era's literature, especially in theatre, The political shift had a dramatic impact on English society, which underwent a shift from the strict moral codes of Puritanism to a culture more open to pleasure, wit, and indulgence. This was also an era marked by scientific curiosity, which was encouraged by the newly established Royal Society and symbolized a spirit of intellectual openness and progress. The literature of the Restoration Age reflects the complexities of this period, embracing both wit and cynicism in response to the shifting social and political landscape. Theatres, which had been closed under Puritan rule, were reopened, and drama flourished. Restoration comedy, often characterized by its sharp wit, satire, and focus on the manners and morals of high society, became immensely popular. Playwrights such as William Congreve, George Etherege, and Aphra Behn wrote comedies of manners that depicted the intrigues, hypocrisies and superficiality of the aristocracy, often with a humorous or satirical tone.In addition to drama, poetry and prose flourished in the Restoration Age, often marked by intellectual clarity, precision, and a sense of irony. Writers like John Dryden, one of the era's most prominent poets and critics, became central figures.

2. An Essay on Dramatic Poesy

- **Introduction**

Dryden's 'An Essay on Dramatic Poesy' published in 1668, stands as a significant critique and defense of drama during a period of transition in English literature. Written during the period when the English theatre was evolving, the essay serves as a defense of drama and a critique of contemporary theatrical practices. It not only reflects Dryden's ideals but also serves as a commentary on the cultural and artistic landscape of the 18thccentury.

Dryden employs a conversational format to present differing perspectives on dramatic poetry. Through the dialogues between four characters – Neander, Eugenius, Crites and Lisideius; Dryden explores fundamental themes and questions about the nature, purpose and standards of dramatic poetry. The discussion takes place against a pleasant background with each of the characters having their own views with each embodying distinct perspectives on drama. The dialogue form facilitated Dryden to refrain to any single point of view, but to debate the key issues of ancient versus modern, French versus English and blank verse versus rhyme.

The character of Neander can be seen as a representation of Dryden himself. Neander serves as a mediator, synthesizing the arguments of the other characters while defending the value of English Drama. He argues that while classical models provide a foundation for understanding drama, English playwrights such as Shakespeare surpass their predecessors in emotional depth and character development. Neander emphasizes on artistic expression and also on the importance of moral themes in drama. Neander favors the Modern form of drama but also respects the ancient norms inspire of being critical regarding the application of classical unities. It is reflective of Dryden's views concerning innovation and flexibility in dramatic form.

Through the next character Eugenius, Dryden explores the tension between classical and contemporary approaches to drama. Eugenius provides a critical perspective on modern drama, practically focusing on English Plays of the period. Eugenius advocates for the merits of the moderns over the ancients as he considers that contemporary English Drama surpass classical works in its emotional depth and relevance. He argues for the innovative form of the moderns which blends genres, over the ancients.

Lisideius, the third character articulates a defense of French drama, that French playwrights adhere closely to the unities of time, place and action, which according to him create a more coherent and impactful theatrical experience. He considers their structural discipline as essential for maintaining focus and clarity in plot. He criticizes the English tendency towards excess and deviation from these unities, suggesting that this can lead to confusion and a lack of artistic discipline.

Crites represents the classical perspective on drama; emphasizes on the critical principles of drama established by ancient Greek and Roman playwrights. He defines the importance of the classical unities, arguing that these principles ensure a more disciplined and coherent narrative technique. He highlights that deviating from the unities by the Modern English dramatists make it prone to the creation of confusion and dilution of the plot and the moral purpose of drama.

- **Synopsis**

Written as a dialogue among four characters: Crites, Eugenius, Lisideius, and Neander; the essay explores several major debates of the contemporary time, including the relative merits of ancient and modern drama, the differences between French and English theater, and whether rhyme has a place in dramatic works. Through this conversational structure, Dryden not only examines these issues but also subtly reveals his own views on what makes drama successful and meaningful.

The characters converse on a barge floating on the Thames, Dryden allows them to express their ideas through witty and ironic exchanges. This setting is symbolic, reflecting the broader tensions between old and new, as well as between different cultural traditions. Their dialogue addresses the merits of ancient versus modern playwrights, with Crites advocating for adherence to classical unities of time, place, and action These rules, he claims, ensure that plays are coherent, believable, and tightly focused. According to Crites, modern dramatists fail to meet these high standards because they often disregard these principles, leading to plots that feel chaotic and unrealistic. Dryden advocates for a dramatic style that prioritizes immediacy and emotional resonance, illustrating how the ancients successfully navigated the challenges of storytelling within the constraints of the unity of Time.

Eugenius challenges Crites's assertion of the superiority of the Ancients by arguing that Crites has not provided convincing evidence to support the claim that ancient playwrights produced more perfect representations of human life.While he acknowledges the contributions of the ancients, he argues that they are not without fault. He highlights their ability to craft intricate plots and create characters that feel more authentic and relatable. Neander defends the value of English dramas and their complexities that incorporate subplots and a mixture of genres. Lisideius offers a defining statement on drama, suggesting it is "a just and lively Image of Humane Nature," highlighting the idea that modern plays reflect the intricacies of human experience more faithfully than their classical counterparts

Dryden notes that modern plays often deviate from the unity of Action, which dictates a single main plot without multiple, competing storylines. By trying to encapsulate multiple events and journeys, these plays often lack the unity and focus of classical drama, which follows one clear, complete storyline that all elements support.

The discussion then shifts to a comparison of French and English drama, a subject that sparks further disagreement. Lisideius advocates for the French theater, which he views as the epitome of refinement and elegance. He commends playwrights like Pierre Corneille and Jean Racine for their ability to craft plays that are polished, morally instructive, and faithful to the classical unities. Lisideius believes that French drama's emphasis on decorum makes it superior to English drama, which he sees as overly chaotic and superficial. In essence, Dryden's analysis reveals a preference for English theatrical conventions, suggesting that they offer a more potent and engaging reflection of human nature than the more rigid, idealized portrayals of French drama.

Neander supports rhymed drama, seeing it as a distinct opportunity for innovation in English theater, beyond what blank verse or prose could offer. Through the dialogues between Lisideius and Neander, Dryden explores differing philosophies of dramatic presentation and narrative style, particularly regarding how actions and emotions are conveyed on stage.

Neander, who is taken to represent Dryden's own views, offers a defense of English drama. While he agrees that English playwrights often ignore the unities, he sees this as a strength rather than a weakness. By freeing themselves from rigid rules, English dramatists are able to capture the full range of human experience. Neander points to Shakespeare as the greatest example of this approach, praising him as a poet of unparalleled genius. Neander also celebrates Ben Jonson for his craftsmanship and wit, though he acknowledges that Jonson's more rigid adherence to classical forms. In contrast, Neander criticizes French drama for being overly constrained by rules, which often results in plays that feel lifeless and overly formal.

The final topic of the dialogue is the use of rhyme in plays, a controversial issue in Dryden's time. Crites opposes rhyme, arguing that it makes dialogue feel artificial and detracts from the natural flow of conversation. Neander, however, defends it, claiming that rhyme can enhance the beauty and emotional power of a play. He argues that, when used skillfully, rhyme does not diminish the realism of dialogue but instead adds a layer of artistry that elevates the overall effect.

By the end of the essay, no definitive conclusion is reached or found, reflecting Dryden's belief that art is too diverse and subjective to be reduced to a single set of rules. While his admiration for English drama, particularly to writers like Ben Johnson, is clear, he also respects the contributions of the ancients and the French. Dryden's ultimate message is to adhere to the rules and traditions which are important, but they should not restrain creativity or limit the artist's ability to explore new ideas and forms.

- **Analysis**

Dryden's 'An Essay on Dramatic Poesy' written in the form of dialogues between four characters Neander, Eugenius, Crites, Lisideius presents a brief discussion on Neo-classical theory of literature.

The narrative is set against the backdrop of a significant naval battle between the English and Dutch fleets, an event that captivates the attention of the city. The essay opens with a vivid description of the chaos and excitement surrounding the battle, where citizens, alarmed by the noise of cannon fire, abandon their daily activities to follow the sounds of conflict. This establishes a dramatic context for the ensuing conversation among four characters: Eugenius, Crites, Lisideius, and Neander. These characters, representing different critical perspectives, engage in a dialogue that explores the nature of drama and poetry during a time when the London theatres were closed due to the plague.

As they sail along the river, they are drawn to the diminishing sound of battle, which they interpret as a good omen for England's victory. This observation sparks the group's conversation, beginning with Crites, who, though he acknowledges the victory, expresses a satirical concern about the inevitable wave of bad poetry inspired by the event. He criticizes those "eternal rhymers," mediocre poets who seize any opportunity especially major public events to produce shallow, overly patriotic verse. Dryden humorously conveys Crites's disdain for these poets, suggesting they are akin to "Ravens and birds of Prey," drawn to battle scenes for inspiration without any true poetic skill.

Lisideius responds with a clever jest about these opportunistic writers, noting their readiness to celebrate the Duke's bravery with a panegyric or, if things go poorly, to compose elegy mourning his tragic fall. This remark highlights the writers' lack of sincerity, as they prepare to flatter the victor or lament a loss based on the outcome, rather than any genuine emotional response. The group finds this humorous, but Crites remains critical, arguing that such inferior poets should be silenced to preserve the peace and "quiet of all honest people." He relates them to "seditious Preachers," emphasizing his belief that poor poetry is a social disturbance that degrades the art form. Eugenius, however, disagrees, showing his love for poetry by advocating that all who attempt it, even those less skilled, deserve some encouragement or reward for their efforts. He believes that, much like Sylla sparing Cicero, some leniency should be extended to poets, suggesting that poetry as an art should be appreciated—even if not all contributions are of high quality. Here, Dryden subtly supports a tolerant, open-minded view of literary expression, favoring constructive criticism over harsh dismissal.

Lisideius and Eugenius pointout the opportunistic nature of such poets, who might prepare both celebratory and lamenting verses to be ready for any outcome. This exchange underscores the thematic tension between sincerity and opportunism in literature. Eugenius represents a more forgiving perspective, suggesting that any effort to produce poetry, even if mediocre, deserves encouragement rather than suppression. His stance reflects a more modern and open-minded approach to literary experimentation, contrasting with Crites' preference for classical restraint.

Eugenius argues that while he deeply respects the poetry of ancient Greeks and Romans, he believes that the writers of his own era are as capable and, in some ways, even better to the ancients. He cites Horace to validate his point that the ancients themselves valued innovation, and they would likely have admired the accomplishments of the modern age if they were present. Eugenius suggests that while Greek and Roman poetry deserves admiration, English poets have also refined their own style to reach new heights, especially in lyric and epic forms.

However, when Crites responds, he narrows the scope of their debate to dramatic poetry, arguing that in this genre, ancient playwrights surpass modern writers. Eugenius concedes that recent plays might not match those of earlier English writers but maintains that in other forms of poetry, contemporary English writers excel. He refers to poets like Suckling, Waller, Denham, and Cowley as exemplars of this refined English style, stating that English drama and poetry now surpass the French, Italian, and Spanish.

On play

Lisideius then proposes a "definition" of what a play should be to ground their debate. He describes a play as "a just and lively image of human nature," capturing both the emotions and events that shape life, with the aim to entertain and educate. While Crites points out a flaw in this definition, noting it lacks technical precision, the group still agrees it is a good starting point. This sets the stage for Crites to present his case for the superiority of ancient dramatic poets.

On the classical unities:

The concept of the "Three Unities"—Time, Place, and Action emerges from the dialogue of Eugenius. He reflects principles that were highly regarded in French Neoclassical drama, which drew heavily from classical Greek theories, particularly those found in Aristotle's Poetics.

"Out of these two has been extracted the Famous Rules which the French call, Des TroisUnitez, or, The Three Unities, which ought to be observed in every Regular Play; namely, of Time, Place, and Action."

(An Essay on Dramatic Poesy)

The unity of Time dictates that the action of a play should unfold within a single day, creating a sense of immediacy and urgency that keeps the audience engaged with the unfolding events on the stage. The unity of Place requires that the entire action take place in one location, helping maintain focus and clarity, which allows the audience to better understand the interactions and developments within a confined setting. Lastly, the unity of Action asserts that a play should revolve around a single, central plot without the distraction of subplots, enhancing the emotional impact of the drama and allowing the audience to connect deeply with the protagonist's journey. While Eugenius recognizes the value of these unities, Dryden through his character also tries to advocate for the strengths of English drama, which often diverges from the strict adherence to these three principles. He acknowledges that while the unities provide a useful framework for structure, the artistic freedom found in English theatre permits more complex character development and thematic exploration, resulting in a richer narrative experience.

Dryden through the character of Eugenius argues that following the unity of Time is particularly challenging in the context of tragedy, where the emotional stakes are high and the narrative is complex. He notes that ancient playwrights typically begin their plays at a pivotal moment in the story.

"Play is to be thought the nearest imitation of Nature, whose Plot or Action is confined within that time;" (An Essay on Dramatic Poesy)

By doing this, they immerse the audience directly into the action. This technique allows the audience to engage with the narrative without the distraction of preliminary details that could slow down the dramatic momentum. Instead of witnessing the gradual development of the story, the audience is thrust into the crucial moments that define the conflict or action of the play. This approach effectively heightens the dramatic tension, as the audience is compelled to piece together the events happening on stage through the dialogues and interactions of the characters. Dryden appreciates this method, as it serves to captivate the audience's attention right from the start. By eliminating the "tedious expectation" of a slow build-up, the playwright ensures that the audience is engaged and invested in the outcome of the narrative from the beginning itself. Dryden advocates for a dramatic style that prioritizes immediacy and emotional resonance, illustrating how the ancients successfully navigated the challenges of storytelling within the constraints of the unity of Time.

The "Second Unity," the unity of 'Place', Dryden explains that the ancients believed a play should be set in a single location throughout its entirety.

"...the Scene ought to be continued through the Play, in the same place where it was laid in the beginning..."(An Essay on Dramatic Poesy)

This principle stems from the idea that the stage is a singular, physical space, making it unnatural for the audience to accept that the action occurs in multiple, distant locations simultaneously. Dryden acknowledges that modern theatrical techniques, such as the use of painted scenes or backdrops, can create an illusion of different settings. These visual elements can trick the audience's imagination into believing that the action is taking place in various places, provided these settings are depicted with some semblance of probability. However, he argues that the unity of Place is most effectively maintained when the locations are relatively close to one another ideally within the same town or city.

"...yet it still carries the greater likelihood of truth, if those places be supposed so near each other, as in the same Town or City; which may all be comprehended under the larger Denomination of one place: for a greater distance will bear no proportion to the shortness of time..." (An Essay on Dramatic Poesy)

He praises the French for their strict adherence to this principle, noting that in their plays, a scene is never changed in the middle of an act. If an act begins in a specific location such as a garden, street, or chamber; it concludes in the same setting.

"...the Act begins in a Garden, a Street, or Chamber, 'tis ended in the same place;"(An Essay on Dramatic Poesy)

Such consistency not only aids in maintaining the audience's suspension of disbelief but also contributes to a more immersive experience. Dryden points out that the stage is kept lively with characters, ensuring it is never empty. It fosters a sense of continuity, as characters are introduced in relation to one another, with each having a purpose or connection to those already present. Dryden refers to Corneille's concept of 'La Liaison des' Scenes, or the continuity of scenes, which is crucial for a well-constructed play. Thecontinuity enhances the narrative flow, as characters engage with one another in a manner that reveals their relationships and the intertwining of plots. Each character's entrance is appropriately placed to ensure that their interactions are relevant to the ongoing action, thereby creating cohesive relationships that enrich the audience's understanding of the story.

He then discusses the "Third Unity", the unity of 'Action'. Dryden draws a parallel between unity of action and the concept of "Finis" in logic, which refers to the end or purpose of an action.

"As for the third Unity which is that of Action, the Ancients meant no other by it than what the Logicians do by their Finis..."   *(An Essay on Dramatic Poesy)*

He asserts that the unity of Action requires a play to focus on a single, overarching narrative or purpose. This means that all elements within the play: characters, events, and even conflicts, should serve to advance this primary action. Dryden emphasizes that the playwright's objective is to create a "great and complete action" that maintains coherence and clarity throughout the narrative. This central action not only guides the plot but also integrates all components of the play, ensuring that even obstacles or complications encountered by the characters contribute to the progression of this main storyline. When a play revolves around a singular action, it enhances the audience's engagement and emotional investment. By avoiding subplots or distractions that deviate from the central theme, the playwright can create a more powerful and resonant experience for the viewers. This focus allows for deeper exploration of characters and their motivations, as their actions are all aligned toward a common purpose. He further elaborates on the "Unity of Action" by emphasizing that a play must centre on a single, dominant action. Dryden argues that if a playwright were to develop two equally prominent actions, it would undermine the unity of the work, resulting in a disjointed experience that feels more like two separate plays rather than one cohesive work.

While Dryden acknowledges that multiple actions can exist within a play, he insists that these must all serve the primary action that is effectively acting as "under-plots." He illustrates this with an example from Terence's Eunuch, where the relationship dynamics between Thais and Phædria do not constitute the main action but rather support the central plot involving the marriage of Chærea and Chreme's sister. This interrelationship demonstrates how secondary actions can enrich the narrative while remaining subordinate to the principal theme. Dryden quotes Corneille to underscore the importance of having one complete action that allows the audience to feel a sense of resolution and closure.

"...Now the Plots of their Plays being narrow, and the persons few, one of their Acts was written in a less compass than one of our well-wrought Scenes, and yet they are often deficient even in this: To go no further than Terence, you find in the Eunuch, Antipho entering single in the midst of the third Act, after Chremes and Pythias were gone off: In the same Play you have likewise Dorias beginning the fourth Act alone; and after she has made a relation of what was done at the Soldier's entertainment..."(An Essay of Dramatic Poesy)

He emphasizes that achieving the singular focus often requires the incorporation of several minor, imperfect actions that contribute to the overall narrative arc. These subplots create a delightful suspense, keeping the audience engaged as they anticipate how these various threads will converge and ultimately lead to the resolution of the main action.

Dryden reflects on how few modern plays would meet the standards set by classical dramatic rules specifically, the unities of Time, Place, and Action. According to Dryden, these unities, established by the ancients, were designed to create a focused, immersive experience for the audience, concentrating on the emotional impact of the play within a limited scope. He argues that modern playwrights often disregard these rules, and in doing so, dilute the effectiveness of their work. The unity of Time, for example, dictates that the events of a play should take place within a single day. Dryden through Crites criticizes modern dramas for ignoring this, stretching narratives over extended periods even lifetimes rather than focusing on a single, intense moment. By trying to capture a whole life in a play, Crites insists that the dramas lose the immediate impact and tension that comes from condensing action within a shorter time span. Similarly, the unity of Place calls for a single, consistent setting. However, many modern plays transport the audience to multiple locations, sometimes across entire countries, within a single performance. Such lack of a stable setting disrupts the play's cohesion, as the audience struggles to imagine the shifts from one place to another. The frequent changes in location can distract viewers from the story, weakening their emotional connection to the action on stage.

Ancient vs. Moderns

Dryden presents Eugenius's response to Crites, highlighting the ongoing debate between the Ancients and the Moderns. Crites, representing the Ancients, argued in favor of classical dramatists and their adherence to the unities and rules established by Greek and Roman playwrights. He emphasizes that the Ancients provided a solid foundation for all subsequent dramatic works. Eugenius, who represents the Moderns, counters Crites's position by acknowledging the debt modern writers owe to the Ancients.

"...Moderns have profited by the rules of the Ancients, but in the latter you are careful to conceal how much they have excelled them: we own all the helps we have from them, and want neither veneration nor gratitude while we acknowledge that to overcome them we must make use of the advantages we have received from them..."(An Essay of Dramatic Poesy)

He concedes that the Moderns have greatly benefited from the foundational principles laid out by classical playwrights, and he does not deny the value of their contributions. However, Eugenius also suggests that the Moderns have advanced beyond their predecessors by building on these ancient rules and infusing them with new insights and innovations. He argues that it is not enough simply to emulate the Ancients; instead, the Moderns should honor their legacy by surpassing them. Eugenius claims that while the Moderns respect and appreciate the contributions of the Ancients, they also bring their own creativity and diligence to the craft of drama, thus extending and enhancing the tradition. By combining classical techniques with modern perspectives and styles, the Moderns seek to elevate drama to new heights. Through this dialogue, Dryden captures the essence of the debate, suggesting that true artistic progress comes from both learning from the past and contributing something original.

Eugenius continues his argument against Crites by asserting that modern playwrights do not merely replicate the works of the Ancients but rather draw inspiration from nature and the broader experiences of life. He argues that while classical dramatists had great skill and insight, the Moderns possess the advantage of having a more extensive understanding of the world due to the cumulative knowledge and experiences accumulated over time.

Eugenius emphasizes that the Moderns have access to both the wisdom of the Ancients and their own life experiences, allowing them to explore and depict aspects of human nature and life that the Ancients may have overlooked or failed to capture fully.

"...We draw not therefore after their lines, but those of Nature; and having the life before us, besides the experience of all they knew, it is no wonder if we hit some airs and features which they have missed: I deny not what you urge of Arts and Sciences, that they have flourished in some ages more than others; but your instance in Philosophy makes for me: for if Natural Causes be more known now than in the time of Aristotle, because more studied, it follows that Poesy and other Arts may with the same pains arrive still nearer to perfection, and, that granted" (An Essay of Dramatic Poesy)

Eugenius asserts that the goal of drama is to reflect the complexities of real life rather than strictly adhere to ancient conventions. He acknowledges that the arts and sciences have experienced evolution over time and has been of flourishing. He suggests that if advancements have occurred in fields like philosophy, where natural causes are better understood than in Aristotle's time, then the same can be true for poetry and drama. The implication here is that with diligence and study, modern playwrights can achieve a level of artistic expression that rivals or even surpasses that of their predecessors.

Eugenius challenges Crites's claim that Greek poetry and drama reached a state of perfection during the period of old comedy. He begins by asserting that the Greeks, particularly in the era of old comedy, did not achieve the sophisticated structure that is associated with plays of his contemporary, specifically the division into acts.

"Be pleased then in the first place to take notice, that the Greek Poesy, which Crites has affirmed to have arrived to perfection in the Reign of the old Comedy, was so far from it, that the distinction of it into Acts was not known to them; or if it were, it is yet so darkly delivered to us that we cannot make it out." (An Essay of Dramatic Poesy)

Eugenius implies that the ancient Greek tradition lacks clarity and organization compared to contemporary standards. He suggests that if the Greeks did use acts, the details surrounding this practice have been poorly preserved, making it difficult for modern scholars and audiences to fully understand how these plays were structured.

Eugenius mentions that the knowledge of Greek plays largely comes from the singing of the Chorus, a key component of ancient Greek drama. However, he points out that the role and functions of the Chorus are ambiguous, suggesting that there may have been variations in how many times the Chorus sang within different plays.

"...from the singing of their Chorus, and that too is so uncertain that in some of their Plays we have reason to conjecture they sung more than five times..."(An Essay of Dramatic Poesy)

Eugenius discusses Aristotle's analysis of dramatic structure, outlining the integral parts of a play according to classical tradition. He delineates Aristotle's four main components: the Protasis, Epitasis, Catastasis, and Catastrophe, explaining their roles in shaping the narrative and emotional trajectory of a play.

"Aristotle indeed divides the integral parts of a Play into four: First, The Protasis or entrance, which gives light…with the conduct of it."

The Protasis is the introduction, which establishes the characters but does not dive deeply into the plot. It serves primarily to present the individuals involved without providing much context about the unfolding action. This sets the stage for the audience to understand who the characters are but does not engage them with the plot's momentum. The Epitasis follows as the part where the plot begins to develop and intensify. In this section, the stakes are raised, and the audience senses that the action is moving towards a climax, creating anticipation for what is to come .Next, the Catastasis introduces a turning point, where the action becomes complicated and the initial expectations of the audience are challenged. Eugenius uses a metaphor comparing this moment to a violent stream encountering a narrow passage, suggesting that just as the water is forced into an eddy, the plot becomes embroiled in new difficulties, moving the audience further from their previous hopes for resolution. This reflects the common dramatic technique of introducing conflict and obstacles that must be navigated before the story can reach its conclusion. Finally, the Catastrophe or denouement resolves the plot. Here, all elements of the story are brought back to a state of equilibrium, as the conflicts introduced earlier are resolved.

Eugenius emphasizes that this resolution should reflect "truth and nature," ensuring that the audience feels satisfied with how the story concludes. Eugenius acknowledges the effectiveness of Aristotle's structure, stating that it has provided valuable insights for modern playwrights in shaping their works into more structured acts and scenes. However, he points out that while Aristotle articulated these principles, the ancient Greeks did not fully utilize them in their plays, often favoring entrances over clearly defined acts. His critique highlights the lack of sophistication in ancient Greek drama regarding act structure, suggesting that they had a less developed understanding of how to orchestrate the dramatic elements effectively.

Regarding Roman comedy, Dryden criticizes it for its formulaic plots and shallow character portrayals. The plots typically centered around a young girl who gets kidnapped or wandered off as a child; gets raised elsewhere, and eventually ends up pregnant by a reckless young man who, with the help of his quick-witted servant, manages to deceive his father to get out of trouble. When the time comes for everything to be revealed, it happens abruptly without much reasoning.

"In their Comedies, the Romans generally borrowed their Plots from the Greek Poets; and theirs was commonly a little Girl stolen or wandered from her Parents, brought back unknown to the same City, there got with child by some lewd young fellow; who, by the help of his servant, cheats his father, and when her time comes, to cry Juno Lucina feropem [Juno, goddess of

childbirth, bring help—ed.]; one or other sees a little Box or Cabinet which was carried away with her, and so discovers her to her friends, if some God do not prevent it, by coming down in a Machine, and take the thanks of it to himself." (An Essay of Dramatic Poesy)

Dryden compares these predictable plots and one-dimensional characters to Italian architecture, where one can "see through" the whole structure from one side. While these characters do reflect some aspects of real people, they lack the depth or complexity of a full portrait, failing to capture the complexity of a real human personality.

"These are Plots built after the Italian Mode of Houses, you see through them all at once; the Characters are indeed the Imitations of Nature…"(An Essay of Dramatic Poesy)

Dryden through Eugenius notes that the formal structure of five acts was established during the time of Horace, who recommended that comedies should also adhere to this format. By referencing Horace, Eugenius indicates that while the ancient Greeks laid the groundwork for drama, they did not consummate the art form, often operating with a "general indigested notion of a Play." This suggests that their plays were not as well-organized or refined as modern plays, which demonstrate a clearer understanding of dramatic structure.

On the contrary, Crites critiques the "modern plays" of his time for disregarding the ancient unities of time, place, and action. This departure, he argues, can lead to sprawling plots that sometimes take up "an age" rather than a single day, cover multiple locations rather than one, and try to cover a man's life rather than focusing on a single, unified action. For Crites, the ancients' adherence to the three unities embodies a disciplined approach that helps maintain the play's believability and coherence.

Crites' admiration for the ancients extends beyond structure to style and wit. He laments at the loss of key ancient texts, particularly those of the Greek playwrights like Menander and Latin writers like Caeilius and Varius, implying that had these works survived, they could have decisively demonstrated the superiority of ancient drama. He refers to ancient works like those of Aristophanes, Plautus, Euripides, and Sophocles which are still available.

"...This is so plain, that I need not instance to you, that Aristophanes, Plautus, Terence, never any of them writ a Tragedy; Æschylus, Euripides, Sophocles and Seneca, never meddled with Comedy; the Sock and Buskin were not worn by the same Poet: having then so much care to excel in one kind, very little is to be pardoned them if they miscarried in it;" (An Essay of Dramatic Poesy)

Crites insists that even contemporary readers of his time cannot fully appreciate their mastery due to language barriers and lost historical context.

However, Eugenius who represents a more modern view counters Crites' admiration for the ancients by suggesting that the moderns have too indeed improved upon classical drama. While acknowledging the debt that contemporary playwrights owe to ancient rules and examples, Eugenius believes the moderns have moved beyond mere imitation, or drawing inspiration from only nature itself. He argues that, just as scientific knowledge and philosophical understanding have advanced over time, so too has drama, adapting its techniques to capture human nature more fully. He points out that while the Greeks lacked certain structural conventions like dividing plays into five acts which was later standardized by Horace; modern playwrights have refined these aspects, improving on the ancients by adding clear acts and scenes that bring in the narrative's clarity.

Eugenius also critiques ancient dramas for their reliance on entrances and exits of the chorus to signal plot progression, suggesting that such techniques feel "indigested" by comparison to the well-structured acts of modern plays. He acknowledges that even some contemporary dramatists, like the Spaniards and Italians, do not strictly follow the five-act structure, yet they at least limit themselves to three acts. He cites the Spanish "jornadas" that shows more consistency than the Greek plays.

Eugenius directs the course of discussion towards the plots of tragedies. He states about the predictability of ancient tragedies. According to him, these tragedies often relied on well-known myths, like the stories of Oedipus or Medea, where audiences already knew the plot twists and outcomes. Dryden through the character of Eugenius observes that this predictability of the plot and events left audiences with little elements of suspense or surprise.

"...Though I see many excellent thoughts in Seneca, yet he, of them who had a Genius most proper for the Stage, was Ovid, he had a way of writing so fit to stir up a

pleasing admiration and concernment which are the objects of a Tragedy, and to show the various movements of a Soul combating betwixt two different Passions, that, had he lived in our age…"(An Essay of Dramatic Poesy)

Turning to ancient comedies, Dryden observes that they too tended to repeat the same elements as well. He refers to Roman comedies, which were often adapted from Greek sources that featured familiar characters and predictable plots like a young woman stolen or lost, a mischievous servant helping a wayward son, and an old father hoping for his son's marriage.

When discussing plot and character, Eugenius notes that ancient plays were tightly structured with limited scope. The characters were realistic but often too narrowly defined, focusing on one or two traits rather than capturing the entire human essence. He compares this narrow focus to looking at an eye or a hand without seeing the entire face or body. Eugenius criticizes the way ancient plays handled transitions between scenes. The ancient plays tended to be episodic, with characters exiting and entering in a way that could feel disjointed. In contrast, Eugenius feels modern English playwrights often manage scene changes more smoothly.

He then reflects on the use of language in ancient plays. He argues that while classical writers like Plautus sometimes used clever language, their metaphors could appear to be forced or overly complicated.

"…in Plautus; but to speak generally, their Lovers say little, when they see each other, but anima mea, vita mea [my soul, my life—ed.], zōe kai psyche [my life, my soul—ed.], as the women in Juvenal's time used to cry *out in the fury of their kindness: then indeed to speak sense were an offence. Any sudden gust of passion (as an ecstasy of love in an unexpected meeting) cannot better be expressed than in a word and a sigh, breaking on…"(An Essay of Dramatic Poesy)*

Dryden here admires wit that appears in natural, simple language, as it's more universally appreciated and accessible. He contrasts Plautus' ornate style with the English satirist Cleveland, who, in Dryden's view, uses excessively complex language, making it inaccessible interpret for readers. Dryden believes that the best wit is conveyed in clear, straightforward language, allowing the audience to access it without much difficulty. When it comes to comedy, Eugenius acknowledges moments of tenderness in Plautus but suggests that love scenes in the ancient plays lack depth. He notes that English dramatists open up the minds of lovers to engage the audience more intimately, which he sees as strength of modern drama.

Crites, representing a more conservative view, counters Eugenius that although the moderns may have evolved certain styles, it's just an alteration in the form rather than an improvement. He acknowledges the notion that poets adapt to their time but stresses the importance of respecting the "masters" of ancient poetry.

French vs English drama

Lisideius, raises the question of whether English plays should adhere to the stern French rules, particularly Aristotle's unities of time, place, and action, Neander advocates for English drama. Lisideius admires the

French playwrights like Corneille, who adhere closely to classical unities, creating a focused plot without subplots. He argues that French drama provide variety of themes in a controlled way, in contrast to the chaotic intermingling of serious and comic elements in English tragicomedies, which he considers as absurd.

Lisideius critiques English plays for violating unity, arguing that subplots tend to confuse audiences by dividing their emotional investment between multiple stories.

"The unity of Action in all their Plays is yet more conspicuous, for they do not burden them with under-plots, as the English do." (An Essay of Dramatic Poesy)

He observes that English plays lack coherence, often presenting disparate plot elements in the same performance. In contrast, he praises the French for their unified structure, saying this gives them more freedom to develop complex emotions within a single storyline.

The discourse extends to cover historical dramas, where Lisideius harshly critiques the English playwrights, particularly Shakespeare, for compressing lengthy historical events into brief performances.

"On the other side, if you consider the Historical Plays of Shakespeare, they are rather so many Chronicles of Kings, or the business many times of thirty or forty years, cramped into a representation of two hours and a half, which is not to imitate or paint Nature, but rather to draw her in miniature, to take her in little; to look upon her through the wrong end of a Perspective, and receive her Images not only much less, but infinitely more imperfect than the life: this instead of making a

Play delightful, renders it ridiculous." (An Essay of Dramatic Poesy)

He argues that this diminishes the realism and emotional aspect of the events, as the audience sees only a miniature version of them. The French, he asserts that by contrast, blend history with fiction, crafting an engaging illusion that appeals to the audience's sense of moral justice.

Lisideius argues that the French playwrights, like Corneille, excel in restraint i.e. they prefer narration over direct depiction of certain scenes like violent deaths or supernatural transformations. He considers that depiction of such scenes on stage might disrupt the audience's suspension of disbelief or sensibilities. He insists that the French approach as refined, focusing on unity, clarity, and decorum.

Neander, counters Lisideius by valuing the English tradition of lively representation and variety in action. He refers to English dramatists like Ben Jonson and Fletcher who have captured "the soul of Poesy" through a diverse, intricate blend of humor and passion. This, according to Neander, creates a dynamic that captivates audiences in ways that the more restrained French style cannot. Neander also critiques the French notion of delivering long monologues, describing them as tedious and less natural in depicting intense passions. He appreciates the English style, a forits swift, responsive exchange that is more effective at evoking genuine emotion. Furthermore, while acknowledging the virtues of unity in French plots, Neander celebrates the complexity and layered subplots in English drama, asserting that, if well-managed, they offer a "labyrinth of design" that enhances audience satisfaction.

By following the classical rules of unity too closely, the French have, according to Neander, limited themselves to producing dramas that lack variety and dynamism. Neander contrasts this with English plays, which, while often less "regular" in structure, exhibit a broader range of emotions, more engaging plots, and a greater sense of freedom.

He praises English playwrights like Shakespeare and Fletcher, noting that their plays, though sometimes structurally "irregular," contain significant and powerful scenes and depict complex characters that resonate deeply with audiences. He describes Shakespeare, as having a "comprehensive soul," with a natural ability to depict life in a way that feels vivid and immediate. This capacity allows Shakespeare's work to transcend time, despite the occasional flaws of "flatness" or "bombast."

Neander examines Ben Jonson, whom he considers the "most learned and judicious" of English playwrights. Jonson is described as meticulous, especially in his classical influences and structural discipline, and as someone who brought a high level of artistic refinement to the English stage; focused on themes like love or deep passions, focusing instead on humor and satire, particularly of common people.

"As for Jonson, to whose Character I am now arrived, if we look upon him while he was himself, (for his last Plays were but his dotages) I think him the most learned and judicious Writer which any Theater ever had. He was a most severe Judge of himself as well as others.

One cannot say he wanted wit, but rather that he was frugal of it. In his works you find little to retrench or alter. Wit and Language, and Humor also in some measure we had before him; but something of Art was wanting to the Drama till he came. He managed his strength to more advantage than any who preceded him. You seldom find him making Love in any of his Scenes, or endeavoring to move the Passions; his genius was too sullen and saturnine to do it gracefully, especially when he knew he came after those who had performed both to such an height. Humor was his proper Sphere, and in that he delighted most to represent Mechanic [laboring, vulgar—ed.] people. He was deeply conversant in the Ancients, both Greek and Latin, and he borrowed boldly from them...."(An Essay of Dramatic Poesy)

Neander comments that, despite Jonson's technical precision, Shakespeare's work has a more profound and instinctive appeal.

Analysis of Ben Jonson's comedy, The Silent Woman

Dryden provides a detailed analysis and defense of Ben Jonson's comedy, The Silent Woman, emphasizing on its technical aspects, mastery over wit, and relevance in English literature. Dryden begins by commending Jonson's adherence to the classical unities of time, place, and action which according to the ancients are essential principles for organizing a play's plot into a cohesive and efficient structure.

Dryden notes that The Silent Woman spans only a few hours, adhering closely to the concept of a "natural day" and requiring only about three and a half hours performing.

"To begin first with the length of the Action, it is so far from exceeding the compass of a Natural day, that it takes not up an Artificial one. 'Tis all included in the limits of three hours and a half, which is not more than is required for the presentment on the Stage…"(An Essay of Dramatic Poesy)

This strict adherence to a condensed timeline is unusual and noteworthy, allowing the play to focus sharply without distractions from unrelated events. The play's setting is similarly limited, occurring almost entirely within two houses and later within just one, thereby maintaining spatial coherence.

"The action of the Play is entirely one; the end or aim of which is the settling of Morose's Estate on Dauphine." (An Essay of Dramatic Poesy)

Dryden observes that Jonson's play achieves unity of action by centering all events around a single purpose i.e. securing Morose's estate for the character Dauphine. Each subplot and interaction serves this central objective, creating a seamless and interconnected narrative.

Dryden praises Jonson's complex plot structure, which progresses smoothly and with increasing tension until its final resolution. He notes that the story introduces new characters and obstacles in each act, adding suspense and depth, which keep the audience engaged and surprised. Dryden finds this organization remarkable, especially in a comedy where the plot deals with everyday people rather than grand, tragic figures.

"Others say it is not enough to find one man of such an humor; it must be common to more, and the more

common the more natural." (An Essay of Dramatic Poesy)

Dryden emphasizes Jonson's skill in depicting "humors," or exaggerated personal traits that make each character unique. For example, Morose, an elderly man who despises all noise, is portrayed with such specificity that he stands out as a realistic, albeit eccentric, individual. Dryden defends this characterization against critics who argue it's forced, explaining that Jonson based it on a real person and that exaggeration is essential to make the character memorable.

"Besides Morose, there are at least or different Characters and humors in The Silent Woman, *all which persons have several concernments of their own, yet are all used by the Poet, to the conducting of the main design to perfection." (An Essay of Dramatic Poesy)*

Dryden contrasts Jonson's nuanced approach to characterization with the simpler, more generalized figures of ancient Greek comedy and French comedy. He explains that Jonson's approach reflects a specifically English talent for portraying complex, unique individuals who evoke laughter through their distinct characterization traits, rather than generalized or repetitive stereotypes.

On use of rhyme and blank verse

Dryden directs the course of discussion towards rhyme and whether it is appropriate for drama. Crites argues against rhyme in serious plays, claiming it is unnatural as it suggests premeditated speech, which clashes with the spontaneity required in dialogues in a play. Crites maintains that natural conversation does not unfold in rhyme, which is why the use blank verse, which is closer to prose, aligns better with the imitation of real life speech. He cites Aristotle, who preferred forms of verse closest to prose for drama. He further argues that use of rhyme in dialogues of a play can detract from its realism, making it seem as if the characters are colluding to create poetic responses rather than engaging in genuine conversation.

Neander, on the other hand defends rhyme, and advocates for its use in tragedies where grandeur is fitting. He insists that rhyme can be natural if the words are carefully chosen and arranged. He argues that an efficient poet or a dramatist finds ways to incorporate rhyme without forcing it, making their verse both appealing and not feeling superficial or forced. He insists that creating rhymed dialogues for drama requires skill, as the language must feel spontaneous while remaining poetic. To illustrate, Neander references recent English tragedies that successfully used rhyme and gained popularity, claiming that, though the people may initially resist new forms, but gradually adapt to the rhymed plays. He also argues that, since the "genius" of each age changes, contemporary poets are developing a mastery of rhyme that even past playwrights, like Shakespeare or Fletcher, might not have achieved in serious rhymed verse.

Neander dismisses Crites' concerns about spontaneity, suggesting that if rhyme is skillfully managed, it does not hinder the audience's suspension of disbelief. He emphasizes that art should conceal itself ("Arsestcelareartem") and suggests that an excellent playwright can achieve this concealment in rhyme as well as in blank verse.

Neander acknowledges the importance of natural speech in drama but distinguishes regarding its place, between tragedy and comedy since the former portrays noble characters and serious themes and the latter does about common life and ordinary speech.

"...by distinguishing betwixt what is nearest to the nature of Comedy, which is the imitation of common persons and ordinary speaking, and what is nearest the nature of a serious Play: this last is indeed the representation of Nature, but 'tis Nature wrought up to an higher pitch..." (An Essay of Dramatic Poesy)

So tragedy he insists to demand an elevated stylized form like rhymed verse. He suggests that rhyme adds dignity to tragedy, elevating it above common language. He believes rhyme provides necessary structure and polish, which makes tragedy more grand and commendable.

"...will often find in the Greek Tragedians, and in Seneca, that when a Scene grows up in the warmth of repartees (which is the close sighting of it) the latter part of the Trimeter is supplied by him who answers; and yet it was never observed as a fault in them by any of the Ancient or Modern Critics." (An Essay of Dramatic Poesy)

Crites argues in repartees i.e. quick replies is highly unnatural since the respondent would not know the previous line and thus could not complete it in rhyme. Neander counters to it that blank verse has similar limitations, as it often completes thoughts across lines, and points out that Greek tragedians like Seneca also used structured meter without criticism. He compares well-crafted rhyme to a dance in which participants work together to create harmony; rhyme in dialogue he assets is like coordinated steps that create beauty.

"Suppose we acknowledge it: how comes this confederacy to be more displeasing to you than in a Dance which is well contrived? You see there the united design of many persons to make up one Figure: after they have separated themselves in many petty divisions, they rejoin one by one into a gross: the confederacy is plain amongst them; for chance could never produce anything so beautiful, and yet there is nothing in it that shocks your sight…"(An Essay of Dramatic Poesy)

To Crites objection to using rhyme for trivial expressions like is Neander concedes that mundane language can undermine the dignity of verse but suggests poets can handle these moments carefully by starting a line in verse and leaving it incomplete or by using elevated language to make even simple expressions sound grand, as Seneca does. Neander argues that rhyme disciplines the poet's creativity.

"From Replies, which are the most elevated thoughts of Verse, you pass to the most mean ones; those which are common with the lowest of household conversation. In these, you say, the Majesty of Verse suffers. You instance in the calling of a servant, or commanding a door to be shut in rhyme. This Crites is a good observation…."(An Essay of Dramatic Poesy)

He suggests that rhyme encourages precision and conciseness; is a tool that aids even a poet with good judgment, helping keep the poet's creativity balanced and ordered. He however balances the discourse by acknowledging the fact that blank verse can also be effective but also carries the risks of producing lazy writing.

Dryden culminates the discussion as the group of four reached Somerset-Stairs, their intended stop. The group reluctantly parts ways after admiring the moonlit water, which shimmered like quicksilver. They pass cross the crowd of carefree French dancers, unaffected by the earlier noise of gunfire. Each of them head to their respective destinations: Eugenius and Lysideius to a social engagement, and Crites and Neander to their respective lodgings.

3. Probable Questions

1. Access critically Dryden's exploration of classical unities of time, place and action and his arguments for and against their observance in English Drama.

Or

2. Analyse Dryden's comparative discussion of the merits of the classical drama (Ancient Greek and Roman) versus modern drama.

Answer:

In An Essay on Dramatic Poesy, John Dryden through the dialogues of his four characters provides a comparative discussion between classical i.e. Ancient

Greek and Roman and the modern drama. Through his characters particularly Crites and Eugenius, Dryden delves into the formal qualities, thematic ambitions, and stylistic choices that distinguish ancient plays from those of contemporary English playwrights.

Dryden through the character of Crites advocates for the ancients, praising their disciplined adherence to the unities of time, place, and action, which he believes uphold the realism and integrity of the drama. Eugenius, however, argues that modern playwrights have built upon this foundation, refining and even surpassing ancient conventions to create plays that resonate more deeply with contemporary audiences.

Crites acknowledges the classical unities, which dictate that a play should cover a single day, occur in a single location, and center on a single, unified action. For him, these unities are essential for maintaining the audience's suspension of disbelief and their investment on the stage. By confining the scope of the drama, the ancients created intense, focused works that engage audiences by closely mirroring the temporal and spatial limitations of real life. In Crites' view, modern plays, by abandoning these unities, often suffer from a lack of coherence. Their plots become too sprawling, covering years in the span of a single performance, and their settings jump erratically from place to place, undermining the immediacy and credibility that the ancients achieved.

Crites' admiration for the ancients extends beyond structure to style and wit. He laments at the loss of key ancient texts, particularly those of the Greek playwrights like Menander and Latin writers like Caeilius and Varius, implying that had these works survived, they could have decisively demonstrated the superiority of ancient drama. He refers to ancient works like those of Aristophanes, Plautus, Euripides, and Sophocles which are still available.

"...This is so plain, that I need not instance to you, that Aristophanes, Plautus, Terence, never any of them writ a Tragedy; Æschylus, Euripides, Sophocles and Seneca, never meddled with Comedy; the Sock and Buskin were not worn by the same Poet: having then so much care to excel in one kind, very little is to be pardoned them if they miscarried in it;" (An Essay of Dramatic Poesy)

Crites insists that even contemporary readers of his time cannot fully appreciate their mastery due to language barriers and lost historical context.

Eugenius, however, offers a compelling rebuttal, asserting that modern drama has not merely imitated classical techniques but has evolved beyond them to address the tastes and expectations of a different audience.

"... Moderns have profited by the rules of the Ancients, but in the latter you are careful to conceal how much they have excelled them: we own all the helps we have from them, and want neither veneration nor gratitude while we acknowledge that to overcome them we must make use of the advantages we have received from them..." (An Essay of Dramatic Poesy)

He acknowledges that the moderns have benefited from the ancients' models but insists that contemporary playwrights have enriched their work with insights into human nature that were unknown to the ancients. By drawing from both natural human experience and the accumulated knowledge of the past, modern dramatists create characters and plots that resonate more deeply with contemporary audiences.

One of Eugenius's major critiques of classical drama is its lack of structural clarity. Unlike the modern five-act play structure, Greek tragedies often lacked clear divisions, relying instead on the entrances and exits of the chorus to signal shifts in the plot. This approach, Eugenius argues, makes the plays feel "indigested" or poorly organized by comparison with the more systematic structure of modern works. He notes that even the Greeks' successors—the Spaniards and Italians—have adopted a three-act structure, showing that even within the classical tradition, there was room for structural innovation. Eugenius contends that by adapting formal structures to fit new insights into character and plot, modern dramatists have produced works that are more complex and nuanced than their ancient counterparts.

Moreover, Eugenius challenges Crites' claim that modern drama lacks the intellectual depth and stylistic elegance of classical drama. He suggests that, just as scientific and philosophical knowledge has advanced since Aristotle's time, so too has dramatic art. By using the knowledge and techniques passed down by the ancients while also drawing from the lived experiences of modern audiences, contemporary playwrights create characters and narratives that speak more directly to the complexities of human nature. This progress, Eugenius argues, does not diminish the greatness of the ancients but rather honors their legacy by building upon it.

In conclusion, Dryden's comparative discussion of classical versus modern drama is thus a nuanced exploration of tradition and innovation. While he acknowledges the structural rigor, stylistic elegance, and thematic depth of classical drama, he also sees the value in modern plays' emotional complexity, structural flexibility, and responsiveness to contemporary audiences. Through the debate between Crites and Eugenius, Dryden suggests that drama is an evolving art form that gains its strength by respecting the past while adapting to the present. His analysis ultimately reflects a view of drama that balances admiration for the ancients with openness to the creative liberties that define modern theater.

4. References and Suggested readings:

i. John Dryden: An Essay of Dramatic Poesy, Poetry Foundation (https://www.poetryfoundation.org

ii. Dryden's theory of criticism in "an essay of dramatic poesy", Krishma Chaudhary

iii. An Essay of Dramatic Poesy: Main Frame of Dryden's Literary Critisism, Victoria Bilge

iv. Essay of DramatickPoesie(https://en.wikipedia.org)
An Essay of Dramatic Poesy Summary & Analysis (http://englishsummary.com)

UNIT-4

Alexander pope- An Essay on criticism

1. **About the Author**

2. **An Essay on criticism**

   a.   Introduction

   b.   Synopsis

   c.   Analysis

3. **Probable Questions**

   a.   Discuss the qualities that Pope identifies as essential for sound judgment and good taste in literary discourse.

   b.   Provide a critical assessment of Pope's framework for critics.

   c.   Explain the ways in which Pope distinguishes between true knowledge and superficial learning.

4. **References and suggested readings**

1. About the Author

Alexander Pope is a towering figure in English literature, particularly known for his contributions to poetry and literary criticism in the early 18th century. Often regarded as the preeminent poet of the Augustan Age, Pope's influence on English verse and satire set a standard that has endured for centuries. His mastery of the heroic couplet is well acknowledged in the literary world. Pope's works reflect the ideals of the Enlightenment, a period that emphasized reason, order, and clarity.

Alexander Pope was born on May 21, 1688, in London, England. He was the only son of Alexander Pope Sr., a prosperous linen merchant, and his wife, Edith Pope. The family was of Catholic faith, which subjected them to legal restrictions and social disadvantages in a predominantly Protestant England. Due to these restrictions, Pope received limited formal education; he was primarily educated at home by tutors. His early exposure to classical literature and the writings of major poets, including John Milton and John Dryden, profoundly influenced his literary development.

Pope's health was frail throughout his life. He suffered from tuberculosis of the spine, which left him with a hunchback and stunted his growth. Despite these physical challenges, he demonstrated an early talent for writing poetry and began composing verses as a child.

Pope's literary career took off in the early 1700s. In 1704, he published his first major work, "Pastorals," which garnered him attention for its poetic style and thematic depth. His next significant work, "An Essay on

Criticism" (1709), established him as a leading literary figure.

In 1711, Pope published "The Rape of the Lock," a mock-epic poem that satirizes the trivialities of high society. The poem's playful treatment of a minor scandal between two aristocratic families showcased Pope's wit and mastery of verse, and it remains one of his most celebrated works.

Pope continued to produce notable poetry throughout the 1710s and 1720s, including "The Dunciad" (1728), a satirical work that critiques contemporary poets and critics, and "An Essay on Man" (1733-1734), which explores the nature of humanity and the universe. "An Essay on Man" is particularly significant for its philosophical reflections and is structured in a series of epistles that address different aspects of human existence.

In his later years, Pope's health continued to decline, but he remained active in literary circles. He engaged in various literary projects, including translating Homer's "Iliad" (1715-1720) and "Odyssey" (1725-1726), which were highly regarded for their poetic quality. His translations helped to popularize Homer's works in England.

Alexander Pope died on May 30, 1744, at the age of 56. He was buried in the churchyard of St. Mary's Church in Twickenham. Pope's influence extended beyond his lifetime, impacting subsequent generations of writers and poets. His emphasis on form, meter, and the moral dimensions of poetry set a standard for literary excellence, and he is often credited with shaping the modern English literary canon.

His notable works:
Poems:
An essay on criticism (1711)
The Rape of the Lock (1712; revised 1714)
The Dunkaid (1728; revised 17423)
An Essay on Man (1733-1734

---

2. An Essay on Criticism

• Introduction

'An Essay on Criticism' by Alexander Pope, first published in 1709 is a philosophical poem that provides a comprehensive exploration of the nature and principles of literary criticism. The poem emphasizes on the importance of understanding and adhering to the rules of art and nature in criticism. The poem exists primarily in two forms: the original 1709 version and the revised 1711 version.

The poem in the 1709 version comprised of 742 limes. When it was revised and expanded in 1711, the link count remained approximately the same with slight adjustments to individual line sand stanzas.

The poem is written in the heroic couplet and is structured into three main sections, each exploring different aspects of criticism. In the opening section,

Pope discusses the characteristics of a good critic and the principles of effective criticism. He argues that both an understanding of the rules of art and a deep appreciation for nature and originality are the essentials of criticism. He defines what it means to be a critic. In the second part, he explores the qualities that an effective critic must possess. He outlines the virtues such as wisdom, humility, and sense of proportion are essentials of a critic. In the final section, Pope offers his views regarding the potential pitfalls of criticism. He advocates for the balance between classical standards and individual creativity. He considers the role of criticism in shaping literary tradition and the advancement of literature.

- **Synopsis**

Part I

The first part of An Essay on Criticism opens with Pope addressing the complex nature of criticism. He begins by observing that both good writing and good criticism are rare and that the art of judging is often as challenging as the art of writing. He stresses the importance of critics following "Nature" as a guiding principle, where "Nature" represents the order, harmony, and balance that underpin all true beauty in literature and art. Pope believes that Nature provides the standard by which all literary work should be judged, as it reflects universal truths and harmony. For Pope, to judge well, one must understand these natural laws, as they form the essence of good taste.

He also addresses the idea that critics should not rely solely on their personal tastes or opinions, but instead shouldlearn from and respect established literary rules. Pope supports this with references to classical ideals, arguing that great critics follow the timeless principles set forth by figures like Aristotle and Horace. These principles provide the foundation for literary beauty and are to be respected rather than dismissed. In this manner, Pope calls for critics to ground their judgments in these ancient standards rather than imposing their subjective interpretations. Furthermore, Pope warns against overconfidence and superficial judgment, which he sees as major flaws among critics. He criticizes those who pretend to have expertise without true understanding, remarking that a shallow approach to criticism often leads to error and misjudgment.

He implies that only those with deep understanding and experience are qualified to critique others, and he criticizes those who are quick to judge without having achieved any significant understanding themselves. Pope also notes that many critics are more interested in finding faults than in recognizing the talent and the merits of the literary work. He describes these critics as having an overly negative focus, one that prevents them from seeing the whole beauty of a work. He implies that good criticism requires balance the ability to identify both strengths and weaknesses, rather than a sole emphasis on flaws. Pope highlights the need for humility. He suggests that critics should remain aware of their own limitations and not assume that they have absolute knowledge. He advises that critics should aim to guide and enlighten rather than condemn, which, he believes, contributes to the enrichment of literature rather than its detriment.

Part II

In Part 2, Pope shifts from outlining the qualities of a good critic, as seen in Part 1, to exploring the common pitfalls and faults that critics often fall into. He addresses these flaws directly, one by one, highlighting how they harm both critics and the literary world they seek to evaluate. Pope's argument is that bad criticism can be as harmful as bad writing, as it can mislead readers, harm creativity, and promote poor standards. He calls for humility, deep understanding, and respect for the art, criticizing those who approach criticism with shallow knowledge or personal biases.

"A little learning is a dangerous thing;
Drink deep, or taste not the Pierian spring."
(An Essay on Criticism)

Pope warns that critics who possess only a shallow understanding of literature are the most prone to making poor judgments. The "Pierian spring," a reference to the mythological source of knowledge associated with the Muses, symbolizes profound learning. Pope's message is that partial knowledge leads to false confidence, which then leads to hasty, misguided criticism. He encourages critics to "drink deep" from the well of knowledge, implying that they must immerse themselves fully in learning to be qualified judges.

Next, Pope critiques the issue of pride in critics. He sees pride as a primary fault that distorts judgment, causing critics to value their own opinions too highly and to dismiss views or insights that differ from their own. Pope writes,

"For fools rush in where angels fear to tread,"
(An Essay on Criticism)

It suggests that inexperienced critics the "fools" are quick to judge and eager to assert their authority without true understanding. He condemns the critics who judge the literary pieces based on the biography of its respective author.

"Some judge of authors' names, not works, and then
Nor praise nor blame the writings, but the men."
(An Essay on Criticism)

Their pride blinds them to the merits of a work, limiting their ability to offer balanced critiques. Pope contrasts these critics with "angels"—those with true insight—who approach criticism cautiously and respectfully, understanding that rash judgment can lead to error.

Pope goes on to condemn the critic who envies others. Envy, in Pope's view, drives critics to harshly criticize successful works out of jealousy rather than out of objective assessment. He argues that envy leads critics to minimize or undervalue literary talent, which not only hurts the author but also deprives readers of fair guidance. He describes such envious critics as "mean," portraying them as small-minded individuals who would rather tear others down than acknowledge their talent. This criticism is part of Pope's broader call for generosity and respect in criticism, suggesting that a good critic should recognize merit without being influenced by personal feelings of rivalry or resentment.

Another flaw Pope identifies is an excessive focus on specific rules or technicalities at the expense of the overall quality or spirit of the literary work. He notes that some critics become so fixated on classical rules such as unity of time, place, and action that they fail to appreciate works that may deviate from these rules yet still achieve artistic beauty and emotional impact. He criticizes critics who prioritize superficial aspects like clever phrases ("glittering thoughts") over the cohesive beauty of a well-constructed work. Pope argues that rigid adherence to rules can reduce criticism to artificial, where critics become obsessed with minor flaws rather than evaluating the work as a harmonious whole.

Pope also addresses the tendency among some critics to follow trends rather than form their own opinions, warning against the dangers of fashionable criticism. He sees such critics as fickle, chasing popular opinion rather than standing by their true convictions. This approach, Pope implies, undermines the integrity of criticism, making it susceptible to passing fads rather than enduring standards.

"Be thou the first true merit to befriend;
His praise is lost, who stays till all commend."
(An Essay on Criticism)

Pope is advising critics to support quality literature even if it is not yet widely acknowledged, rather than simply waiting until public opinion has deemed it worthy of praises. Towards the end of Part II, Pope revisits the importance of humility and self-awareness in criticism.

He again implies that good critics should recognize their limitations and avoid making absolute judgments, as literature is complex and open to multiple interpretations. He is cautioning against critics who view their opinions as final and unimpeachable, which leads to arrogance and intolerance. Pope suggests that criticism should be a reflective, respectful practice rather than an assertion of authority.

Part III

In Part 3, Pope shifts from discussing the pitfalls of critics to offering guidance on how critics can achieve true wisdom and judgment. This section is a culmination of Pope's advice, underscoring the qualities of an ideal critic who combines humility, taste, and moral integrity. By reflecting on the importance of patience, self-control, and reverence for classical standards, Pope completes his vision of a balanced, virtuous critic, grounded in both intellect and moral character.

Pope introduces the idea that critics need more than just intellectual understanding; must also exhibit moral virtues like fairness, patience, and humility. By implying that criticism requires both wisdom and virtue, Pope situates criticism as a moral task, one where critics must hold themselves to high ethical standards in order to avoid causing harm to authors or misleading readers. This theme of moderation continues throughout Part 3, with Pope advocating for a balanced approach to criticism. For him, the critic's task is not merely technical; it also involves a moral responsibility to uphold fairness, honesty, and respect. By grounding criticism in morality, Pope suggests that a true critic does not simply dissect a work but rather seeks to elevate it, helping both authors and readers gain a deeper appreciation for literature.

Pope next emphasizes the importance of patience in criticism. He advises critics to avoid being overly harsh, particularly with young or inexperienced writers, whose "modesty might mend what folly blame." Pope insists that criticism should encourage growth rather than discourage potential. By exercising patience and kindness, critics can inspire writers to improve rather than demoralizing them. Pope suggests that a critic should show restraint and sensitivity, understanding that too much censure can harm a writer's development. Moreover, Pope argues that this patience reflects wisdom, as a patient critic is more likely to recognize a work's deeper qualities rather than rushing to judgment. He cautions against a quick dismissal of works that may not be perfect, acknowledging that art can take time to reveal its true worth. By fostering a patient, encouraging environment, critics can promote creativity and foster the growth of new talent.

Pope continues by advising critics to avoid personal biases, stressing the need for objectivity and honesty. He writes,

" 'Tis not enough, taste, judgment, learning, join;
all you speak, let truth and candour shine."
(An Essay on Criticism)

Pope argues that critics should base their judgments on a sincere appreciation for the truth, rather than on personal preferences or grudges. He calls for honesty and integrity reflect his belief that criticism is a virtuous service meant to guide readers and writers, not to promote the critic's own agenda.

One of Pope's most famous pieces of advice that appears in this section is that critics should approach each work with the same "spirit" in which it was written. He argues that a true critic should seek to understand the author's intentions, perspective, and artistic aims rather than imposing their own interpretations.

For Pope, criticism should not be an exercise of power or authority; instead, it should involve a genuine effort to connect with the author's vision. By adopting this "spirit," the critic can provide more insightful and meaningful critiques, recognizing the work's strengths and weaknesses in their proper context. This approach emphasizes the need for humility, as it requires critics to set aside their own biases and assumptions, allowing them to appreciate the work on its own terms.

In the closing lines of the section Pope reaffirms "nature" as the ultimate standard for beauty and truth. He compares "true expression" to the "unchanging sun," suggesting that genuine artistry has a clarity and purity that illuminates and enhances everything it touches. For Pope, "nature" represents an ideal of order, balance, and universality, providing a timeless standard by which all literature can be judged. He sees "nature" as the foundation of both good writing and good criticism, as it embodies the qualities of harmony, simplicity, and truth. This return to Nature emphasizes Pope's belief that critics should seek universal principles rather than personal preferences or trendy opinions. By aligning themselves with Nature's standards, critics can achieve a more balanced and objective perspective, enabling them to recognize genuine beauty and excellence in literature.

- **Analysis**

The poem is divided into three distinct sections each focusing on different aspects.

Part I

Pope begins with his assessment of the issue that whether poor writing or poor criticism is more problematic. While the former can only cause annoyance to the readers, the later can mislead the readers which is more dangerous.

"Tis hard to say, if greater want of skill
Appear in writing or in judging ill;"
(An Essay on Criticism)

These opening lines set the argument about the role of criticism, and its nature. He begins with a reflection on the challenges of both writing and criticism, and suggests that it is difficult to determine whether poor writing or poor judgement in criticism is worse. The next lines (3-8) provide the differences to be considered while deciding on the issue. He argues that fault and misguided criticism is more problematic for the readers towards true understanding rather than misleading them. He asserts that while few individuals may "err" in writing many more criticize poorly. The hyperbolic comparison here underscores the prevalence of flawed criticism compared to faculty writing.

Pope proceeds in his argument that both poets and good critics are very rare on the literary discourse. He argues that true criticism requires both an understanding of the rules of art and a deep appreciation for a nature and originality. He advises the critics to avoid letting their personal judgements overshadow their assessments but at the same time defends the arrogance of the poet who is partial to his wit and the critic who is proud of his judging ability. He highlights the delicate balance required in literary judgement.

"Authors are partial to their wit, 'tis true
But are not critics to their judgement too?"
(An Essay on Criticism)

Pope defends the poets as more tolerate towards the works of other poets than the critics, since they are guided by a sense of poetic composition and the principles of order and harmony. In comparison to the poets, his tone for the critics is rather satirical. He mocks the critics who have failed as poets and addresses such critics as 'fools'. He mocks them that they have no knowledge of the poetic or literary traditions and are entangled between the various forms. Pope ridicules such men to have lost their poetic sensibility, which had led them to turn themselves as critics to judge the works of other poets and authors. He terms such men of criticism as false learners.

"Some are bewilded in the maze of schools
And some made coxcombs nature meant but fools
In search of wit these lose their common sense
And then turn critics in their own defence"
(An Essay on Criticism)

Critics of such are composed to minor poets who try to mimic the classical traditions. He alludes to "Maevius scribble in Apollo's spite" which suggests the careless or poor writing that undermines quality art. Pope here satirizes the decline of literary standards and the dull critics who failed as poets.

Pope illustrates the career trajectory of some individuals who start as wits or poets but eventually become critics, only to end up as "plain fools." This progression highlights the idea that not everyone who attempts to critique literature possesses the requisite understanding or skill, and many ultimately fail to contribute meaningfully to the discourse. Pope further contrasts those who can neither be classified as wits nor critics with "heavy mules," emphasizing their mediocrity and lack of distinctive qualities.

"Some neither can for wits nor critics pass,
As heavy mules are neither horse nor ass.
Those half-learn'd witlings, num'rous in our isle"
(An Essay on Criticism)

This metaphor serves to underscore the notion that true literary talent is rare, while those who lack both the creative spark of a poet and the discerning eye of a critic occupy an unremarkable position in the literary landscape. By comparing these individuals to "half-learn'd witlings" and "half-form'd insects," Pope suggests that they are incomplete and unrefined, existing in a state of uncertainty regarding their identity and purpose.

Pope addresses aspiring critics, offering them guidance on how to navigate the delicate balance between ambition and self-awareness in their critical endeavors.

"But you who seek to give and merit fame,
And justly bear a critic's noble name,"
(An Essay on Criticism)

He indicates that the responsibility of a critic is significant. Critics hold the power to influence public perception and the reputation of authors and their works, thus their role is both noble and demanding.

Pope emphasizes the importance of self-knowledge, urging critics to be aware of their own abilities:

"Be sure your self and your own reach to know,
How far your genius, taste, and learning go."
(An Essay on Criticism)

Here, he advocates for an honest assessment of one's skills and limits. This idea of self-awareness is crucial; critics must understand their strengths and weaknesses to evaluate others effectively. Critics should not overextend themselves into areas where they lack expertise or understanding. The metaphor of "launching" suggests the dangers of venturing too far into the depths of criticism without a solid foundation.

"Nature to all things fix'd the limits fit,
And wisely curb'd proud man's pretending wit,"
(An Essay on Criticism)

It suggests that nature has established inherent boundaries for all things, including human intellect.

Pope implies that despite mankind's aspirations and ambitions, there are natural limits to what one can achieve or comprehend, a critique of human arrogance in the face of these limitations.
The metaphor comparing land and ocean illustrates this concept further.

"As on the land while here the ocean gains,
In other parts it leaves wide sandy plains"
(An Essay on Criticism)

It indicates that while knowledge may expand in one area, it diminishes or leaves gaps in another. This analogy emphasizes the idea that mastery in one field can often come at the expense of understanding in another, reflecting the complex relationship between knowledge and ignorance.

Pope highlights the tension between memory and understanding; as one becomes more reliant on memory, the deeper understanding of concepts may fade.

"Soul," asserting that "while memory prevails",
(An Essay on Criticism)

He reinforces the idea that human capability is inherently limited. Each individual may excel in a specific discipline or area of knowledge, but the breadth of human art and thought is too vast for any one person to master entirely. This notion of specialization is crucial in understanding how knowledge is often compartmentalized.
"One science only will one genius fit;
So vast is art, so narrow human wit,"
(An Essay on Criticism)

Pope indicates that even within a specific field, individuals may only grasp fragments or particular aspects rather than achieving comprehensive mastery. This suggests that even specialized knowledge has its own boundaries.

"Not only bounded to peculiar arts,
But oft in those, confin'd to single parts,"
(An Essay on Criticism)

Pope establishes the doctrine that nature should serve as the ultimate guide for artistic and critical endeavors. Pope suggests that nature, as a constant and universal reference point, provides an objective standard against which art can be measured. Pope describes nature as "Unerring," "divinely bright," and "One clear, unchang'd, and universal light," attributing to it a sense of purity and constancy that is essential for creative expression. By stating that nature is "the source, and end, and test of art," he implies that all artistic endeavors should originate from natural principles and ultimately strive to reflect the beauty and force found in nature. This reinforces the idea that art should not be overly extravagant or artificial rather, it should arise organically from the truths of the natural world.

Pope highlights that true art draws upon the foundational truths of nature. It is characterized by subtlety and authenticity, avoiding superficial embellishments. He illustrates this point by comparing the relationship between art and the soul: just as the soul informs and animates the body, art should infuse vitality into its creations. The metaphor implies that genuine artistry operates beneath the surface, visible through its effects rather than through ostentatious displays.

He introduces a critique of those who possess great natural talent or wit but lack the ability to apply it effectively. Pope acknowledges that while some individuals may be endowed with extraordinary gifts, they may still struggle to harness those gifts constructively.

"Some, to whom Heav'n in wit has been profuse,
Want as much more, to turn it to its use"
(An Essay on Criticism)

He underscores the tension between creative inspiration "wit" and the discerning judgment necessary for effective expression.

Pope further develops this theme by emphasizing the importance of restraint in artistic creation.

"'Tis more to guide, than spur the Muse's steed;
Restrain his fury, than provoke his speed,"
(An Essay on Criticism)

The "Muse's steed" symbolizes creative inspiration, and Pope suggests that the true role of the poet or artist is not merely to incite creative passion but to channel and regulate it effectively. By advocating for restraint over provocation, he implies that wisdom in artistry comes from knowing when to temper the impulses of creativity, allowing for a more focused and refined expression.

Pope alludes with the striking image of the "winged courser, like a gen'rous horse," which "Shows most true mettle when you check his course." This metaphor reinforces the idea that true artistic expression is characterized by balance and control.In essence, he is suggesting that the best art arises when the creative spirit is both liberated and disciplined, resulting in work that is grounded in the truths of nature and exemplifies genuine beauty.

Pope reflects on the relationship between nature, artistic creation, and the rules of poetry and criticism.

"Those RULES of old discover'd, not devis'd,
Are Nature still, but Nature methodis'd,"
(An Essay on Criticism)

He establishes the foundational argument that the principles governing good poetry are derived from nature itself rather than being arbitrary inventions. Pope suggests that true artistic rules do not contradict nature; rather, they seek to understand and organize it, transforming raw inspiration into structured expression. By comparing nature to liberty, Pope highlights that both are subject to constraints that ultimately enhance their beauty and functionality. Just as liberty requires certain laws to flourish, artistic creation thrives under guidelines that preserve its essence while allowing for creativity. This duality underscores a central theme in Pope's work, that order and structure do not stifle creativity but rather provide the framework within which it can thrive.

Pope continues by discussing the role of ancient Greece in shaping artistic rules:

"Hear how learn'd Greece her useful rules indites,
When to repress, and when indulge our flights."
(An Essay on Criticism)

He portrays ancient Greece as a model of artistic excellence, where the ancients understood when to exercise restraint in their creative endeavors and when to allow their imaginations to soar. The reference to Parnassus, the mountain associated with the Muses, evokes the idea of high achievement in art, and the "immortal prize" symbolizes the ultimate recognition of artistic greatness.

Pope implies that the ancients drew inspiration from divine sources, establishing rules based on the natural order and exemplifying the ideals of beauty and excellence in their works. In this sense, criticism is elevated to a noble purpose; it serves not merely to evaluate but to inspire and elevate both poets and audiences. The "gen'rous critic" fuels the poet's creativity and encourages appreciation for art, demonstrating the symbiotic relationship between the critic and the creator. Pope introduces a critical perspective on modern critics and poets. He observes that "

"following wits from that intention stray'd;
Who could not win the mistress, woo'd the maid."
(An Essay on Criticism)

This metaphor suggests that critics, unable to capture the essence of poetic inspiration, instead focus on the form and rules, thus losing sight of the true purpose of criticism, which is to enhance the understanding and appreciation of poetry. The image of the critic wooing the maid (the Muse) instead of the mistress (the true art) reflects a failure to engage with the core of artistic creation. The comparison to "modern 'pothecaries" illustrates Pope's disdain for those who attempt to practice criticism or poetry without a genuine understanding of the craft. Pope asserts that these critics often produce work that lacks substance or originality, as indicated by phrases like

"write dull receipts how poems may be made."
(An Essay on Criticism)

They focus more on adhering to formulas than on fostering genuine creativity, resulting in lifeless poetry devoid of meaning and innovation. He critiques both uninspired critics and poets who fail to engage meaningfully with their work.

Poet emphasizes the necessity of understanding the historical and cultural context of classical authors before attempting to critique the works. Pope begins by addressing the reader directly, instructing those who seek to guide their judgment in literary criticism to gain a comprehensive understanding of each ancient author's "proper character." This implies that a critic must be familiar with not only the works themselves but also the backgrounds and circumstances that shaped these authors and their writings. The mention of "fable, subject, scope in ev'ry page" highlights the various dimensions of a literary work that critics must consider while providing criticism regarding a literary work. Each of these elements contributes to the overall meaning and significance of a text, and understanding them is crucial for an informed critique. Furthermore, by including "Religion, country, genius of his age," Pope emphasizes on the importance of situating a work within its historical and cultural framework. He makes the observation that theauthor's background influences their perspective and thematic choices, and recognizing this context allows critics to appreciate the work's nuances rather than simply imposing contemporary standards or values onto it. Pope suggests that without a comprehensive understanding of these various factors, any criticism offered will be superficial or misguided.

Pope advises critics to make the works of Homer a central part of their studies, stating,

"Be Homer's works your study and delight."
(An Essay on Criticism)

Homer, as one of the most revered figures in classical literature, represents the pinnacle of poetic achievement, and engaging deeply with his texts is essential for any aspiring critic. The phrase'

"Read them by day, and meditate by night",
(An Essay on Criticism)

 reflects the idea that a thorough and contemplative approach to reading is necessary for fully grasping the richness of Homer's works.
He explores the complex relationship between artistic creativity, rules, and the nature of beauty in poetry and music. Pope acknowledges the existence of qualities in art that cannot be neatly defined or codified by rules, emphasizing that some aspects of beauty are inherent and cannot be fully articulated through precepts.

Pope draws a parallel between music and poetry, asserting that both art forms share "nameless graces" that a master artist can evoke but that cannot be taught through systematic methods. This idea reflects the belief that while techniques and rules can guide artists, the most profound and moving aspects of art often stem from an intuitive understanding that goes beyond formal training.

"If, where the rules not far enough extend,
(Since rules were made but to promote their end)"
(An Essay on Criticism)

He implies that rules should serve a purpose, enhancing the creative process rather than constraining it. Therefore, if an artist successfully breaks a rule for the sake of expression or beauty, that deviation can be justified and regarded as a valid "licence." Pope uses the metaphor of Pegasus, the mythical winged horse associated with poetic inspiration, to illustrate the notion that true creativity can involve straying from conventional paths. Pope acknowledges that even the ancients, who are often revered for their adherence to rules, occasionally bent or broke those rules, much like kings who dispense with their own laws. However, he cautions modern artists, urging them to be wary when deviating from established precepts.

"Moderns, beware! or if you must offend
Against the precept, ne'er transgress its end"
(An Essay on Criticism)

He emphasizes the importance of maintaining the intention behind artistic rules. If a modern artist chooses to break a rule, they should do so infrequently and out of necessity, ensuring that their actions still honor the original purpose of those rules. Pope warns that critics may impose their own rigid standards on artists who do not adhere to established norms, potentially undermining their reputation:

*"The critic else proceeds without remorse,
Seizes your fame, and puts his laws in force."
(An Essay on Criticism)*

This suggests that a critic's judgment can be harsh and unyielding, holding artists accountable for deviations from expected norms without regard for their artistic intentions or the emotional impact of their work.

Pope acknowledges the complex nature of beauty in art and how perception can influence judgment. He reflects on how certain artistic expressions, when viewed from a limited perspective, can appear flawed and "monstrous". Pope suggests that these perceived flaws often arise from a lack of understanding or the failure to appreciate the broader context of a work. Pope shifts his focus to the enduring legacy of ancient poets, emphasizing their timelessness and the reverence they command.

*"Still green with bays each ancient altar stands"
(An Essay on Criticism)*

He invokes imagery of 'laurel wreaths', symbols of triumph and honor, indicating that the works of these poets are still celebrated and respected.

*"Secure from flames, from envy's fiercer rage,
Destructive war, and all-involving age"
(An Essay on Criticism)*

He asserts that the great works of the past are protected from the destructive forces of time and human malice, indicating their immortality in the realm of art. Pope emphasizes that scholars and admirers from all over the world bring their respect and admiration to these ancient works.

"See, from each clime the learn'd their incense bring!"
(An Essay on Criticism)

He reflects on a universal recognition of the value of ancient literature, where learned individuals pay homage to the greatness of poets like Homer, ensuring that their contributions continue to resonate through time.
By addressing the classical poets as "immortal heirs of universal praise," he emphasizes that their contributions to literature will endure across generations, and their honors will grow over time, much like rivers that become larger as they flow:

"Whose honours with increase of ages grow,
As streams roll down, enlarging as they flow."
(An Essay on Criticism)

This metaphor suggests that as time passes, the recognition of their greatness only deepens, reflecting the idea that true art transcends its era. He envisions a future in which their names will be celebrated by "nations unborn," and even worlds yet to be discovered will "applaud" their achievements. This notion of timelessness highlights the enduring relevance of the great poets, suggesting that their influence will persist well beyond their lifetimes.

Part II

Alexander Pope explores the theme of pride and its impact on human judgment. He argues that pride is one of the primary causes that "blind man's erring judgment" and misleads the mind. According to Pope, pride exerts a powerful influence over those with "weak heads" people lacking true insight or intelligence. For these individuals, pride acts as a substitute for wisdom, a "never-failing vice of fools" that prevents them from seeing their own limitations. Pope suggests that when Nature denies a person wit or ability, it compensates with "needful pride." This pride, he says, serves as a kind of self-protective mechanism, filling the "mighty void of sense" left by a lack of genuine intellect.

Pope warns of the perils of superficial knowledge.

"A little learning is a dang'rous thing;
Drink deep, or taste not the Pierian spring:
There shallow draughts intoxicate the brain,
And drinking largely sobers us again."
(An Essay on Criticism)

He argues that shallow understanding can lead to overconfidence and misguided conclusions. He uses the metaphor of the "Pierian spring", a mythical source of knowledge and inspiration associated with the Muses to illustrate his point. Pope advises that one should either "drink deep" from this spring, committing to thorough study, or avoid it altogether, since only a small amount of learning can "intoxicate the brain." In other words, incomplete knowledge can lead to arrogance and false confidence, whereas a deeper, fuller understanding fosters humility.

Pope describes how, in "fearless youth," many are excited by the first taste of knowledge and enthusiastically pursue "the heights of arts." However, because their understanding is limited by the "bounded level" of their minds, they don't yet realize the vastness of knowledge that remains.

"In fearless youth we tempt the heights of arts,
While from the bounded level of our mind,
Short views we take, nor see the lengths behind,
But more advanc'd, behold with strange surprise
New, distant scenes of endless science rise!" (An Essay
on Criticism)

As they gain more insight, they become aware of how much more there is to learn, experiencing "strange surprise" as "new, distant scenes of endless science rise."

Pope compares this journey of learning to climbing the Alps. At first, the ascent is exhilarating; as one reaches certain heights, it seems like they've nearly conquered the mountains, with clouds and peaks left behind.

"Sopleas'd at first, the tow'ring Alps we try,
Mount o'er the vales, and seem to tread the sky;"
(An Essay on Criticism)

But upon reaching one peak, a person realizes that higher mountains lie ahead, creating a sense of wonder and even intimidation.

Pope discusses the qualities of an ideal critic and how they should engage with works of literature. He asserts that a "perfect judge" approaches each literary piece with the same passion and spirit that its author put into it, emphasizing the importance of understanding the work in its entirety rather than fixating on minor faults.

"A perfect judge will read each work of wit
With the same spirit that its author writ,
Survey the whole, nor seek slight faults to find,"
(An Essay on Criticism)

The phrase "survey the whole" suggests that a good critic should appreciate the overall impact of a work, especially when it is infused with emotion and creativity, as indicated by "where nature moves, and rapture warms the mind."

Pope criticizes a narrow-minded approach to criticism that focuses on trivial errors, which he describes as "malignant dull delight." This perspective detracts from the "gen'rous pleasure" that comes from appreciating wit and artistry. In essence, he argues that a critic should be open to the ideas and charms of a work instead of letting a quest for perfection overshadow that the enjoyment of its beauty.

Pope reflects on the nature of artistic creation and criticism, challenging the idea that a flawless piece of writing exists. He emphasizes the importance of considering the writer's intentions, stating,

"In ev'ry work regard the writer's end."
(An Essay on Criticism)

He believes that the purpose behind a work is crucial in assessing its merit. Since no author can achieve more than they aim for, the effectiveness of the means they employ and the integrity of their intentions are what truly matter. He states that if an author's methods are sound and their execution is honest, then the work deserves "applause, in spite of trivial faults." Pope advocates for a more forgiving and contextual approach to criticism, suggesting that minor flaws should not overshadow the overall effectiveness of a piece. Pope critiques the overly meticulous critics who become preoccupied with "the rules each verbal critic lays." He suggests that ignoring trivial details can sometimes be a virtue, as it allows for a greater appreciation of the work as a whole.

"Neglect the rules each verbal critic lays,
For not to know such trifles, is a praise."
(An Essay on Criticism)

This commentary highlights a tension between rigid adherence to rules and the creative spirit of literature. He notes that many critics, acquainted with specific artistic techniques, often make the overall quality of a work depend on its adherence to those individual aspects, such as grammar or form.

Pope critiques certain types of critics and their superficial approach to literature and art. He observes that some critics possess less judgment and more caprice, suggesting that their evaluations are driven more by personal whims than by a sound understanding of artistic quality. This "curious not knowing" leads them to form "short ideas," which are simplistic and incomplete, causing them to offend both in art and manners due to their overly detailed focus on specific parts rather than the whole.

Pope observes that some critics confine their taste to mere conceit, valuing superficial or clever expressions over substance. They delight in works where coherence and appropriateness are lacking, resulting in what he describes as one glaring chaos and wild heap of wit. This illustrates his disdain for writing that prioritizes cleverness or spectacle over meaningful content and structure, as it ultimately leads to a lack of artistic integrity.

He then draws a parallel between poets and painters, asserting that both can fall into the trap of being "unskill'd to trace", the nature and the grace of aesthetics. He suggests that both groups may attempt to mask their deficiencies in craftsmanship by over-embellishing their work with excessive decoration "with gold and jewels cover ev'ry part." This is a critique of artists who use ornamentation as a substitute for genuine skill, hiding their lack of artistic depth behind superficial flourishes.

In contrast to this approach, Pope argues that true wit involves presenting "nature to advantage dressed." This means that authentic wit should enhance and clarify the inherent beauty or truth of an idea rather than obscure it. He defines true wit as something that captures "what was thought, but ne'er so well expressed," suggesting that the best expressions resonate with familiar thoughts but are articulated with such clarity and skill that they feel fresh and enlightening.

Pope critiques those who judge poetry solely by its rhythm and melody rather than its intellectual or emotional content.

"But most by numbers judge a poet's song;
And smooth or rough, with them is right or wrong:"
(An Essay on Criticism)

He argues that many "tuneful fools" admire a poem's musicality without understanding or valuing its deeper meaning. Such readers are like people who go to church not to learn from the doctrine but merely to enjoy the music, focusing on superficial aspects rather than seeking enlightenment.

Pope satirizes critics "fools" who judge poems based on metrics like smoothness or syllable count, failing to see beyond the aesthetic to the poem's substance. They are content with rigid, predictable patterns and "equal syllables," which can make poetry sound monotonous, especially when poets overuse unnecessary filler words or create lines that, despite meeting syllable counts, add nothing meaningful to the poem's message. He describes such verse as repetitive, where "ten low words of creep in one dull line," and predictable rhymes add nothing to the poem's artistry.

Pope addresses the dangers of self-love and excessive pride among writers and critics.

"And while self-love each jealous writer rules,
Contending wits become the sport of fools:"
(An Essay on Criticism)

He observes that "self-love" often leads writers to view each other with jealousy, turning their rivalry into a spectacle for others to mock. He suggests that bad writers are typically bad friends, offering insincere praise out of self-interest rather than genuine admiration.

This "sacred lust of praise" pushes people toward shallow, self-centered behavior, degrading their integrity and turning them into lesser versions of themselves.

Pope warns critics not to let their drive for judgment overshadow their humanity, urging them to approach their task with "good nature and good sense." He highlights the value of forgiveness, immortalized in his line,

"To err is human; to forgive, divine."
(An Essay on Criticism)

Pope here suggests that making mistakes is a natural, unavoidable part of being human. All people are prone to errors, driven by limitations in knowledge, perspective, and judgment. He urges the critic to have the essence of being empathetic while dealing with criticism of a work. This speaks to Pope's belief in balancing judgment with compassion

He acknowledges, however, that it is natural for even noble minds to hold some bitterness or "spleen." If critics must release their disdain, Pope suggests that they must target truly harmful subjects, specifically "vile obscenity" and moral degradation, which he compares to an "impotence in love" ineffectual and shameful. He criticizes the cultural decay he perceives during the Restoration period, a time when, he says, superficial pleasure and wealth fostered moral corruption.

Pope laments the influence of his contemporary period on both literature and society, as preachers adapted to secular tastes, neglecting moral instruction to win favor, and writers published irreverent or even blasphemous works with little restraint. He encourages critics to direct their criticism toward these "monsters" of obscenity and blasphemy, but warns them to avoid overzealous judgment, as those who are "scandalously nice" or overly critical can see vice where there is none like a person with jaundice who sees everything as yellow. Pope advises a balanced perspective, recognizing real faults without projecting any kind of personal prejudice onto every work.

Part III

Alexander Pope elaborates on the moral responsibilities of critics in their pursuit of literary evaluation. He begins by asserting that understanding and knowledge are only part of a critic's role:

"Learn then what morals critics ought to show,
For 'tis but half a judge's task, to know."
(An Essay on Criticism)

He asserts that a critic must not only possess knowledge of taste and judgment but also embody a moral framework that informs their critiques.

Pope emphasizes the importance of truth and candor in criticism, stating,

"In all you speak, let truth and candour shine."
(An Essay on Criticism)

This insistence on honesty suggests that the integrity of a critic's evaluation carries much importance. A responsible critic should aim not only to express personal opinions but also to foster a sense of understanding within the readers:

"That not alone what to your sense is due,
All may allow; but seek your friendship too." (An Essay
on Criticism)

Here, Pope underscores the need for critics to build relationships and community through their critiques, rather than merely asserting authority based on their personal taste.

"Be silent always when you doubt your sense;
And speak, though sure, with seeming diffidence."
(An Essay on Criticism)

Pope encourages critics to exercise caution when uncertain about their judgments, implying that doubt should lead to silence rather than unwarranted assertions. The contrast between "speak, though sure, with seeming diffidence" highlights the idea of maintaining an appearance of modesty, even when confident in one's opinions as it fosters an atmosphere of respectful dialogue rather than dogmatic assertion. He then critiques those who are stubbornly opinionated:

"Some positive, persisting fops we know,
Who, if once wrong, will needs be always so."
(An Essay on Criticism)

Pope identifies a type of critic as belonging to those who refuse to acknowledge their mistakes and instead cling to their inappropriate judgments. In contrast, he advocates for a more reflective approach:

"But you, with pleasure own your errors past,
And make each day a critic on the last."
(An Essay on Criticism)

He calls for self-awareness and growth, suggesting that critics should take joy in recognizing and learning from their previous misjudgments, allowing for continual improvement in their critical assessments. Pope's vision of a critic is that who combines knowledge, humility, and moral integrity. He presents criticism as a collaborative effort grounded in truth, emphasizing on the importance of open-mindedness and the willingness to learn from one's mistakes.

Pope elaborates on the delicate balance required in criticism, particularly concerning the delivery of truth and the manner of advising others.

"'Tis not enough, your counsel still be true;
Blunt truths more mischief than nice falsehoods do,"
(An Essay on Criticism)

He suggests that while honesty is vital, the manner in which it is presented can significantly impact its reception. Pope implies that overly blunt or harsh truths can cause more harm than gentle, perhaps even false, reassurances. The effectiveness of criticism relies not just on the content but also on the approach taken to convey it. Pope continues with the idea that critics should be subtle in their teaching methods: "

Men must be taught as if you taught them not;
And things unknown proposed as things forgot."
(An Essay on Criticism)

He states that a critic should guide others without appearing overtly didactic, allowing individuals to discover truths for themselves. By framing new concepts as if they are merely forgotten rather than entirely unknown, critics can engage their audience more effectively, fostering a sense of discovery rather than imposition.

Pope argues that without an appropriate level of decorum, even the most accurate criticisms may be rejected. This reinforces the idea that a critic's demeanor plays a crucial role in the acceptance of their insights. A respectful and gracious approach can enhance the appeal of sound judgment, making it more likely to be embraced by others. Pope then emphasizes the importance of generosity in providing advice:

"Be niggards of advice on no pretence;
For the worst avarice is that of sense."
(An Essay on Criticism)

He condemns the reluctance to share knowledge, suggesting that withholding valuable insights is a form of intellectual capability. Critics should feel a responsibility to share their understanding generously. He suggests that true critics should not refrain from providing critical assessment, even if it may provoke displeasure among the learned. This reinforces the notion that those who are deserving of praise will also be receptive to constructive criticism.

"Fear not the anger of the wise to raise;
Those best can bear reproof, who merit praise."
(An Essay on Criticism)

It indicates a belief in the resilience and humility of true scholars, who can handle criticism without taking offense, viewing it as an opportunity for growth.

Pope critiques the dangers and limitations faced by critics, especially when dealing with sensitive figures or "honourable" individuals who are protected by their status.

"Like some fierce tyrant in old tapestry!
Fear most to tax an honourable fool,"
(An Essay on Criticism)

He begins by acknowledging that in an ideal world, critics would have the freedom to express their views honestly. However, he points out that figures like "Appius" react with anger and defensiveness when confronted with criticism, as if they were tyrannical figures in old tapestries, menacing and intimidating. Pope then advises critics to be cautious about criticizing "an honourable fool" someone of high social status but limited intellectual ability since society often shields such figures from open criticism. He implies that these individuals are granted an implicit "right" to be "dull," or uninspired, without consequence. Here, he is also criticizing poets and writers who, lack genuine talent or learning, but still receive respect or praise due to their connections or rank, much as some people gain degrees without truly earning them.

Pope suggests that critics should avoid tackling "dangerous truths" or sharp critiques directly. Instead, he advises critics to leave these potentially risky observations to "unsuccessful satires," which are less likely to be taken seriously or to flatterers who heap insincere praise on the powerful.

"Leave dangerous truths to unsuccessful satires,
And flattery to fulsome dedicators,"
(An Essay on Criticism)

Pope advises critics to sometimes hold back their harsh judgments, especially when dealing with writers who lack talent or originality. He suggests that it may be better to allow such writers the comfort of their vanity rather than actively criticize them. Pope argues that remaining silent can be more effective than open criticism, as criticizing these writers may actually encourage them to keep producing their poor work.

"Tis best sometimes your censure to restrain,
And charitably let the dull be vain:
Your silence there is better than your spite,"
(An Essay on Criticism)

Pope uses the image of dull writers as spinning tops that continue to whirl in their repetitive, uninspired writing despite being "lash'd" or criticized repeatedly. Instead of stopping, they simply carry on, dull and unchanging, like tops that spin even when hit.

"And lash'd so long, like tops, are lash'd asleep.
False steps but help them to renew the race,"
(An Essay on Criticism)

He explains that for some writers, making mistakes" steps" doesn't discourage them instead, it spurs them on, much like tired horses ("jades") that regain energy after stumbling.

Pope turns his focus from poor writers to equally misguided critics. He highlights that there are critics who are just as "mad" and "abandon'd" as the shameless, talentless poets he described earlier.

"Such shameless bards we have; and yet 'tis true,
There are as mad, abandon'd critics too.
The bookful blockhead, ignorantly read,"
(An Essay on Criticism)

These critics, whom Pope describes as "bookful blockheads," are people who may be well-read but lack genuine understanding. Instead of true knowledge, they carry "learned lumber" in their minds useless information that doesn't contribute to any real insight.

Pope emphasizes that these critics love to hear themselves talk, constantly "edifying" their own ears with their opinions, as though they are more interested in their own voices than in meaningful critique. They read a wide range of works, from the ranging from Dryden's Fables to the trivial like Thomas Durfey's Tales, and attack them all indiscriminately though misguided criticism. Pope states that these critics accuse many authors of either plagiarizing or paying others to write their works, reflecting a suspicious, dismissive attitude. For instance, Pope references Sir Samuel Garth's popular poem The Dispensary, implying that some critics baselessly claim Garth didn't actually write it.

Pope also notes the hypocrisy and inconsistency of these critics. They may befriend a playwright or poet, point out their flaws, and yet never offer constructive feedback that leads to improvement—possibly because they enjoy highlighting faults rather than encouraging artistic growth. He describes these critics as being so intrusive that no place is safe from their opinions, not even sacred spaces like St. Paul's Cathedral. They invade even the most holy places to the point of overwhelming others, talking incessantly and uninvited, where even the wisest ("angels") would hesitate.

"No place so sacred from such fops is barr'd,
Nor is Paul's church more safe than Paul's churchyard:"
(An Essay on Criticism)

Pope's view that unwise and presumptuous people often intrude into matters they lack the insight to handle properly.

"For fools rush in where angels fear to tread,"
(An Essay on Criticism)

He accuses such critics, to be full of superficial knowledge and self-importance; impose their views recklessly, failing to recognize their own limitations. Pope's critique highlights the arrogance, ignorance, and meddling nature of such critics, who bring more confusion than clarity to the field of literature.

Pope praises the Roman poet Horace, contrasting his graceful approach to writing and criticism with the flawed methods of contemporary critics. Pope admires Horace for his "graceful negligence", the effortless, natural style that communicates deep insights without rigid structure or formality. Horace's writing is like a casual conversation with a friend, conveying "the truest notions in the easiest way." Pope suggests that Horace's charm lies in his ability to instruct without seeming didactic, presenting complex ideas in a simple, relatable manner.

Pope emphasizes that Horace had both wit and judgment, which allowed him to critique others boldly while maintaining fairness and composure. He states that Horace could:

"Yet judge with coolness, though he sung with fire,"
(An Essay on Criticism)

It means that while his poetry was passionate and spirited, his criticism was calm and thoughtful. For Pope, Horace embodies the ideal critic who demonstrates through his own works the very principles he advocates, thus,

"His precepts teach but what his works inspire."
(An Essay on Criticism)

In contrast, Pope criticizes his contemporaries, who fall into "a contrary extreme." Unlike Horace, who balances judgment with creativity, these critics are excessively harsh in their judgments "judge with fury" but lack energy and originality in their writing "write with fle'me," or phlegm, meaning sluggishness or dullness. Pope's criticism suggests that these critics are quick to condemn others, yet their own work lacks the passion and vitality they expect from the works they critique.

Pope also points out that just as Horace's poetry is often misrepresented by poor translations, as the modern critics are equally misrepresented by inaccurate or inappropriate quotations from their works.

"Nor suffers Horace more in wrong translations
By wits, than critics in as wrong quotations." (An Essay
on Criticism)
Pope praises Longinus, as an ideal critic, inspired by "all the Nine" Muses, meaning he is blessed with poetic insight as well as critical skill.

"Thee, bold Longinus! all the Nine inspire,
And bless their critic with a poet's fire."
(An Essay on Criticism)

He states that such an unique blend of talents allowed Longinus to critique with "a poet's fire," suggesting that his passion and creativity bring life to his criticism. Pope admires Longinus for his enthusiasm and dedication to truth, describing him as an "ardent judge" who is passionate "with warmth" yet "always just" in his assessments. Pope emphasizes that Longinus' example reinforces the principles he sets out in his criticism. Longinus doesn't simply dictate rules but embodies the very "great sublime" he describes, modeling his own ideals through his work. The minor critics who follow the principles laid by Aristotle, Horace, Quintilian, and Longinus flourish in their art of criticism.

"Whose own example strengthens all his laws;
And is himself that great sublime he draws"
(An Essay on Criticism)

Pope's admiration reflects his belief that the best critics are not just rule-makers but also practitioners who elevate literature and demonstrate the qualities they advocate.

Pope comments on the broader role of critics through history. He notes that "succeeding critics justly reign'd," suggesting that later critics upheld and refined the standards Longinus set, using criticism to curb excess "licence repress'd" and establish "useful laws" for writers. Pope links this growth in criticism with the rise of Rome's influence, implying that as Rome's empire expanded, so did the reach and authority of literary principles.

"Learning and Rome alike in empire grew,
And arts still follow'd where her eagles flew;"
(An Essay on Criticism)

Just as Rome extended its dominance through its "eagles" which is a symbol of Roman power, the spread of the Roman Empire allowed the ideals of learning and criticism to flourish. However, Pope acknowledges that both Rome and learning eventually faced decline, meeting their "doom" from the same forces.

Pope reflects on the qualities of two exemplary critics, the Earl of Roscommon and William Walsh, praising both their virtues and their contributions to literature.

Pope reflects on his own approach to writing and criticism, emphasizing on humility, moderation, and honesty as the guiding principles. He describes himself as attempting "short excursions" in poetry, modest and "in low numbers," which suggests that he is cautious and self-aware about his literary ambitions. Pope asserts that his goal is not grand fame or public acclaim, but rather to offer guidance to different readers: for the unlearned, to help them see where they might lack knowledge, and for the learned, to remind them of what they already understood. Pope explains that he is "careless of censure" and "not too fond of fame," showing that he values sincere expression over public approval.

He aims to strike a balanced tone, "pleas'd to praise, yet not afraid to blame," meaning he will commend what is worthy and criticize what falls short, with fairness and integrity. Unlike the flatterers or those who harshly judge others, Pope maintains a middle ground, "averse alike to flatter, or offend."

In his closing lines, Pope admits his own fallibility:

"Not free from faults, nor yet too vain to mend."
(An Essay on Criticism)

Pope thus, advocates for an approach to criticism that values honesty, balance, and self-improvement over harsh judgment or blind praise, reflecting a mature and deep understanding of both literature and human nature.

3. **Probable Questions**

1. Discuss the qualities that Pope identifies as essential for sound judgement and good taste in literary discourse.

OR

2. Provide a critical assessment of Pope's framework for critics.

Answer:

In 'An Essay on Criticism', Alexander Pope defines the essential qualities required to be a good critic. He defines a critic as a person who blends intellect, humility, patience, and respect for classical standards. Pope's advice to the critics reflects his belief that criticism is as much an art as the works it appraises, requiring not only knowledge but also a strong moral compass and empathy. Throughout the poem, he describes a good critic as someone who judges fairly, aiming to elevate literature and assist both writers and readers in understanding the depth of a work.

Pope starts by drawing distinction between writing and criticism, suggesting that while few may fail as writers, many fail as critics. This exaggerated contrast emphasizes the widespread problem of flawed criticism, which is more common than poor writing. Pope continues by arguing that both poets and good critics are rare, as true criticism requires a profound knowledge of artistic principles and a deep appreciation of nature and originality.

Pope questions which is worse whether poor writing or poor criticism. He insists that while bad writing may only annoy readers, bad criticism can mislead them, which Pope views as more harmful. He starts with the lines,

"'Tis hard to say, if greater want of skill
Appear in writing or in judging ill," (An Essay on Criticism)

It sets up his inquiry into the role and nature of criticism. Pope acknowledges the difficulty in deciding whether faulty writing or poor critical judgment causes more harm. He argues that misguided criticism as more damaging to readers' understanding.

Pope provides his guidelines with an admonition against superficial knowledge, warning that

"A little Learning is a dang'rous Thing."
(An Essay on Criticism)

He believes that a critic's understanding should go beyond surface knowledge, encouraging them to "Drink deep" from the "Pierian Spring," a symbol of true intellectual depth. This implies that shallow familiarity with literary concepts or classical rules leads to misguided judgments, while deep understanding is essential for insightful criticism. For Pope, a knowledgeable critic who has studied the classics, understands poetic form, and appreciates the importance of harmony in both structure and content. He is wary of critics who judge based on limited knowledge, suggesting that they often overestimate their grasp and mislead readers and writers alike.

Humility is another defining quality of a good critic in Pope's view. He warns against rash judgment with the line,

"Fools rush in where Angels fear to tread,"
(An Essay on Criticism)

It reflects his belief that a good critic must approach each work with caution and respect. This line suggests that only the foolish judge hastily, while wise critics understand the limits of their knowledge and are careful not to overstep their understanding. Pope's emphasis on humility also extends to how critics present themselves; they should be aware that their role is to illuminate the work, not overshadow it. By exercising humility, critics avoid projecting their own egos onto the work and instead focus on an honest appraisal that respects the author's intent.

For Pope, true understanding means going beyond simply following or repeating established ideas without real insight. Critics who imitate popular opinions or classical rules without fully comprehending them fail to capture the essence of what makes a work valuable or flawed. He criticizes such critics for approaching literature without proper knowledge of rules as they fail to cultivate an authentic appreciation for the complex ideas, emotions, and artistry within a text. In Pope's view, shallow critics look only at the "shell" of the work, unable to interpret or acknowledge the intricacies of an artistic work that makes it successful or flawed.

Pope acknowledges that some aspects of art are beyond strict rules or definitions, advising critics to appreciate qualities that "no precepts can declare." By recognizing that certain beauties in art come from an intuitive "happiness" rather than calculated effort, Pope suggests that good critics must be open to recognizing value in works that may not strictly adhere to classical rules. Such flexibility allows critics to appreciate originality and genius, qualities that cannot always be measured by traditional standards. In this way, Pope warns against rigid criticism, encouraging critics to celebrate innovation and creativity, which he views as vital to the progression of literature.

Pope also emphasizes the importance of empathy, encouraging critics to approach each work "with the same Spirit that its Author writ." He implies that a good critic seeks to understand the author's intentions, viewing the work from the author's perspective. By doing so, the critic avoids imposing their own interpretations or biases, instead aiming to assess how effectively the author has realized their vision. Pope's insistence on empathy underscores his belief that criticism should not distort a work's meaning; rather, it should honor the author's creative effort by evaluating it within its intended framework. This empathy also fosters a more accurate understanding of the work's strengths and weaknesses. Although Pope criticizes certain critics harshly, he holds poets in a more forgiving light, viewing them as individuals guided by a sense of harmony and order in poetic composition. This respect for the complexity of literary creation suggests that Pope believes critics should be patient and understanding, rather than overly harsh or dismissive. This tolerance, however, does not excuse critics from abandoning rigorous standards; rather, it calls for a measured approach that recognizes the art forms.

Pope regards a good critic in the role as a guide who helps readers and writers appreciate literature's complexity. He believes that true criticism is a service to both the art form and the audience, enhancing their understanding of literature's nuances. Pope criticizes both the privileged who react poorly to critique and those who flatter and enable them, highlighting the difficulty of honest criticism in a society where truth is often overshadowed by status and empty flattery. Pope critiques these writers as trapped in a cycle of superficiality, unable to recognize their own lack of talent. Rather than encourage them through criticism, he suggests it's sometimes better to leave them to their vanity, as their relentless but uninspired efforts reveal the emptiness of their work.

Pope suggests that critics should avoid tackling "dangerous truths" or sharp critiques directly. Instead, he advises critics to leave these potentially risky observations to "unsuccessful satires," which are less likely to be taken seriously or to flatterers who heap insincere praise on the powerful.

"Leave dangerous truths to unsuccessful satires,
And flattery to fulsome dedicators, "
(An Essay on Criticism)

Pope advises critics to sometimes hold back their harsh judgments, especially when dealing with writers who lack talent or originality. He suggests that it may be better to allow such writers the comfort of their vanity rather than actively criticize them. Pope argues that remaining silent can be more effective than open criticism, as criticizing these writers may actually encourage them to keep producing their poor work.

Thus, Pope's concept of a good critic in "An Essay on Criticism" is deeply rooted in both intellectual rigor and moral integrity. The ideal critic possesses not only extensive knowledge but also humility, fairness, patience, and empathy.

3. Explain the ways in which Pope distinguishes between true knowledge and superficial learning.

Answer:
In An Essay on Criticism, Alexander Pope distinguishes true knowledge from superficial learning by contrasting genuine insight with superficial learning and shallow understanding.

Pope emphasizes the importance of truth and humility in criticism, stating,

"In all you speak, let truth and candour shine"
(An Essay on Criticism)

He states that the integrity of a critic's evaluation is of great importance. A responsible critic should aim not only to express personal opinions but also to foster a sense of understanding within the readers. Pope describes how, in "fearless youth," many are excited by the first taste of knowledge and enthusiastically pursue "the heights of arts." However, because their understanding is limited by the "bounded level" of their minds, they don't yet realize the vastness of knowledge that remains.

"A little learning is a dangerous thing;
Drink deep, or taste not the Pierian spring."
(Part II An Essay on Criticism)

Pope warns that critics who possess only a shallow understanding of literature as they are the most prone to making poor judgments. The "Pierian spring," he makes a reference to the mythological source of knowledge associated with the Muses, symbolizes profound learning. Pope's message is that partial knowledge leads to false confidence, which then leads to hasty, misguided criticism. He argues that shallow understanding can lead to overconfidence and misguided conclusions. He encourages critics to "drink deep" from the well of knowledge, implying that they must immerse themselves fully in learning to be qualified judges. Pope cautions the critics and readers alike, warning against the pitfalls of "a little learning," which he describes as a shallow grasp of knowledge that can mislead individuals into arrogance and faulty judgments. In other words, incomplete knowledge can lead to arrogance and false confidence, whereas a deeper, better understanding fosters humility.

Pope identifies the type of critics who belong to those who refuse to acknowledge their mistakes and instead cling to their erroneous judgments. In contrast, he advocates for a more reflective approach:

"But you, with pleasure own your errors past,
And make each day a critic on the last."
(An Essay on Criticism)

To Pope, superficial learning is characterized by a limited or surface-level understanding that prioritizes displaying knowledge rather than truly comprehending it. In contrast, Pope holds up true knowledge as a deep, sincere pursuit that requires humility, patience, and an awareness of one's limitations. He believes that those who are genuinely wise understand the value of self-critique and are cautious in their judgments.

He condemns the reluctance to share knowledge. Critics should feel a responsibility to share their understanding generously, as the sharing of wisdom enriches the readers. He suggests that true critics should not refrain from providing critical assessment, even if it may provoke displeasure among the readers. This reinforces the notion that those who are deserving of praise will also be receptive to constructive criticism.

In conclusion, he calls for self-awareness and growth, suggesting that critics should take joy in recognizing and learning from their previous faults, allowing for continual improvement in their critical faculties. Thus, Pope's vision of a critic is that who combines knowledge, humility, and moral integrity. He presents criticism as a collaborative effort grounded in truth, emphasizing on the importance of open-mindedness and the willingness to learn from one's mistakes.

4. References and Suggested Readings:

i. Alexander Pope: An Essay on Criticism Poetry foundation (https://www.poetryfoundation.org)
ii. An essay on criticism, (https://en.wikipedia.org)
iii. An Essay on Criticism Project Gutenberg, (https://www.gutenberg.org)
iv. Alexander Pope An Essay on Criticism, (http://olympos.cz)
v. Alexander Pope- Understanding The Essay of Criticism, Dogac Kutlu
vi. Adams, Hazard. Critical Theory Since Plato. Rev.ed. Fort Worth: Harcourt, 1992. Print.

UNIT-4

Samuel Johnson: "On Metaphysical Wit", From Life of Cowley

1.   **About the Author**

2.   **Life of Cowley**

   a.   Introduction

   b.   Synopsis

   c.   Analysis

3.   **Probable Questions:**

   a.   How does Johnson assess the achievements of Cowley as a Metaphysical poet? Elaborate.

   b.   Examine Johnson as a biographer and critique of Abraham Cowley in his essay "Life of Cowley".

   c.   Johnson's views on the Metaphysical poets.

   d.   Johnson's assessment of Metaphysical wit.

4.   **References and suggested readings**

5.

   1.   **About the Author**

Samuel Johnson (1707-1784), often referred to as Dr Johnson was a towering figure in the 18th century English literary landscape. He was an influential poet, writer, essayist, biographer, moralist and lexicographer recognized for his substantial contributions to English literature and language. He was one of the leading literary figures of the Neo-classical age or the age of Enlightenment.

Johnson was born on September 18,1707 in Lichfield, Staffordshire, England. His father was a bookseller named Michael Johnson. His family was financially modest. Johnson suffered from severe health issues since birth, that left him with scars and impaired vision. Despite his ailments, Johnson emerged as a an exceptional and excelled in his education at Lichfield Grammar School. Later he attended Pembroke College, Oxford but due to financial difficulties, had to drop from his studies before getting a degree.

After leaving Oxford, Johnson struggled with his financial instability for much of his early life. Eventually he moved to London, in search of literary work and started to earn a living by writing fir various publications such as the Gentleman's Magazine, and translating books. In 1735 he married Elizabeth Tetty Porter.

Johnson was deeply religious and his Christian faith played a significant role in his early life and his works often reflected it through the morals and spiritual matters. His most famous ties were with James Boswell, a Scottish lawyer and writer who later composed "The life of Samuel Johnson" that biographical Johnson's legacy. Roswell recorded many of Johnson's conversations, providing insight into his complex character, opinions and sense of humor.

In his later life, Johnson achieved considerable fame and financial stability particularly after the wide success of his Dictionary. The publication of his dictionary made him a central figure in London's literary culture and social circles. He wrote drama, fictional speculations on the emptiness of worldly pursuits as well as numerous essays in periodicals such as 'The Rambler', 'The Idler'. One of his famous poems is 'The Vanity of Human Wishes'. His through examination of literature is reflected in his work, 'The Lives of Eminent Poets', where he critiques many eminent poets and literary figures.

Johnson continued to write until the end of his life, through his health steadily declined. He suffered from a stroke and respiratory problem. He died at the age of 75 in London on 13 December, 1784, leaving back his wide legacy and lasting influence on the development of English literature.

- **His notable works:**
  Poems:
  The Vanity of Human Wishes (1749)
  London(1738)
  On the Death of Dr. Robert Levet(1783)
  Drama:
  Irene(1749)
  Johnson's widely acclaimed work:
  A Dictionary of the English Language
  Criticism and essays:
  The Lives of the Eminent Poets(1779-1781)
  The Preface to Shakespeare (1765)

The Idler (1758- 1760)
Periodicals:
The Adventurer (1752-1754)
The Rambler(1750-1752)

---

2. Life of Cowley

•   Introduction

'Life of Cowley' by Samuel Johnson is a biographical essay on Abraham Cowley. It provides a detailed and critical examination of Cowley's life and his literary works. This essay written in 1770, belongs to Dr Johnson's biographical series on poets named: 'The Lives of Most Eminent Poets'(1779-81).

'Life of Cowley' like his other essays belonging to the collection is structured to offer insight into both the personal and public aspect of Cowley's life exploring how his experiences shaped his works and reputation. Johnson's assessment is organized chronologically and thematically. It begins with an overview of Cowley's early life, then moves to his education, professional achievements, political activities and finally his later years and works of literature.

Johnson provides a critical analysis of Cowley's works and mostly his use of "Metaphysical wit" acknowledging Cowley's role in the Metaphysical movement. The title of the essay in some sense can be considered as misleading as it offers mostly the views of Johnson regarding Metaphysical poetry and poets through Cowley as a medium.

<table>
<tr><td>

The Lives of Most Eminent Poets (1779-81)

"The Lives of Most Eminent Poets" is an influential work by Samuel Johnson that he started publishing in 1779. This collection consists of biographical and critical essays on significant English poets from the 16th to the 18th centuries. Johnson provides detailed accounts of the lives of various poets, exploring their backgrounds, personal struggles, influences, and the socio-political contexts in which they wrote. This biographical approach gives readers a deeper understanding of the poets as individuals and how their experiences shaped their work. In addition to biographical sketches, Johnson offers critical assessments of each poet's style, themes, and contributions to literature. His evaluations often include discussions of their poetic techniques, strengths, and weaknesses. Johnson's critiques are known for their sharpness and thoughtfulness, setting a standard for literary criticism. The work also reflects the cultural and intellectual currents of Johnson's time, including the rise of Romanticism and the shift away from classical forms.

</td></tr>
</table>

- **Synopsis- Analysis**

Johnson starts with his criticism of Dr. Sprat's portrayal of Abraham Cowley, arguing that it resembles a panegyric rather than a comprehensive biography. Johnson notes that while Sprat's eloquence and admiration for Cowley are evident, his work lacks the essential details needed to provide a clear understanding of Cowley's life and contributions. He emphasizes that the biography presents Cowley in broad strokes, failing to capture the nuances of his character and the complexities of his experiences. This lack of specificity leads to a narrative that is "confused and enlarged," obscuring the subject through grandiose language and vague generalities rather than illuminating Cowley as an individual.

Johnson starts to detail Cowley's early life and education. Born in 1618 in London, Abraham Cowley was the son of a wealthy merchant. After his father's death, Cowley was raised by his mother and received a good education at St. Paul's School in his young age. At the age of 15, he was admitted to Trinity college, Cambridge. There he excelled in his studies and began writing poetry. By 1633, Cowley published his collection 'Poetical Blossoms' which had five poems. He also wrote a pastoral drama in 1638, 'Naufragium Loculare' in his early years. His time at Cambridge was formative; he immersed himself in the study of classical literature and philosophy which significantly influenced his later works. Cowley's academic career at Cambridge was interrupted by the English Civil War (1642-1651). Due to the political challenges England, as a Royalist Cowley faced political challenges and had to eventually go into exile. During his time in exile, Cowley lived in various European countries including France and the Netherlands. Johnson asserts that his exile however did not halt his literary production; rather, it provided him with new experiences and perspectives that influenced his work. Cowley returned from his exile in 1656 but was apprehended and put into arrest as he was under the suspension of being a loyalist of the monarch. After his release, he established himself as a physician at Oxford in 1657. The Restoration of Charles II in 1668 allowed him to return to a more suitable environment and favorable for his literary activities. During this period, Johnson observes that Cowley focused on writing essays and philosophical works.

Johnson reflects on Abraham Cowley's contributions to botany and poetry, highlighting the intersection of his scholarly pursuits and literary output. Johnson notes that although Cowley may not have actively practiced as a physician, his studies in botany were significant enough to honor his country. This engagement with plants and nature fostered a creative transformation within Cowley, as his botanical interests became a source of poetic inspiration. Johnson elaborates on Cowley's Latin works on plants, which include various books that explore the qualities of herbs, the beauty of flowers, and the uses of trees through different poetic forms. Johnson addresses Cowley's hopes for recognition and reward during the Restoration period, highlighting the disappointment that accompanied the era's general optimism. Despite Cowley's loyal service and his expectations for a prominent position, such as the Mastership of the Savoy previously promised by both Charles I and Charles II he faced delays in receiving any substantial acknowledgment. Johnson attributes this setback to "certain persons, enemies to the Muses," suggesting that Cowley's literary aspirations were obstructed by individuals who undervalued the arts.

Johnson delves into the disappointments Cowley faced in his later career, particularly highlighting his attempts to revive his old comedy, "The Guardian," which he reworked and presented as "The Cutter of Coleman-street." Despite his efforts, the play received a harsh reception on stage and was criticized as a satire targeting the royalty reflecting the sensitive political climate of the time. Johnson notes that this neglect and criticism from the court was not Cowley's only source of frustration; it compounded his feelings of disappointment regarding his artistic endeavors. Johnson recounts an anecdote involving John Dryden and Mr. Sprat, who witnessed Cowley's reaction to the poor reception of his play. Dryden's observation of Cowley's response indicates that the poet did not exhibit the expected resilience in the face of adversity. While Johnson does not provide specific details about the nature of Cowley's reaction, he implies that the man's disappointment was severe and perhaps more profound than what his stature might suggest. Despite Cowley's defense, it is indicated that the play was widely perceived as a satire targeting the Royalists, which contributed to its poor reception. In an effort to articulate his frustrations and seek clarity regarding his situation, Cowley published an ode titled "The Complaint," where he adopts the persona of the "melancholy Cowley." However, rather than garnering sympathy for his plight, Johnson observes that this ode received ridicule, suggesting that his complaints fell on deaf ears and were met with more mockery than compassion.

Cowley's reputation suffered due to a perceived failure in both his creative endeavors and his attempts at self-promotion. Ultimately, these experiences led Cowley to desire retirement more frequently. Disillusioned by the lack of opportunities and frustrated by the success of others, he withdrew to Surrey, highlighting his increasing discontent and isolation. Johnson's account portrays Cowley not only as a talented poet but also as a figure grappling with the complexities of artistic ambition, loyalty, and the harsh realities of public reception in a politically volatile environment.

Johnson observes that initially, Cowley's living conditions were modest, but he soon secured a more stable financial situation through the support of influential patrons, such as the Earl of St. Albans and the Duke of Buckingham. This newfound security allowed him to enjoy a comfortable lifestyle while still maintaining his distance from the court life. Johnson reflects on the final years and legacy of the poet Abraham Cowley, who died in 1667 at the age of 49. Johnson notes that Cowley did not experience long periods of solitude, having passed away shortly after retreating from public life to Chertsey. His death is marked by significant recognition, as he was buried with great ceremony near literary giants Geoffrey Chaucer and Edmund Spenser, which underscores his esteemed position in English literature. Johnson quotes King Charles, who remarked that Cowley left behind no better man in England, suggesting a high regard for Cowley's character and contributions.

"...king Charles pronounced 'That Mr. Cowley had not left a better man behind him in England." (Life of Cowley)

Johnson then shifts to the next segment of his essay, where he tries to access the Metaphysical poets and wit. He critiques the metaphysical poets of the early seventeenth century, positioning their work as an example of how narrow views in poetry can lead to inconsistent praise and neglect.

He introduces the metaphysical poets as a distinct group characterized by their emphasis on showcasing their learning rather than crafting genuine poetry.

"The metaphysical poets were men of learning, and to shew their learning was their whole endeavour" (Life of Cowley)

Johnson critiques their approach, suggesting that their desire to demonstrate intellectual prowess led them to prioritize 'form' over substance, resulting in verses that lack the musicality and emotional resonance typically associated with poetry. He asserts that their choice to express their knowledge through rhyme results in compositions that lack the essential qualities of poetic art. He notes that their works often fail to engage the ear, highlighting that their focus on rhyme and syllable count detracts from the overall poetic experience.

"...they only wrote verses, and very often such verses as stood the trial of the finger better than of the ear..."(Life of Cowley)

In essence, Johnson's critique underscores a significant disconnect between intellectual ambition and the art of poetry.

Johnson critiques the metaphysical poets by invoking the authority of Aristotle, who defined poetry as an imitative art. Johnson argues that the metaphysical poets fall short of this definition because they do not successfully imitate nature or human life in their work. He emphasizes that true poetry should reflect the real world and the complexities of human experience, but these poets instead seem detached from the essential elements. Johnson acknowledges a distinction made by some critics who, despite denying the metaphysical poets the title of "poets," still regard them as "wits." He refers to John Dryden, who admits that he and his contemporaries do not match the wit of the metaphysical poet, John Donne. This admission suggests that while Johnson although critiques the metaphysical poets' failure to adhere to the principles of poetry, he recognizes that they possess certain intellectual capabilities to write. Johnson's argument here indicates that while the metaphysical poets lack the qualities necessary to be considered true poets, they still engage with wit and intelligence. He implies that wit alone does not to elevate their work to the level of genuine poetry, which must engage with the complexities of human emotion and the natural world. Johnson critiques the metaphysical poets' understanding and execution of wit, comparing their work to the definition provided by Alexander Pope, who suggests that wit is "that which has been often thought, but was never before so well expressed." Johnson asserts that the metaphysical poets fail to achieve this standard of wit because they prioritize originality in thought over clarity and elegance in expression. He argues that while they aim for singularity in their ideas, they often neglect the importance of diction and form, resulting in a disconnect between their innovative thoughts and effective communication. However, Johnson contends that Pope's conception of wit is flawed because it reduces the essence of wit from a profound strength of thought to merely a pleasing arrangement of language.

"But Pope's account of wit is undoubtedly erroneous; he depresses it below its natural dignity, and reduces it from strength of thought to happiness of language." (Life of Cowley)

He offers a more elevated understanding of wit as something that is both "natural and new," that resonates with the reader as immediately just and recognizable. According to this definition, true wit should not only be original but also feel inherent and obvious upon first encounter. He suggests that true wit is characterized by its ability to be both "natural and new," meaning that it should resonate with the audience as immediately valid, even if it is not obvious at first glance. This form of wit evokes a sense of recognition, making the reader wonder how they could have overlooked such insights. However, Johnson argues that the metaphysical poets rarely achieve this standard; while their ideas may be innovative, they often lack the natural quality that makes them relatable or accessible. Instead of sparking curiosity or wonder in their audience, their work frequently leaves readers perplexed, questioning how such complex thoughts were ever produced.

Johnson then provides a more philosophical definition of wit as "Discordia Concors," a harmonious blend of contrasting images or a revelation of hidden similarities between seemingly separate things. He acknowledges that the metaphysical poets excel in creating this kind of wit; they skillfully combine a diverse range of ideas and draw on extensive learning to craft their poetry. However, this very complexity often alienates the readers, who may appreciate the intellectual effort involved but feel that the reward is not worth the struggle. Johnson notes that while readers may admire the poets' intellect, but they are "seldom pleased," indicating that the enjoyment of poetry should not only come from its cleverness but also from its ability to engage and resonate with the audience. Johnson acknowledges that despite the shortcomings of the metaphysical poets, their labour and intellectual efforts are not entirely in vain. While he criticizes their tendency to indulge in "false conceits" and exaggerated imagery, he concedes that they occasionally produce "unexpected truth." Johnson suggests that the metaphysical poets' reliance on intricate and superficial conceits can sometimes yield valuable insights, even if the journey to those insights is complex. He emphasizes that achieving the level of a metaphysical poet requires considerable effort, one cannot simply become such a poet through imitation or mere skill with language. Instead, it requires a depth of reading and contemplation.

"No man could be born a metaphysical poet, nor assume the dignity of a writer by descriptions copied from descriptions, by imitations borrowed from imitations, by traditional imagery and hereditary similes, by readiness of rhyme and volubility of syllables." (Life of Cowley)

Johnson implies that the intellectual engagement required to navigate their works makes the experience worthwhile, even if the immediate pleasures of poetry, such as emotional resonance or aesthetic delight are not always present.

Johnson reflects on the evolution of poetic style during the time of the metaphysical poets and their immediate successors. He suggests that the intricate and intellectual style prevalent among the metaphysical poets was largely influenced by the works of Giambattista Marino and his followers, as well as by John Donne, who is recognized for his extensive knowledge and unique approach to poetry. Johnson notes that Ben Jonson also shares some similarities with Donne, particularly in the ruggedness of his lines, although their sentiments differ significantly. Johnson points out that these poets inspired a wave of imitators, though many of these have since been forgotten. He names a few key figures of the next generation, including Sir John Suckling, Edmund Waller, John Denham, Abraham Cowley, John Cleveland, and John Milton. Waller and Denham are noted for their efforts to enhance the harmony and musicality of English verse, seeking a different path to literary fame. Johnson observes that while Milton experimented with the metaphysical style in a limited capacity evidenced by his poem about Hobson the Carrier, Johnson argues that Cowley truly embraced and surpassed his predecessors in this style. Cowley, according to Johnson, possessed a wealth of sentiment and greater musicality, demonstrating a mastery of the intricate conceits that characterized the metaphysical tradition.

Johnson then shifts to discuss Cowley's "Miscellanies," a collection that showcases Cowley's diverse poetic abilities. He observes that the diverse elevated nature of these compositions, which range from light-hearted to serious and grand themes. Johnson acknowledges the difficulty of choosing a single standout piece from such a varied collection, noting the challenge critics face when attempting to elevate one work above others. He mentions the opinions of scholars like Scaliger, who praised certain odes in Cowley's oeuvre, but ultimately expresses a personal preference for Cowley's first piece, emphasizing that the title is essential for clarity. Johnson critiques literary works that lack sufficient context or completeness, referencing Alexander Pope's practice of writing epitaphs that are unnamed and therefore lack full significance. Johnson then examines Cowley's "Ode on Wit," noting that it stands out as a significant work that contributed to the evolution of the concept of 'wit' during Cowley's time. He explains that the term "wit," which originally referred to intellect and reasoning as opposed to will, began to take on its modern connotations around this period, illustrating Cowley's role in this linguistic and conceptual shift.

The next collection of poems that Johnson examines is 'The Mistress'. Johnson critiques the collection acknowledging both its strengths and weaknesses. He points out that all the poems in this collection share a uniformity of style, characterized by an abundance of wit and extensive learning. Johnson quotes Sprat's observation that Cowley's knowledge flows into his writing, often surprising readers with new insights. However, despite this intellectual richness, Johnson asserts that The Mistress ultimately fails as love poetry. He argues that the verses lack the emotional resonance which is expected from romantic poetry, describing them as neither "courtly" nor "pathetic," devoid of the gallantry and tenderness typically associated with expressions of love.

Johnson offers a critical analysis of Cowley's poetic style, particularly focusing on his use of diction and versification. Johnson notes that Cowley's works often lack appropriate epithets, which are essential for creating vivid imagery and enhancing the emotional impact of poetry. Instead of a thoughtful selection of language that fits the subject matter, Cowley's diction appears haphazard and generic, influenced more by the subject itself than by the poet's careful choice. Johnson contrasts Cowley's treatment of different poetic forms, highlighting that his diction does not significantly differ between his lighter, more playful pieces and his serious, heroic poetry. This lack of variation suggests a failure to adapt his language appropriately to the emotional weight or tone required by different genres. For example, Johnson points out that Cowley uses similar diction for both the gentle themes of Anacreon and the grand themes associated with Pindar, which can diminish the distinctiveness of each style. Regarding Cowley's versification, Johnson asserts that it seems to lack meticulous attention. Johnson points out that Cowley frequently uses weak rhymes, often employing pronouns or insignificant particles to complete his rhymes. By relying on unimportant words for rhyme, Cowley detracts from the overall energy and effectiveness of his poetry. Johnson criticizes Cowley's use of varied meters, claiming that the combination of different measures can be dissonant and unpleasing. When the rhythm of one verse does not transition smoothly into the next, it disrupts the flow of the poem and can lead to a jarring reading experience. This lack of musicality further detracts from the enjoyment of the poetry.

Johnson notes that Cowley was likely the first poet to freely mix Alexandrines (twelve-syllable lines) with the standard heroic couplet of ten syllables.

"...the first poet that mingled Alexandrines at pleasure with the common heroick of ten syllables..."(Life of Cowley)

This practice was later adopted by Dryden, who viewed the Alexandrine as a majestic form of verse, especially suitable for conveying the voice of the Supreme Being. Cowley's willingness to innovate with verse structure shows his creative approach to poetic form. Johnson emphasizes that Cowley's prose essays are distinct from his poetry, noting that no other author has kept such a significant distance between the two. He praises Cowley's prose for its natural thoughts and smooth, equable style, which remains accessible and engaging without being trivial. Johnson references Felton's observation that Cowley excelled in various poetic forms but notably did not attempt tragedy. He acknowledges Cowley's broad mastery of poetic genres and his ability to rival classical poets.

Johnson in his concluding lines of the essay asserts that Cowley infused English poetry with both the grandeur of the greater ode and the lightness of the lesser ode, showcasing his versatility. While Johnson praises Cowley's capacity for original thought, noting that his sentiments were distinct and personal, he also observes that Cowley often shared a similar manner of expression with other poets.

4. Probable Questions:

1. How does Johnson assess the achievements of Cowley as a Metaphysical poet? Elaborate.

OR

2. Examine Johnson as a biographer and critique of Abraham Cowley in his essay "Life of Cowley".

Answer:

Samuel Johnson in "Life of Cowley" provides a complex assessment of Abraham Cowley as a metaphysical poet, both acknowledging Cowley's intellectual abilities and critiquing the limitations of metaphysical poetry as a whole. Johnson portrays Cowley as a poet of extensive learning and wit, setting him apart from his contemporaries, yet he also critiques Cowley's frequent deviations from natural poetic expression, which often result in an excess of forced conceits.

Johnson's assessment of Cowley begins with his thorough investigation of Cowley's early and later life and then as a literary figures. Johnson demonstrates Cowley journey from his birth, education, profession, culminating with his death.In terms of Cowley's literary contributions, Johnson begins with the Metaphysical poets. The Metaphysical poets were a group of 17th-century English poets known for their complex imagery, philosophical themes, and innovative use of language. He introduces the metaphysical poets as a distinct group characterized by their emphasis on showcasing their learning rather than crafting genuine poetry.

"The metaphysical poets were men of learning, and to shew their learning was their whole endeavour" (Life of Cowley)

Johnson critiques the metaphysical poets for their lack in qualities of poetic compositions. In light of his views regarding the metaphysical poets Johnson examines Cowley's literary works.

Samuel Johnson offers a refined analysis of Cowley's poetic capabilities, assessing both his emotional range and intellectual capability as a Metaphysical poet. Reflecting on Cowley's elegy on the death of his friend Hervey, Johnson points out that while Cowley gives generous praise to Hervey's virtues, but falls short in conveying genuine sorrow. Johnson observes that Cowley admires and vividly describes Hervey's qualities particularly those nurtured in a life of scholarly solitude and reflection but seems emotionally distant when attempting to inspire grief in the reader. Johnson highlights an instance where Cowley, rather than expressing personal grief, shifts to an intellectual image of how his hypothetical crown of laurels would "crackle in the fire," focusing on the scientific observation that bay leaves crackle when burned. This detail, though accurate, Johnson insists that it reflects Cowley's tendency to approach poetry intellectually rather than with deep feeling, suggesting his ease of mind even in moments meant to be sorrowful.

Johnson praises 'The Chronicle', calling it a uniquely lively and imaginative piece, marked by Cowley's unusual wit, smooth expression, and vibrant imagery. Cowley's genius, Johnson suggests that it lies in his intellectual agility and capacity to weave diverse ideas seamlessly within even light-hearted poetry. This combination of wit and depth, Johnson argues, sets Cowley apart from contemporaries such as Suckling, who had gaiety but lacked erudition, or Dryden, who possessed insight but could not match Cowley's playful lightness. Focusing on Cowley's 'Anacreontiques', Johnson argues that these poems, written in a light and celebratory style inspired by the Greek poet Anacreon, retain their original charm because they rely on this familiar, straightforward language. Johnson believes that Cowley was naturally inclined toward this kind of writing, excelling in the "familiar and the festive" where clarity and simplicity are essential. This style as Johnson observed allowed Cowley's work to capture the joy of celebration and lightheartedness in a way that continues to delight readers long after his time.

The next collection of poems that Johnson examines is 'The Mistress'. Rather than analyzing each of the individual poems, Johnson argues that these pieces share similar strengths and weaknesses throughout. On one hand, Johnson acknowledges the wit and abundant learning displayed in 'The Mistress', noting that Cowley's knowledge often surprises the reader with insights that might inspire intellectual growth. However, as love poetry, Johnson finds the collection lacking the passion required for the genre. He asserts that these poems fail to convey the genuine emotions of a lover, as they lack the sincerity, charm, and affection one would expect in romantic verse. Instead, Johnson remarks that Cowley's language is overly elaborate and exaggerated, with frequent metaphors of "darts and flames" and "wounds and death," which Johnson finds too artificial to inspire real emotion. Johnson contends that Cowley's approach to love poetry is overly elaborate and superficial, with each stanza filled with imagery of "darts and flames, with wounds and death, with mingled souls, and with broken hearts." This abundance of exaggerated metaphors, rather than conveying the genuine emotions of a lover, instead comes across as detached, even cold, and more concerned with cleverness than with heartfelt expression. To Johnson, these excessive images don't evoke real essence of love rather they seem too calculated, and artificially constructed to invoke true empathy or emotional engagement.

A significant issue Johnson identifies is Cowley's reliance on "conceits" which are complex, sometimes extravagant metaphors often used in metaphysical poetry. In 'The Mistress', Cowley frequently expresses love through the metaphor of fire, but he takes the metaphor to extremes, creating images that Johnson finds both inventive and unnatural. For instance, Cowley considers his lover's cold gaze as both icy and fiery by imagining her eyes as "burning-glasses made of ice." Johnson borrows Addison's term "mixed wit" to describe Cowley's conceits, explaining that "mixed wit" combines two senses of a word in a way that is logically inconsistent being true in one sense, but not in the other. Johnson's critique ultimately portrays 'The Mistress' as a collection that prioritizes intellectual display over emotional truth. Johnson suggests that the poems in 'The Mistress' are more about showing off Cowley's wit and learning than about conveying authentic affection or devotion.

Johnson reflects on Cowley's poetic abilities in relation to the esteemed Greek poet Pindar, who is celebrated for his grand and elevated style, particularly in his odes. Johnson opens with skepticism, suggesting that it is difficult to believe that someone of Cowley's intellectual caliber, who was known for his wit and learning, could ever think he was successfully imitating Pindar when his poetry often features "feeble diction" and "minute morality." Johnson critiques Cowley for what he perceives as a lack of strength in language and an overly simplistic approach to moral themes, implying that Cowley's poetry sometimes lacks the gravity and eloquence necessary to evoke the lofty spirit of Pindar's work. However, Johnson acknowledges that in some of Cowley's original odes, where he selects his own subjects, Cowley does achieve a level of dignity that is reflective of Pindar's style. He cites Clarendon's view that Cowley "took a flight beyond all that went before him" and mentions Milton's claim that Cowley was among the three greatest English poets, alongside Spenser and Shakespeare. This recognition illustrates Cowley's prominence and the high regard in which he was held by his contemporaries.

In the final section of the essay Johnson offers a critical analysis of Cowley's poetic style, particularly focusing on his use of diction and versification. He observes that Cowley's poetry often lacks carefully chosen epithets, which are vital for creating vivid imagery and deepening the emotional impact of poetry.

"His diction was in his own time censured as negligent." (Life of Cowley)

Rather than selecting language that aligns with his themes, Johnson observes that Cowley's diction often appears random and generic, driven more by the subject than by deliberate poetic choice. Johnson contrasts Cowley's handling of various poetic forms, noting that his language remains largely the same across both light-hearted and serious works. This uniformity suggests a failure to adapt his diction to suit the emotional tone or gravity of different genres. For instance, Johnson remarks that Cowley employs similar language for both Anacreon's gentle themes and the more elevated themes linked with Pindar, which diminishes the unique character of each style. As for versification, Johnson argues that Cowley appears to lack precision. He points out that Cowley often uses weak rhymes, relying on pronouns or insignificant particles to complete his lines. This habit falls short of the strength and impact expected in refined poetry, leaving the reader or listener dissatisfied. By depending on unimportant words for rhyme, Cowley reduces the overall energy and effectiveness of his verses. Johnson also critiques Cowley's varied meter, asserting that the inconsistent measures can feel dissonant and unappealing. Johnson insists that when one line's rhythm does not transition smoothly to the next, it disrupts the poem's flow, creating a jarring experience that detracts from the musical quality and enjoyment of the poetry.

Johnson notes that Cowley was likely the first poet to freely mix Alexandrines (twelve-syllable lines) with the standard heroic couplet of ten syllables.

"...the first poet that mingled Alexandrines at pleasure with the common heroick of ten syllables..." (Life of Cowley)

This practice was later adopted by Dryden, who viewed the Alexandrine as a majestic form of verse. Johnson asserts that Cowley's willingness to innovate with verse structure shows his creative approach to poetic form. He emphasizes that Cowley's prose essays are distinct from his poetry, noting that no other author has kept such a significant distance between the two. He praises Cowley's prose for its natural thoughts and smooth, equable style, which remains accessible and engaging without being trivial.

In conclusion, Johnson's analysis revolves around Cowley's technical innovations, his intellectual complexity, and his occasional faults to maintain clarity and natural sentiment; acknowledging Cowley's versatility in handling various poetic forms; considers that during his lifetime, Cowley was regarded as an exceptional poet.

3. Johnson's views on the Metaphysical poets.

OR

4. Johnson's assessment of Metaphysical wit.

Answer:

The Metaphysical poets were a group of 17th-century English poets known for their innovative and complex use of language, their exploration of abstract themes, and their unique style that often combined the intellectual with the emotional. The term "Metaphysical" was first used by Samuel Johnson in the 18th century to describe a style characterized by intricate conceits, philosophical themes, and a blend of personal reflection with universal questions.

In 'Life of Cowley' Johnson introduces the metaphysical poets as a distinct group characterized by their emphasis on showcasing their learning rather than crafting genuine poetry.

"The metaphysical poets were men of learning, and to shew their learning was their whole endeavour" (Life of Cowley)

Johnson critiques their approach, suggesting that their desire to demonstrate their intellectual capability led them to prioritize 'form' over substance, resulting in verses that lack the musicality and emotional resonance typically associated with poetry. He asserts that their choice to express their knowledge through rhyme results in compositions that lack the essential qualities of poetic art. He notes that their works often fail to engage the ear, highlighting that their focus on rhyme and syllable count detracts from the overall poetic experience.

"...they only wrote verses, and very often such verses as stood the trial of the finger better than of the ear..." (Life of Cowley)

Johnson critiques the metaphysical poets by referring to Aristotle, who defined poetry as an imitative art. Johnson argues that the metaphysical poets fall short of this definition because they do not successfully imitate nature or human life in their work. He emphasizes that true poetry should reflect the real world and the complexities of human experience, but these poets instead seem detached from these essential elements.

Johnson critiques the metaphysical poets' understanding and execution of wit, comparing their work to the definition provided by Alexander Pope, who suggests that wit is "that which has been often thought, but was never before so well expressed." Johnson asserts that the metaphysical poets fail to achieve this standard of wit because they prioritize originality in thought over clarity and elegance in expression. He argues that while they aim for singularity in their ideas, they often neglect the importance of diction and form, resulting in a disconnection between their innovative thoughts and effective communication.

Johnson suggests that true wit is characterized by its ability to be both "natural and new," meaning that it should resonate with the audience as immediately valid, even if it is not obvious at first glance. This form of wit evokes a sense of recognition, making the reader wonder how they could have overlooked such insights. However, Johnson argues that the metaphysical poets rarely achieve this standard; while their ideas may be innovative, they often lack the natural quality that makes them relatable or accessible. Instead of sparking curiosity or wonder in their audience, their work frequently leaves readers perplexed, questioning how such convoluted thoughts were ever produced.

Johnson observed that the Metaphysical poets struggled to achieve both the sublime and the emotional appeal in their work. Sublimity, refers to a vast and awe-inspiring quality in art and literature, is characterized by generality and the ability to evoke broad, profound thoughts. In contrast, Johnson argues that the Metaphysical poets focus on particularities of their thoughts, which is prone to dilute the grandeur of their ideas.

Johnson then provides a more philosophical definition of wit as "Discordia Concors", a harmonious blend of contrasting images or a revelation of hidden similarities between seemingly disparate things. He acknowledges that the metaphysical poets excel in creating this kind of wit; they skillfully combine a diverse range of ideas and draw on extensive learning to craft their poetry. However, this very complexity often alienates the readers, who may appreciate the intellectual effort involved but feel that the reward is not worth the struggle. Johnson notes that while readers may admire the poets' intellectual capability, they are "seldom pleased," indicating that the enjoyment of poetry should not only come from its cleverness but also from its ability to engage and resonate with the audience.

In conclusion, Johnson suggests that the flaws in metaphysical poetry stem from a conscious departure from natural expression in favor of novelty and strangeness, which often results in improper or superficial writing that fails to delight the audience, as these poets prioritize evoking admiration over genuine engagement.

4. References and Suggested Readings:

i. Samuel Johnson, 'Life of a Cowley', from 'The Lives of Eminent Poets'
ii. Martz, Louislohr (1991), 'From Renaissance to Baroque: Essays on Literature and Arts', University of Missouri Press
iii. Harry Blamires: A History of Literary Criticism

Additional Questionnaire

1. Briefly discuss on the demerits of imitative art as defined by Plato. Refer to 'The Republic', book X.

2. Evaluate on Aristotle's notion of art in contrast to his predecessor Plato with specific reference to the context.

3. *"Tragedy is an imitation of an action, and the action is performed by certain agents."* Explain.

4. *"Tragedy has everything that epic does…"* Evaluate on how Aristotle defines tragedy to be superior to epic

5. Critically access Horace's adherence to the classical norms of art and poetry.

6. Explain with reference to the context:

   a. *"If a painter had chosen to set a human head*
   On a horse's neck, covered a melding olimbs.
   Everywhere, with multi-coloured plumage, so.
   That what was a lovely woman, at the top,
   Ended repulsively in the tail of a black fish:
   Asked to a viewing, could you sniffle laughter,
   my friends?"

   b. *Either follow tradition, or invent consistently.*
   If you happen to portray Achilles, honoured,
   Pen him as energetic, irascible, ruthless,
   Fierce, above the law, never downing weapons

   c. *"Poets wish to benefit or to please, or to speak*
   What is both enjoyable and helpful to living.

> *When you give instruction, be brief, what's quickly*
> *Said the spirit grasps easily, faithfully retains:*
> *Everything superfluous flows out of a full mind."*

d. *"An honest, sensible man will condemn lifeless verse,*
> *Fault the harsh, smear the inelegant with a black*
> *Stroke of the pen, cut out pretentious adornment,*
> *Force you to elucidate where it's not clear enough,*
> *Denounce the ambiguous phrase, mark amendments,"*

e. *"He's mad: like a bear, that's broken the bars of its cage*
> *The pest puts all to flight, learned or not, with reciting:*
> *Whom he takes tight hold of, he grips, and reads to death,*
> *A leech that never looses the skin, till gorged with blood."*

7. Access critically Longinus' concept of sublimity and on how it can be achieved.

8. Evaluate on Sidney's treatment of poetry as an elevated literary form.

9. Discuss briefly on Dryden's views regarding rhyme and use of blank verse in 'An Essay on Dramatic Poesy'.

10.Prepare a critical assessment on the merits of English drama with contrast the French. Give reference to context from 'An Essay on Dramatic Poesy'

11. Prepare an explanatory note regarding Dryden's examination of 'The Silent Women'.

12. Explain with reference to context:

 a. *"A little learning is a dang'rous thing;*
   Drink deep, or taste not the Pierian spring:
   There shallow draughts intoxicate the brain,
   And drinking largely sobers us again."

 b. *"Tis hard to say, if greater want of skill*
   Appear in writing or in judging ill;"

13. Critically examine pope's advice to the critics. Give reference to context.

14. Access Samuel Johnson as a biographer with specific reference to his essay 'Life of Cowley'

[324]